Promoting Reasonable Expectations

Promoting Reasonable Expectations

Aligning Student and Institutional Views of the College Experience

Thomas E. Miller

Barbara E. Bender

John H. Schuh

and Associates

JOSSEY-BASS
A Wiley Imprint
www.josseybass.com

Published by Jossey-Bass
A Wiley Imprint
989 Market Street, San Francisco, CA 94103-1741   www.josseybass.com

Jossey-Bass books and products are available through most bookstores. To contact Jossey-Bass directly
call our Customer Care Department within the U.S. at 800-956-7739, outside the U.S. at 317-572-3986
or fax 317-572-4002.

Jossey-Bass also publishes its books in a variety of electronic formats. Some content that appears in
print may not be available in electronic books.

Library of Congress Cataloging-in-Publication Data

Miller, Thomas E., 1948 Nov. 25-
    Promoting reasonable expectations : aligning student and institutional views of the college
experience / Thomas E. Miller, Barbara E. Bender, John H. Schuh, and Associates.
        p. cm.
    Includes bibliographical references and index.
    ISBN 0-7879-7624-5 (alk. paper)
    1. College student development programs—United States. 2. Student affairs services—
United States. 3. College students—United States—Attitudes. I. Bender, Barbara E.
II. Schuh, John H. III. Title.
    LB2343.4.M55 2005   2004025496

Printed in the United States of America
FIRST EDITION
HB Printing   10 9 8 7 6 5 4 3 2 1

The Jossey-Bass Higher and
Adult Education Series

The National Association of Student Personnel Administrators (NASPA) is the leading voice for student affairs administration, policy, and practice and affirms the commitment of student affairs to educating the whole student and integrating student life and learning. NASPA represents a wide range of student affairs professionals committed to serving college students by embracing the core values of diversity, learning, integrity, service, fellowship, and the spirit of inquiry.

With 8,500 members at 1,400 campuses, and representing 29 countries, NASPA is the largest professional association for student affairs administrators, faculty, and graduate students. NASPA members serve a variety of functions and roles including vice presidents and deans for student life as well as professionals working within housing and residence life, student unions, student activities, counseling, career development, orientation, enrollment management, racial and ethnic minority support services, and retention and assessment.

For more information about NASPA publications and professional development programs contact:

National Association of Student Personnel
    Administrators (NASPA)
1875 Connecticut Ave. Suite 418
Washington, DC 20009-5728
202-265-7500
E-mail: office@naspa.org
Web site: www.naspa.org

Contents

Preface

The very beginnings of this project arose following discussions about the Joint Statement of Rights and Freedoms of Students upon its reconsideration and reissuing in 1992 as part of the 25th anniversary of the original publication by the American Association of University Professors (AAUP, 1968). A group of representatives of higher educational associations convened over a period of years to reconsider the Joint Statement and evaluate it to determine the extent that it accurately represented current thought and language regarding student rights. The result was a slightly reframed Joint Statement, with updated language and references to court decisions and other relevant developments since its original issuance. The Joint Statement is widely recognized as a useful and necessary contribution to higher education. In the context of the higher educational climate in its original iteration, it was an essential statement to protect students and inform the higher educational community about the norms for their rights. However, in the months following the publication of the 1992 version, leaders of the National Association of Student Personnel Administrators (NASPA) hosted a series of conversations about it, and the sense of student affairs professionals was that, although it was an essential statement, it did not provide a very high test for institutional performance. The thinking was that protecting the rights of students was not a useful measure for establishing how well institutions were doing, nor a very good benchmark for assessing the quality of relationships between colleges and students. Conversations turned from considering the rights of students to the expectations they held for the college experience.

As a result, in the summer of 1993, the NASPA Board of Directors commissioned a group to explore an approach intended to clarify the relationships between students and institutions of higher learning and to enhance student and institutional productivity. At the core of the discussion was the matter of what students expect of higher education and what, in turn, institutions expect of students. The persons serving on this group were George Kuh, of Indiana University; James Lyons, from Stanford University; Jo Anne Trow, from Oregon State University; and Thomas Miller, from Canisius College. They met several times over a two-year period, and the product of their work was the "Reasonable Expectations" document, followed by a series of workshops and programs at conferences and on college campuses.

The document was a pamphlet-length piece that used the expectations that students have of institutions (and that institutions have of students) to provide a lens through which their relationships could be viewed. The text divided expectations into five categories: teaching and learning, the curriculum, institutional integrity, the quality of institutional life, and educational services. In each area, a sampling of expectations was presented to help the reader see how that "lens" can inform the relationships that colleges and universities have with students.

In the years that followed, NASPA hosted various workshops and programs around the student expectations theme. Also, there was some interest in the higher educational research community about student expectations. In the fall of 2002, the NASPA Board of Directors authorized the appointment of a group to explore a new consideration of the Reasonable Expectations project. A design team of the following persons was convened:

Barbara E. Bender, Rutgers University

Evelyn Clements, Middlesex Community College

George D. Kuh, Indiana University

Thomas E. Miller, University of South Florida

Gregory Roberts, University of St. Thomas

John H. Schuh, Iowa State University

This book is the product of the work of that design team, as well as many other persons who wrote sections of chapters, generated or culled research reports, and contributed in other ways to the production of the manuscript.

Purpose of the Book

The principal goal of this book is to examine student expectations and compare them with the realities of the student experience, exploring points of dissonance and contrast. That contrast, which could be characterized as "unmet expectations," results in a series of observations and recommendations addressed to the higher education community. The book includes a review of how student expectations vary by institutional type and by individual differences. Further, the text addresses the expectations of constituents outside of the higher education community, such as parents, media, government, neighborhoods, and so forth.

The book is intended to stimulate interest in student expectations among higher education leaders. It is premised on the belief that too little attention has been given to the subject and that the failure of higher educational institutions to understand student expectations has led to dissonance and, to some extent, failure. The writers hope that wider understanding of student expectations and comparisons with how those expectations resonate with real experiences of students will inform practice, decision making, and planning in the higher educational community.

Institutions that discover gaps between the expectations and experiences of students can consider strategies to address those gaps. It may be that better information about the college experience should be shared with prospective students, so they can frame expectations that are accurate and reasonable. On the other hand, some student expectations may be quite reasonable, and institutions may need to consider how to perform better to match student experiences with expectations. This can occur at the widest level, with broad consideration of students as a class or group, but it can also be highly individual and frame conversations in academic advising, career planning, and course learning activities.

Intended Audience

This text is targeted to the higher education community, including presidents, faculty members, and administrators. Although it has been sponsored by a national student affairs association, it is not narrowly intended for just the audience of student affairs professionals. We hope that such persons will be interested in it, but we also hope their colleagues with other duties and responsibilities, particularly campus academic officers and executives, will find appeal in its topics. The intention is that it will resonate with those who have interest in college students and how they interact with and relate to institutions of higher learning. The book proposes strategies for addressing how expectations can be better matched with real experiences.

Acknowledgments

The writers who contributed to this project represent a wide array of institutions and characteristics. They are a mixture of professional administrators, many working in student affairs areas, and faculty members and scholars in the higher education industry. Their work on this text stands independently from that of others, and I am very grateful for their hard work, thoroughness, and attention to detail.

Barbara Bender and John Schuh were of immense help in reviewing the submissions and framing the thoughts of our writers in ways that were best coordinated and consistent. Gwen Dungy helped to get the project started when she suggested to me that a follow-up to the original Reasonable Expectations project would be timely. The support from the NASPA Foundation for the purchase of research was a crucial contribution to the effort. David Brightman, representing the publisher of the book, was consistently encouraging, supportive, and responsive. Colleagues at the University of South Florida, particularly Wilma Henry, made my allocation of time to this project possible, and her encouragement and support were absolutely essential. The students in graduate classes that I teach were helpful and engaged with the project, and I appreciate their interest and enthusiasm. Staff in the office of the dean of students regularly managed the affairs of the office in my absences while the project was unfolding, and I am grateful for their independence and self-sufficiency. Melissa and Jason Spratt, Melanie Rago, and John Moore helped with research and production tasks, and Lynne Dalton and Chiqui Aldana coordinated several management functions that helped the project unfold as it did. Finally, I close with a note of appreciation and affection for Carol Lesher Miller, my favorite editor, dance partner, and best friend.

February 15, 2005   Thomas E. Miller
                                                      University of South Florida

Reference

American Association of University Professors. (1968). *Joint statement on rights and freedoms of students.* Washington, D.C.: American Association of University Professors.

The Authors

Frank P. Ardaiolo has been the Vice President for Student Life at Winthrop University in Rock Hill, South Carolina, since 1989, where he oversees a broad portfolio of student-related areas at this public comprehensive institution. His doctorate was received from Indiana University in higher education, student affairs, political science, and African studies, and his bachelor's is from Assumption College. He is also an associate professor in education and has taught undergraduate and graduate courses ranging from freshman seminars to African politics to college legal issues at varying institutions. He has published more than 25 monograph chapters, articles, and essays on legal issues, quality improvement, adult learners, student affairs–academic affairs collaboration, and African politics.

Barbara E. Bender is Associate Dean of the Graduate School–New Brunswick, and Director of the Teaching Assistant Project at Rutgers University in New Brunswick. She earned her bachelor's degree at State University of New York (SUNY) Cortland, her master's degree at SUNY Albany, and her doctorate at Teacher's College, Columbia University. She has worked professionally in numerous capacities at both public and independent institutions for the past 25 years in such roles as associate provost and dean of students and has taught a wide variety of courses in higher education. At Rutgers University, she founded the Teaching Assistant Project in 1987, as well as the Academic Leadership Program, a professional development program for academic department chairs.

Gwendolyn J. Dungy has been Executive Director of the National Association of Student Personnel Administrators (NASPA) since 1995, after serving as the Associate Director of the Curriculum and Faculty

Development Network for the Association of American Colleges and Universities. Her campus experience includes being a senior administrator at the County College of Morris (New Jersey), Montgomery College (Maryland), and Catonsville Community College (Maryland) and a member of the faculty at St. Louis Community College in the Department of Counseling. She has served on the ACE Commission on Government Relations and as a trustee at several colleges and universities. She earned B.S. and M.S. degrees from Eastern Illinois University, an M.A. degree from Drew University in New Jersey, and a Ph.D. from Washington University in St. Louis.

Robert M. Gonyea is Associate Director of the Center for Postsecondary Research. He has presented at several national and regional conferences on student engagement, assessment of institutional quality, student expectations about college, and the contribution of student affairs to student learning. He has previously worked as a student affairs administrator at the University of San Francisco, University of Wisconsin, and Northern Michigan University. He has a B.S. in psychology and a master's of labor and industrial relations from Michigan State University, and is a doctoral candidate in higher education and student affairs at Indiana University with a minor in educational inquiry.

Wilma J. Henry is Associate Professor in the Department of Psychological and Social Foundations and Associate Professor of Educational Training Programs in the Department of Student Health Services at the University of South Florida (USF) in Tampa. Additionally, she serves as Director of the College Student Affairs M.Ed. degree program. Previously, she was Associate Vice President for Student Life and Wellness at USF. She has also served as Associate Professor and Assistant Dean in the College of Education at Wright State University, Dayton, Ohio. She held other student affairs administrative posts at Fayetteville State University in North Carolina, Texas A&M University–Commerce, and the University of Georgia.

Jeffrey A. Howard is a Professor of Developmental and Personality Psychology at Eckerd College, a small, four-year liberal arts college where faculty work very closely with undergraduate students. He has been professionally engaged in activities with first-year students for nearly 20 years. He was the Director of the Freshman Honors Program for 10 years. His Leadership and Self-Discovery Practicum, an intensive January Term program exclusively for first-year students, is in its eighth year. He regularly teaches in the year-long, general education freshman seminar at Eckerd. In 2000, he was awarded the Robert A. Staub Distinguished Teacher Award. His recent research has revealed how psychological attachment theory can predict which students may be at risk for a poor adjustment to college.

Susan R. Komives is Associate Professor at the University of Maryland. She is former president of the American College Personnel Association (ACPA) and former vice president for student development at Stephens College and the University of Tampa. She is coeditor of *Student Services* (Jossey-Bass, 1996, 2003), and coauthor of *Exploring Leadership* (Jossey-Bass, 1998) and *Management and Leadership Issues for a New Century* (Jossey-Bass, 2000). She is a senior scholar diplomate with ACPA and senior scholar with the Burns Academy of Leadership. She is the 2004 recipient of the Robert H. Shaffer Award Graduate Faculty Member Award from the National Association of Student Personnel Administrators (NASPA) and the ACPA Esther Lloyd Jones Professional Service award.

George D. Kuh is Chancellor's Professor of Higher Education at Indiana University Bloomington. He directs the Center for Postsecondary Research, which is home to the National Survey of Student Engagement (NSSE) and related surveys for faculty members and law school students, the NSSE Institute for Effective Educational Practice, and the College Student Experiences Questionnaire Research Program. A past president of the Association for the Study of Higher Education, Kuh has written extensively about student engagement, assessment, institutional improvement, and college and university cultures and has consulted with more than 150 educational institutions and agencies in the United States and abroad.

John Wesley Lowery is Assistant Professor of Higher Education and Student Affairs in the Department of Educational Leadership and Policies at the University of South Carolina. He earned his doctorate at Bowling Green State University in higher education administration. Before beginning his doctoral work, he was Director of Residence Life at Adrian College in Michigan and university judicial administrator at Washington University in St. Louis. He is a frequent speaker and author on topics related to student affairs and higher education, particularly legislative issues and judicial affairs. He has a master's degree in student personnel services from the University of South Carolina and his undergraduate degree in religious studies is from the University of Virginia.

Thomas E. Miller is the Dean of Students at the Tampa campus of the University of South Florida, where he has served since 2001. Before that time he served as the Senior Student Affairs Administrator at Eckerd College and held a similar post at Canisius College. He has also worked in student affairs positions at Indiana University and at Shippensburg University. He holds a bachelor's degree from Muhlenberg College and master's and doctoral degrees from Indiana University. He serves as a member of the boards of directors of BACCHUS/GAMMA Peer Education Network and of the National Consortium for Academics and Sports.

Larry Moneta is Vice President for Student Affairs at Duke University, and he previously worked in a similar capacity at the University of Pennsylvania. He received his Ed.D. and his B.S. from the University of Massachusetts and his M.Ed. from Springfield College. He is an active member of the National Association of Student Personnel Administrators (NASPA), serving most recently as a member of its National Academy for Leadership and Executive Effectiveness Board and as a member of the NASPA Foundation Board. His publications include *The Influence of Technology on the Management of Student Services,* and *Future Issues in Serving Students at Metropolitan Universities* (both New Directions in Student Services monographs, 1998) and *Future Trends in Student Affairs* for NASPA's Leadership Exchange.

Harold L. Nixon became the Vice President for Student Affairs at the University of South Florida in 1994. He is a graduate of Fisk University and the University of North Carolina at Chapel Hill. He also completed the Higher Educational Management Institute at Harvard University. Dr. Nixon's experience also includes positions as Vice President for Student Affairs at Wright State University, Dayton, Ohio; and Fayetteville State University, Fayetteville, North Carolina. His 35 years in higher education have been spent providing leadership in creating and fostering programs and facilities that have enabled students to benefit from a more comfortable learning and living environment.

Elizabeth M. Nuss retired as Vice President and Dean of Students from Goucher College in Baltimore, Maryland, in 2001. She earned the bachelor of arts from the State University of New York at Albany, the M.Ed. from the Pennsylvania State University, and the Ph.D. from the University of Maryland. Prior to Goucher College, she served as Executive Director of the National Association of Student Personnel Administrators (NASPA). She previously worked at Penn State, the University of Maryland College Park, and Indiana University. She received NASPA's Dissertation of the Year Award in 1982 and the Fred Turner Award for Outstanding Service to NASPA in 1996.

Patricia A. Rissmeyer serves as the Vice President for Student Affairs at Emmanuel College in Boston. She has held positions at Canisius College in Buffalo, New York; Saint Mary's College in Notre Dame, Indiana; and the University of Massachusetts at Amherst. She holds a bachelor of science in education from the University of Hartford, a master of education from the University of Massachusetts, and a doctor of philosophy from the University at Buffalo. Currently, she serves on the editorial board of the *Journal of the National Association of Student Personnel Administrators* and on the Coordinating Council of the Colleges of the Fenway.

Gregory Roberts is the Executive Director and Senior Operating Officer of ACPA: College Student Educators International after serving as Vice President for Student Affairs at the University of St. Thomas–Minnesota for nearly 11 years. He is former president of the American College Personnel Association and has served on the boards of several civic organizations. He has been a long-standing member of several professional societies, including Omicron Delta Kappa and Phi Delta Kappa. He holds bachelor's and master's degrees from Indiana University–Bloomington, an educational specialist (Ed.S.) degree from University of Missouri–Kansas City, and a certificate in educational management from Harvard University Graduate School of Education.

Leah Ewing Ross is a doctoral student in educational leadership and policy studies at Iowa State University and also serves as the Managing Editor of the *Journal of College Student Development*. Prior to enrolling at Iowa State, she was Director of the NASPA National Academy for Leadership and Executive Effectiveness, and has worked in admissions for Randolph-Macon Woman's College, Vanderbilt University, and Agnes Scott College. Leah has a bachelor's degree in English from Mount Holyoke College and a master's degree in higher education from Florida State University.

John H. Schuh is Distinguished Professor and Chair of the Department of Educational Leadership and Policy Studies at Iowa State University. He is the author, coauthor, or editor of more than 200 publications. Currently he is Editor-in-Chief of the New Directions for Student Services Series and is Associate Editor of the *Journal of College Student Development*. Schuh has received the Contribution to Knowledge Award from the American College Personnel Association, and the Contribution to Research or Literature Award from the National Association of Student Personnel Administrators. Schuh received a Fulbright award to study higher education in Germany in 1994.

Julie M. Williams is a Project Associate with the Indiana University Center for Postsecondary Research. Her work with the center includes client information and data support for the College Student Expectations Questionnaire, the College Student Experiences Questionnaire, and the Beginning College Student Survey. She has worked previously in admissions/enrollment services and student development. She earned a B.A in business administration from Alma College, in Alma, Michigan, and an M.Ed. in college student personnel from Loyola University Chicago. She recently earned a post-master's certificate in institutional research from Indiana University, where she is a doctoral student in the Higher Education and Student Affairs program with a minor in Philanthropic Studies.

Penelope H. Wills has been recognized regionally and nationally for her contributions in student affairs. Her expertise is primarily in community colleges, while her career also includes liberal arts colleges and research universities. She has continued to teach at both the un-

dergraduate and graduate levels throughout her career. Her experience draws upon her involvement in communities in the southwest,
northwest, southern, and midwestern regions of the United States.
She is currently president of Northeast Iowa Community College.

Chapter One

Introduction

Thomas E. Miller

Colleges in the United States have usually had success conveying to students the institutions' expectations of student performance. There are many examples of how colleges do this. Institutions publish codes of conduct that establish standards of behavior for students and sets of rules, regulations, and procedures for addressing violations. Students entering college are given clear indications by their institutions regarding how they are expected to behave.

Institutions also make clear what standards must be met by students to attain degrees. Students are informed about how many courses they need to take, as well as which ones are needed for particular degrees. In the classroom, students receive syllabi that establish what instructors expect of students, what academic exercises will be conducted, and what performance levels will lead to various grading outcomes. In their academic work, in the residence halls, and on athletic fields, students are informed about what they are expected to do and how they are expected to perform. One might argue that students may not always pay careful attention to the expectations that institutions establish for them, but it seems clear that colleges articulate them, whether they are heeded or not.

Although the relationship between students and colleges is important to both, the explication of anticipated behavior may be a bit one-sided. Institutions expend considerable effort detailing what they expect of students, but it appears as though much less energy goes into determining what students expect of institutions. How does an institution go about determining what students expect? How do expectations of students affect their performance, and how does the performance of colleges compare to what students expect?

Nobody wants to deny that individuals sometimes have rather romantic notions about their futures. The optimism often associated with new ventures, like buying a car, starting a new job, getting married, or beginning college, helps one feel good about the risks involved in taking on new things. The aspirations of students should not be denied to them. The principles of aiming high and being personally ambitious are laudable ideas. However, some students have what would be considered unreasonable expectations of college and of themselves.

There are students who move into residence halls thinking that their roommates will become their lifelong friends. Residence hall administrators know that this is usually not the case. The optimism associated with the start of the first semester may have some students anticipating close, warm, and supportive relationships with their instructors and expecting wondrous stimulation in the classroom. Those conditions may unfold, but often they do not. Some students expect to be able to handle the academic responsibilities of college in a way similar to how they did in high school.

The preceding establishes that part of the challenge is to inform students about the realities of college and negotiate with them to help them form expectations that are sound. Colleges need to help students develop realistic pictures about the college experience. However, a necessary step is to determine what exactly students do expect. Institutions can hardly correct unrealistic notions of the experience without knowing they exist.

One of the most important sources of data for this project has been the College Student Expectations Questionnaire (CSXQ), a project managed at Indiana University. Institutions voluntarily participate in the project and administer a questionnaire to incoming students before they begin classes. The study helps institutions establish what their incoming students believe will occur in their college-going experience. It provides a glimpse into the ways in which students are uninformed or misinformed about college life and learning and allows institutions to frame programs and activities to adjust how students are prepared for their experiences. The background and research reliability of CSXQ are explained in Chapter 3 by George D. Kuh and colleagues.

Another useful institutional research tool is the Cooperative Institutional Research Program (CIRP), managed by the Higher Educational Research Institute at the University of California at Los Angeles. Several items in the CIRP survey point to information about what students might expect of the college experience, but one in particular collects responses about the likelihood, in the mind of the students, that they will have certain experiences, such as dropping out, getting a job, or participating in a sports team. The technical details of the CIRP research are explained in Chapter 9 by Gwendolyn J. Dungy, Patricia A. Rissmeyer, and Gregory Roberts.

One of the limitations of this project has been that available research is incomplete. Not much data are available regarding expectations held across the full range of student and institutional characteristics. Little is published about the expectations of students over 30 years old or for students who are attending college part time or those engaged in distance learning. In particular, there is little to compare the expectations of students with those characteristics with those who recently graduated from high school and attend residential colleges.

This project also focuses entirely on undergraduate students. Even were we inclined, the design team could not have included graduate and professional school students in its analyses, because studies about their expectations for their learning and educational experiences were not readily available.

Clearly, the landscape of higher education has changed, but research about the thinking of students regarding what they will encounter in college has not kept pace with those changes. We found little information about students pointed toward educational experiences that differ from historically traditional colleges and universities. We do not know much about the expectations of students attending trade or vocational schools or for those enrolled at proprietary institutions. There may be research about those institutions and those students, but we did not locate any that related to student expectations as compared to other types of colleges and universities.

Where do unreasonable expectations arise? What are the conditions under which students come to believe that their experiences will differ from what is known about college life and learning? Part of the answer is that the enrollment management process, beginning with the recruitment of students, is highly competitive. College recruiters are often evaluated on their ability to successfully enroll students and persuade them that a particular college will meet their needs and help them realize their dreams. Admissions and recruitment staff are less apt to be rewarded on the basis of how well they match student interests with college realities or on how well the students they recruit persist to degrees. This is a phenomenon with which higher education needs to come to grips.

At the same time, institutions should also evaluate carefully how well they meet the needs of the students they admit. The persistence rates we have observed clearly point to a problem, and it is short-sighted for colleges to see attrition as a problem (or failure) of the student. Action is needed to address these concerns. Enrollment management is a broad principle that guides many institutions and may help inform this issue. The principles of enrollment management involve broad engagement with students across the entire time of their connection with institutions, not just at recruitment. Institutions that subscribe to that notion may find better, more lasting connections with their students.

Another issue facing college admissions staff members is related to the nature and character of the high school generation now coming to college. Those coming directly from high school are certainly not the only student constituency that colleges serve; they are not even the majority, but they do form a cohort of sorts. The "new millennials" are different from previous generations and need to be understood by recruiters, administrators, and faculty members alike. Their interests, backgrounds, and nature give rise to new sorts of expectations, and those expectations must be understood. The institution that behaves as if students are the same as they were 10 or 20 years ago will be poorly prepared for the reality of this generation (Howe & Strauss, 2003).

Although it would be a worthy subject, this book does not address what institutions and faculty expect of students. That is a useful notion, and articulating clear (and high) expectations of students is one way in which institutions can affect what students expect of themselves and of their college-going experience. Establishing expectations is a way for institutions to engage students, set terms for their experiences, and reframe expectations that might be unreasonable or unrealistic. Therefore, although it is not the subject of this book, it is a worthy notion and not unrelated to the process of framing reasonable student expectations.

Contents and Organization

This book intends to describe what is known about the expectations of students in various aspects of their relationships with colleges, including the classroom setting, student services, campus life, and so forth. After discussion of those expectations, what is known about the real experiences of students is presented. The dissonance between expectations and real experiences is discussed, followed by suggestions, where appropriate, about what institutions might do to close any demonstrated gaps between expectations and experience. In recognition of the diversity of American higher education, there are two chapters that address how student expectations vary, respectively, by individual characteristics and by institutional type. The text also addresses how the expectations of other constituencies affect the student-institution relationship. Before the Conclusion is a collection of essays written from interviews with a collection of college presidents and leaders of professional associations of the higher educational community.

Chapter 1 presents the framework and collection of principles that guided the design of the text. Chapter 2 was written by Jeffrey A. Howard, a member of the psychology faculty at Eckerd College, with a contribution from Robert M. Gonyea of Indiana University. Howard explores the psychological premise of expectations, how unmet expectations affect us, and why it is useful for us to consider them in the context of student relationships with higher educational institutions. He describes the psychological framework for the establishment of expectations and the stress that we encounter when things do not turn out as we had expected. Howard explains the ways in which our expectations affect human behavior. His chapter is largely pointed toward the expectations associated with late adolescence, so aspects of his work apply best to students coming to higher education directly from high school, but many of the principles he presents are applicable to older students, also.

Chapter 3 was written by George D. Kuh, Robert M. Gonyea, and Julie M. Williams, all of Indiana University. They focus on research about student expectations relative to the teaching and learning environment and how those expectations differ from what actually happens. Indiana University is the home for the College Student Expectations Questionnaire (CSXQ), a study used at an increasing number of institutions to help them understand the exact nature of the expectations of their incoming students. Indiana is also the host for the College Student Experiences Questionnaire (CSEQ), an instrument that formed the basis for the CSXQ and which is easily used to compare expectations with experiences. Kuh, Gonyea, and Williams relied heavily on their own research to report how student expectations, particularly as related to learning, match up with what is known about their experiences.

Chapter 4 was written by Larry Moneta of Duke University and George D. Kuh. It addresses expectations regarding campus life and the environment. Moneta and Kuh establish that student expectations of the campus environment are most apt to be inaccurate and that colleges have substantial work to do to help create student expectations that are reasonable while also attempting to meet those that are fair. The writers also address expectations related to diversity issues as an area where higher education has much work to do.

Chapter 5 was written by Frank P. Ardaiolo of Winthrop University; Barbara E. Bender of Rutgers University; and Gregory Roberts, Executive Director of the American College Personnel Association (ACPA). It focuses on student expectations regarding services. While Chapter 4 described expectations regarding the culture of the campus or the environment in which students find themselves, this chapter addresses another aspect of the campus experience that is important to students: the services that support their learning and the college experience. Student expectations regarding everything from health services to career services to counseling services or even parking and transportation services all lead to some anticipation regarding service. Those expectations are not always reasonable, and they often come at a very high cost, as Ardaiolo, Bender, and Roberts explain.

Chapter 6 is by John H. Schuh and Leah Ewing Ross of Iowa State University, and it addresses expectations and realities regarding the cost of higher education. The rising cost of a college education has attracted much attention in recent years. Schuh and Ross explore how the expectations of students and their families compare with the reality of college costs. The research they describe points to the fact that students and their families overestimate the cost of college attendance, but that overestimation has little to do with decisions about attending college. The authors point out that their analysis is limited to the subset of the student population that is dependent on their parents. That limitation is driven in part by the tremendous complexity of the balance of the student population and the difficulty in reaching useful conclusions and making generalizations about them.

Chapter 7 was written by Thomas E. Miller, and it is on student persistence and degree attainment and how expectations differ from realities. Degree attainment is a fundamental goal of most, but not all, college students, and this chapter explores how far short of that expectation is the reality. The chapter presents a series of recommendations for action to help close the gap, all related to improving institutional performance rather than lowering student expectations.

Chapter 8 is by Susan R. Komives of the University of Maryland and Elizabeth M. Nuss, former Executive Director of the National Association of Student Personnel Administrators (NASPA). They write about expectations related to outcomes of college other than degree attainment. They use a set of outcomes from college adapted from previous work of Hamrick, Evans, and Schuh (2002). The outcomes they detail are that students become educated persons, skilled workers, life skills managers, self-aware and interpersonally sensitive individuals, and democratic citizens. Nuss and Komives describe how the college experience induces those outcomes and how they relate to the expectations of students.

Chapter 9 is by Gwendolyn J. Dungy, the Executive Director of NASPA; Patricia A. Rissmeyer of Emmanuel College; and Gregory Roberts. They write about how student expectations vary by individual demographic type. One of the key aspects of this project has been the acknowledgment of the great diversity of the students engaged in American higher education and the awareness that much of what we write involves broad generalizations that capture only an aspect of the population of enrolled students. This chapter explores some of the ways in which expectations vary by individual student characteristic.

Chapter 10 is by Wilma J. Henry and Harold L. Nixon of the University of South Florida and Penelope H. Wills, recently appointed President at Northeast Iowa Community College. They address how expectations of students vary by institutional type. In addition to the diversity of the student community described in part in Chapter 9, another condition of American higher education is the great diversity in institutional type. There are far more types of institutions than we were able to study, but this chapter does describe ways in which students attending two-year institutions differ in their expectations of college from those going to four-year schools. The chapter also reviews how expectations vary between the public sector of colleges and universities and the private sector, and it concludes with a review of the unique expectations of students enrolling at historically black colleges and universities.

Chapter 11 is by Barbara E. Bender, John Wesley Lowery, and John H. Schuh from the University of South Carolina. They write about the expectations of higher education held by other constituencies, such as government, communities, parents, the media, and so forth. Over the past decade the expectations of parents for colleges and universities have elevated and become more specific, as have the expectations of government and legislators. The interests of alumni and donors have had a growing impact on interactions that institutions have with students. The employment community also has dynamic, changing expectations of institutions. For many institutions, relationships with surrounding communities and neighborhoods can have a dramatic effect on how they interact with students. All of these relationships are laden with expectations of performance by institutions, and all of them affect how institutions relate with students. This chapter explores the complexity of those expectations.

Chapter 12 was written by Thomas E. Miller and Barbara E. Bender and is a summary of comments gathered from conversations with college presidents and executives of higher educational professional associations, following their review of the principles of the text and an early prepublication edition of this book. When the early drafts of the manuscript were completed, each was sent to one of 12 leaders in higher education. After their review of the text and its principles, the reviewers were interviewed for their reactions. The essays that resulted were reviewed by them prior to being published, and the chapter is a compilation of those essays. The writing team is deeply indebted to those 12, for their time, attention, and diligence.

Chapter 13 was written by Thomas E. Miller; it is the Conclusion of the text and summarizes the key issues presented in the book. It points toward the substantial value of institutional study of student expectations and analysis of performance against those expectations.

Conclusion

The writing team hopes that this book will stimulate interest in understanding student expectations on the part of higher educational institutions and their leaders. If what students think will occur in college has the sort of effect we think it does on the relationship between those students and their institutions, it is worth our attention. When the expectations of students are not reasonable, institutions have an obligation to negotiate better ones with them. When student expectations that are reasonable are still not met, institutions have a performance obligation that should be addressed.

References

Hamrick, F. A., Evans, N. J., & Schuh, J. H. (2002). *Foundations of student affairs practice: How philosophy, theory, and research strengthen educational outcomes.* San Francisco: Jossey-Bass.

Howe, N., & Strauss, W. (2003). *Millennials go to college.* Great Falls, VA: LifeCourse Associates.

Chapter Two

Why Should We Care About Student Expectations?

Jeffrey A. Howard

Imagine that you are planning to host a large party. You plan a generous budget and even ask friends to contribute, which they gladly do. You are going to leave no detail to chance, because you want the party to be a great success. You have put a lot of thought into the amenities, food, tables and chairs, music, games, and fun activities, and various kinds of entertainment. You have hired a staff to set up and to make certain that the guests' needs are met. When the guests arrive, everyone swings into action, and everywhere you look, guests are laughing, having a great time, participating in the interesting activities that you had arranged, and introducing themselves to the other guests.

Well, not everywhere. As you survey the activities, you spot a number of guests who appear to not be engaged in the festivities. They are milling around, clearly not having the time of their lives. Some seem bored. Some seem upset. Many are leaving. As you make your way over to these guests, you can't help but wonder what the problem is. Was the staff rude? Has something been overlooked? Your anxiety grows, fearing that these new friends have been treated badly and are feeling angry or hurt.

Note: The editors acknowledge a contribution by Robert M. Gonyea, of Indiana University, to this chapter.

As you finally catch up with several guests who are leaving, you ask simply, "What's wrong? Was someone unkind? Were you mistreated in some way?" "No," they respond. "Nothing like that. Your people were very nice." The guests search for a way to articulate exactly what they are feeling. Their eyes scan the party scene absently and then one, speaking for the group, remarks, "It just wasn't what I had expected."

You are stunned. "Not what they had expected?" What did they expect? Why did they not understand what they were coming to do? Had you contributed, in some inadvertent way, to their false expectations? What are they thinking and feeling? You stand there, watching the backs of their heads fade away, and wonder what it means to have a successful party. Part of you feels that the party suddenly is much less successful. Another part of you wonders: Is it fair to have my party judged by how many guests leave early?

When it comes to understanding why people do what they do, the incredible complexity of human motivations and behavior becomes highly salient. Where does one start? Fortunately, a number of theorists have provided us with useful tools to understand the relationships among past experiences, the development of mental representations of these experiences, and the use of these schemas to perceive and evaluate the world around us when we decide how to act. When our schemas fail to help us function effectively in our world, there are both cognitive and emotional consequences. The ongoing task of perceiving and operating in our world is no less than the necessity of adapting and adjusting to each day's challenges. When the challenges involve major life changes, we are tasked to change our "self" as well as our behaviors. Even when the life changes are positive, like starting a new job or going off to college, we are faced with figuring out the demands of the new situation and adjusting our behavior to meet those demands. When our past experiences, our cognitive and emotional resources, and our self-perceived abilities seem to be inadequate for success, anxiety and stress reactions are inevitable. We now know that how adequately we cope with these stressors has an impact on our mental and physical health. Can we use these theoretical tools to identify strategies that will help us to better understand and respond to the disaffected guests?

A thorough discussion of the psychological theories and empirical research related to the relationships between thought and actions would require a book in itself, and that is not the purpose of this chapter. Rather, we can safely assume that the actions that we choose, and the reactions that we have to new experiences, are not random and capricious, but are inextricably linked to an internal accumulation of knowledge, beliefs, understandings, and resultant expectations that we have acquired over a lifetime and bring along with us to every situation. In the chapters to come, the specific contents of these expectations as they relate to higher education are discussed in detail. This chapter is intended to orient us to the nature and function of expectations, how they play a role in behaviors, and the well-understood psychological outcomes of expectations that fail to match up with reality.

The Meaning of Expectations

In everyday conversation, of course, we use the word *expectations* to refer to all those things that our past experiences have taught us to realistically anticipate. Expectations are not "hopes" in the sense that sometimes we hope for things that we don't realistically expect to actually happen. We might hope to win the lottery, but if we understand the odds of winning, we don't realistically expect that we will. Expectations are based on our best understanding of our past experiences. In fact, our expectations are so fundamentally what we *predict* will actually turn out to be the case that we are surprised if they don't turn out as we anticipated. We have expectations for ourselves, for others, and for the world in which we live. We know that sometimes others "let us down," but nonetheless, we continue to have expectations. We have expectations for what behaviors are appropriate in various situations. We have expectations about the things that will happen to us. We have expectations that investments will yield certain returns. Of course, students have expectations about college life. The new college student arrives full of anticipations or expectations for every aspect of college life. These will likely be partly fantasy and idealistic, but they are more than just hopes. The new student will be oriented to questions like, "Is this what I expected, or not?" "Can I be successful here?" "Is this a good fit for me?" And in egocentric mode, "How does this apply to me?" Before considering the psychology of expectations and how they function to guide behavior, however, it is useful to understand the thinking processes of adolescents and young adults.

Characteristics of Late-Adolescent Thought

To better understand the nature of the thinking that goes on in the head of the new traditional-age college student, we must first examine what is known about the cognitive capacities, abilities, and limitations of the late adolescent. Understanding that there is a wide range of intellectual powers and an even wider range of educational preparation for higher education represented in every freshman class, it is still possible to explore the universal characteristics of adolescent thought with the goal of identifying key factors that will shape their perceptions of their world and their responses to it.

Starting at least with Jean Piaget in the 1920s, developmental psychologists have known that the thinking of the late adolescent or young adult is much more nuanced, capable, and complex than that of younger children. Young adults can think abstractly, systematically, and scientifically, in a manner that is necessary for higher education. For example, if you ask a 10-year-old, "What is love?" or "How do you know when someone loves you?" the child will probably answer with something like, "Love is when someone cares for you." "When Mom takes care of me I know that she loves me." The same questions put to a 17-year-old would result in different responses. He or she might reply that "there are different kinds of love that apply to different kinds of relationships. Furthermore, it's difficult to know when you love someone and when they love you. Sometimes people love you and they don't tell you, and sometimes people will tell you that they love you but they really don't." Not only do young adults understand qualitative differences in the nature of the concept, but they understand the contextual, or relative, meaning of the concept. They may have had personal experiences, even painful ones, that have taught them to pay attention to certain cues from others in order to decode the other's true motivation. Such sophistication of thought is due, in part, to more years of experience. But to a greater extent it is the result of a maturation process in the brain (after puberty) that creates new capacities for thought that the 10-year-old can't yet imagine. For the younger child, the world is a fairly straightforward place, and when adults tell you that the answer to a question is "complicated," it simply means that they don't know the answer. For the late adolescent, the new capacity to see shades of gray can be overwhelming, as the world suddenly becomes a much more involved and confusing place than it was a few years earlier.

Research illuminating the nature of adolescent thought has identified the dramatic accomplishments in intellectual ability of adolescents relative to younger children. Keating (1990) identified four distinctive characteristics of adolescent thought: reasoning hypothetically, thinking about thinking, planning ahead, and thinking beyond conventional limits. These new abilities enable the young college student to engage in new levels of thinking that can transcend the immediate situation. They can think systematically and more abstractly. They can identify and determine the implications of all possible combinations of a set of variables. They can rethink fundamental issues of relationships, morality, religion, and politics, and often see the glaring discrepancy between the ideal and the real. They tend to be critical of the status quo and keen to point out conditions of unfair or hypocritical policies. Together, these cognitive abilities create the intellectual potential to engage in advanced academic activities.

Reasoning hypothetically allows the late adolescent to generate and consider both possible and impossible scenarios. Unlike younger children, who are more bound to thinking about things as they are, adolescents can imagine conditions that have not yet happened or are contrary to fact. This ability allows the college student to consider, for example, whether going to a party might result in people getting drunk and out of control. By being able to anticipate possible scenarios, the chance to be prepared to handle them improves. As the student anticipates the future, possible scenarios will be imagined and mentally played out as a cascading series of unfolding events. The student has the ability to hold a given scenario in mind and mentally play it against other possible scenarios, and to determine the alternative outcomes. That the student can do this, of course, doesn't necessarily mean that he or she always does so, much to the consternation of parents and teachers. Indeed, from the student's perspective, "thinking too much" becomes a danger to be avoided, as imagined hypothetical realities can easily spin out of control, and, given their lack of experience in the "real" world, students can become overwhelmed and fearful in the face of imagined (however implausible) outcomes. The common experience of the "imaginary audience," the feeling that everyone is watching your every move and laughing behind your back at your every miscue, is largely due to this capacity to leap mentally to possible outcomes and the failure to accurately screen out implausible ones.

The ability to mentally project into the future, to plan ahead, may lead the adolescent to take on much more ambitious projects, to get a job to earn money for a goal, and to conspire with friends. Educators understand that this new ability, like any new tool, is not used skillfully at first, and requires training and practice to be able to do well. High schools typically teach students to use daily planners or agendas to physically plot out future assignments and to use planning skills to juggle multiple tasks. At the college level, the situation radically changes. Unlike the high school teachers who told students what was due for tomorrow's homework, college professors distribute a syllabus that typically expects the students to determine what work needs to be done to prepare for exams and assignments and to decide for themselves when to do it. This is a significant challenge for most students and is known by that dreaded phrase *time management*.

The idealism of youth has been a subject of discussion and analysis since the times of Plato and Cicero, and probably earlier. The capacity to think outside of conventional limits brings a naive sense of the ideal in conflict with a realization that the real world often falls short. Late adolescents may become cynical and hypercritical of the adults who are currently running the world. They may passionately embrace environmental or political causes. They may pine for the "perfect man" or "perfect woman" in the face of numerous imperfect specimens around them. They may imagine the perfect college, with the perfect major, with perfect caring professors who embody the highest wisdom, and cheering on their college sports team, which, of course, has a perfect season. What's been called the "personal fable," an unrealistic belief in one's own specialness and destiny, is an interesting upshot of this thinking (Elkind, 1979). For the prospective college student in such a state, a dose of realism is both necessary and actively resisted. The risk is too great that one would "stop dreaming" or "resign oneself" to the mediocre life that they observe in so many adults. The late adolescent is a natural risk taker, and why not reach for more, now that one can imagine it?

That young college students mentally minimize the possible negative outcomes of risky behaviors is well known. It is undeniably a necessary condition for the late adolescent to leave home and venture into an uncertain world. If the college student really understood how inexperienced and unprepared he or she was for the tasks of adulthood, and how dangerous the world can be, he or she would probably never leave home. Students engage in so many dangerous behaviors, experimenting with lifestyle alternatives, drinking, sexuality, and the like, that it's easy to question whether they have achieved any of the higher-order thinking skills discussed previously. They know, intellectually, the dangers of smoking, not wearing a seat belt, drinking too much, STDs, and not getting enough sleep, but they behave as if they are "bullet proof." Unconsciously, they may exaggerate their own abilities to handle difficult and risk-filled situations. Many studies of late adolescents have revealed just this kind of feeling. There is a dark side to these newly acquired cognitive abilities.

Juxtaposed against these impressive cognitive abilities is the observation that late adolescents don't use these mental capacities as much as they should. They fail to anticipate the consequences of their actions. They fail to take into account others' perspectives. They don't plan ahead. They focus not on important world affairs but on pop culture and the latest cool style. And they seem so focused on "self" that older adults refer to them as "the Me generation" or "self-centered" youth. They certainly are more focused on "self," but *selfish* is not the appropriate word. Indeed, late adolescents today generate a huge number of volunteer hours in service to others in their communities.

A more appropriate way to see this pervasive emphasis on self is as a temporary resurgence of egocentrism. Egocentrism, in the preschool child, is the inability to see perspectives other than one's own. With the adolescent's new cognitive abilities comes the recognition that the world is an overwhelmingly complex place. Not to mention the hypothetical possibilities! One can't begin to attend to, much less process, all of the many stimuli received through the senses. One has to narrow down the stimuli to the essential ones, namely, "only those relevant to me."

The egocentric reaction of late adolescence is a self-defense mechanism, and reminds us that the complexity of the world—which older adults can "put in perspective," "prioritize," and which is so familiar that it is "taken for granted"—is not so manageable for the new intellectual. From the student's viewpoint, it makes good sense to focus exclusively on the things that matter to me and my life. The compression of reality through the filter of personal relevance is frustrating to professors who try to interest the freshman in great books, and faculty members bemoan the paucity of philosophical debate in dorm life. But the activities that are taking place in the new student are profound in a different sense, and they underscore the importance of college as a truly developmental institution. In this focus on self is the active process of sorting out the personal significance and relevance of all of the adolescent's daily experiences. With the transition to college comes the need to adapt to the new environment. With it comes the explicit expectation that the student will grow and change into whatever he or she will be in the future.

Search for Adult Identity

The older adolescent or young adult is on a passionate quest to answer the "Who am I?" question. In the 1950s, Erikson identified this as the fundamental psychosocial task of adolescence. He defined identity largely in terms of one's vocational role in adult society and the ideological commitment to one's adult value system. Since then, the concept of personal identity has expanded to be only partially related to work role and has become a self-definition with much more expansive ambitions. Erikson (1968) used the term "identity crisis" to communicate that the need to have an acceptable answer to the "Who am I?" question takes an urgent and compelling place in the consciousness of the adolescent.

There are additional forces at work in today's students that also force the issue of identity and go beyond those discussed by Erikson. One such factor is the financial and emotional independence that traditional-age students experience when they go away to college and don't have parents to supervise and structure their activities. They are also freed from the behavioral expectations of those in their old high school crowd and have the opportunity to "revision" themselves in a place where no one knows them and they can, theoretically, be whatever they want to be. The many choices are arrayed right before their eyes, especially if they attend a college with a high degree of diversity. They may discover that others have traits that they admire and would like to emulate. The new college student experiences encouragement to be open-minded, break free of other's expectations in the past, and proactively create a new identity.

Another factor in forcing identity resolution is the mobility of students today. They find themselves in new, unsupervised situations where behavior choices have moral and value implications. Invitations from peers to engage in new activities require decisions revolving around a central concern: "Is this me or not me?" Students do things and then ask themselves, "Why did I do that?" Without a values "compass" (Covey, 1989) that a secure sense of identity affords, one is subject to peer pressure and the whim of the moment. When one can't decide who one is at a core level, no integrity is possible. The judging mind of the student finds this difficult.

When all of these pressures are examined, the overarching factor in the need to resolve the identity crisis is the student's capacity to think abstractly about the nature of identity itself, and in particular to think reflectively about the self, using the new cognitive abilities discussed earlier. The capacity to entertain the possibility of alternative "selves," the ability to weigh different hypothetical outcomes against each other systematically, the need to reconcile desired, "ideal," and possible future selves with an appraisal of one's actual skills and potential, all force the late adolescent to feel the need to sort out options and move forward in a direction that is personally relevant.

This quest for identity, motivated by factors that push toward resolution of conflicting views of the self, is a journey or a process. Although the student is moving toward achieving a mature sense of his or her own, unique, personal identity, not all students of the same age will be at the same point in the journey as they begin college. Marcia (1980) has studied this process and has discovered four distinct types of students who are at qualitatively different points in the process. He refers to these four types as one's "identity status." The four status categories result from crossing two variables: exploration and commitment.

Those who have done a significant amount of exploration of possible identities and have matured to the point where they can choose a direction for themselves and commit to it are in the category of *identity achievement*. These students have come to strive for their own internalized goals and to rely on their own abilities to handle the daily tasks of college life. They have made well-thought-out commitments to occupational trajectories and to personal values. As a result, they seem more mature to others, and in a certain sense, they are.

Students who are in the *moratorium* status are still actively exploring possible future selves and resist commitment. They don't know who they are and they know it. Since they are actively exploring opportunities, they also seem relatively mature and are likely to make a commitment fairly soon. Like identity achievers, they are apt to hold highly individualistic conceptions of themselves and are mostly comfortable with their progress.

Those who commit to an adult identity without much exploration are in the category called *foreclosure*. The pre-vet student, who made a decision as a first grader who loved animals to grow up to be an animal doctor, may be in this category if no other career alternatives were ever considered. Erikson (1968) viewed this as a premature crystallization of the identity process, and it often involves an acceptance of traditional values internalized without question and deference to authority figures. Marcia (1980) has found that, as a result, these students may appear to be the best behaved.

The last category is the *identity diffusion* status. These are students who are neither committed to a chosen personal identity nor are they actively exploring. With no strong commitments to the past or to a specific future, they tend to drift along without much direction. They behave in a manner that looks like withdrawal, and they tend to report feeling out of place and socially isolated. One can wonder about the psychological underpinnings of students in this identity status, and speculate about their past experiences that left them with little connection to their past and little interest in planning for a particular future. They are certainly a vulnerable group, especially in a program that challenges students to excel and to become engaged in campus life.

Another important distinction among college students emerges from identity research by Berzonsky (1992). He demonstrated that students also have different identity styles that affect how they engage in college life. Some students are characterized by the *informational* style. They actively pursue new information and are eager to grow their nascent identities by adding new learning experiences. They are quick to become involved in such opportunities as they stretch their wings in new ways. The students with a *normative* style seek to fit in. A conformist tendency marks these students, and they will quickly try to be assimilated into the campus culture. Rather than trying to be unique and pursue internalized goals, they strive for acceptance and will be highly attuned to the implicit rules of the campus. The third style is the *diffuse/avoidant* group. Like Marcia's identity diffusion status (Marcia, 1980), they resist efforts to engage them in a developmental process.

Lessons from Research

The students arrive on campus with the mental equipment to fly to scholarly heights, but they are likely to be much more focused on issues seen as personally relevant to the developing self. There is a tremendous heterogeneity of skill level with these cognitive capacities among the new students. Some will be fairly dualistic, "black and white" thinkers, while others will be flaming relativists (Perry, 1970). Some will be impatient to get on with the courses in their major (decided on long ago), while an increasing number will be content to remain "undeclared." Some will be grateful for college efforts to engage them, while others will resist in active or passive ways. The importance of sorting out one's identity has a powerful impact on the emotional life and behavior of the student. All of this is a reminder that we may generalize only very carefully to the whole freshman class. In some ways, they are all alike. In other ways, we can identify subgroups with common characteristics. In still other ways, each student embodies a unique set of experiences and resultant expectancies. Knowledge of these can lead to strategically designed programs and sensitive interventions. A "one size fits all" approach will inevitably fit some better than others.

Perceptions, Expectations, and Outcomes

The discussion of adolescent thought and the primacy of their search for an adult identity is important as a context from which to understand new students' perceptions of the college environment and their assessment of how it fits their needs. The academic and social tasks undertaken by new college students, however, involve the same mental processes that older adults use in everyday situations, and these are the precise focus of many psychological theories. Theories, especially psychological theories, are most helpful when they identify key variables and allow interventions that can effectively direct a complex process to a desired outcome. A number of theoretical approaches are useful to understand the nature of expectations and how they operate to shape perceptions and evaluations, and to energize and direct behaviors.

When we look backward in time, we remember what we have experienced and interpret the meaning of those experiences through this framework. When we look to the future, the framework of schemas guides, shapes, and even provides our anticipations. A common way to say this is that our past experiences create expectations of what will happen in the future.

Psychologists have studied these cognitive processes in precise detail; it is beyond the scope of this chapter to review the many approaches that comprise modern cognitive psychology. A couple of examples, however, will illustrate how the expectations that individuals bring with them to a new situation completely determine their perceptions and evaluations of their new experiences. Modern psychology has revealed exactly how "one's perceptions are one's reality." If we want to understand how the departing guests experienced the party, we need to understand the primary importance of their preconceived expectations.

How does one decide how to act in a situation? Fifty years ago, Kelly (1955) claimed that people fundamentally act like scientists. Kelly thought that, in any given situation, people will analyze their experiences in similar situations encountered in the past and then form a plan of action, a hypothesis if you will, which would be "tested" in the present situation. For example, if a particular behavior was successful in the past and produced a result that I now want, I predict that if I do it now, the same thing should happen. Before contemporary cognitive science proved him correct, Kelly theorized that past experiences were used to create a system of constructs that captured the important meanings of past experience. If the hypothesized behavior was successful, the constructs worked as intended. If the behavior was a failure, the constructs failed. This would require revising the constructs. It would also result in significant levels of anxiety, since one's best guess how to act in a situation was proven wrong or inadequate.

If you want to predict a person's behavior in a given situation, what do you need to know about that person? Mischel (1979), a social learning theorist, discounted dispositional "traits" (for example, extroversion) for predicting behavior. Instead, he wanted to know what the person had learned in previous similar situations. Among the variables that he assessed are two that are relevant for our purposes: subjective values and expectancies. *Values* are worth assessing to find out if certain conditions or outcomes are important to the person or not. *Expectancies* include the anticipated outcome of a specific behavior in a situation, but also a person's confidence that he or she will be able to perform a specific behavior in a particular situation. Especially if a desirable outcome (for example, graduating) is highly valued, the confidence that one is able to perform the required behaviors is critical to persisting at the task.

Bandura's self-efficacy theory has become the most widely accepted articulation of the role of self-confidence in a specific situation. *Self-efficacy* is the belief that one can successfully carry out the behaviors necessary "to deal with prospective situations containing many ambiguous, unpredictable, and often stressful elements" (Bandura & Schunk, 1981, p. 587). In his review of the literature, McAdams concludes, "Research has suggested that self-efficacy judgments help determine whether we undertake particular goal-directed activities, the amount of effort we put into them, and the length of time that we persist in striving for the goals in particular situations" (2001, p. 207). One may feel highly self-efficacious in one realm, like schoolwork, and feel relatively incompetent and be low in self-efficacy in another, such as social life. High or low levels of self-efficacy are related to relative feelings of empowerment and control. Since these beliefs have been linked to stress and health outcomes, the expectations of self-efficacy are more than just trivial beliefs, and they relate to college experiences across age differences.

One essential additional point is that expectations are not merely rational, mental representations of past experiences. At one level, they surely are, and determining what the student has "learned to expect" from school is an important data source for predicting student reactions to college. At another level, the affective, or emotional, components of past experiences also factor into the student's ability to engage in the life of the institution and the challenges of the new environment—both academic and social. These affective components are deep in the psyche of the individual and have been shown to yield a hardiness in the face of stressors for some individuals as well as certain vulnerabilities in others.

Expectations are always in flux and are continuously revised in the face of new experiences. They can be viewed along a continuum from fairly superficial (for example, I expected class sizes to be smaller in my advanced courses in my major) to a core belief system about what to expect from others and from oneself (for example, I expect other people to keep promises, to be generally cooperative, and to return phone calls). It follows, then, that some expectations would be easily revised in the face of new information or conflicting experiences, whereas others would not. Although making such accommodations in one's schemas requires some effort, they are, after all, the essential task of learning. This would be especially true in institutions of higher education, where the explicit task is to "stretch" students to revise their earlier views and to challenge them to rethink truth statements that they held as they entered. Learning is not merely the adding of new knowledge in an attempt to beat back ignorance; it is the quest for new understandings. Sometimes those new understandings cut to one's core positions and beliefs. Such beliefs were not formed capriciously, but over a lifetime of experiences. As a result, some of them are highly salient, powerful, and relatively resistant to change. These might include a view of oneself that was prompted by a remark made by one's third grade teacher that still resonates in one's mind, or an experience of betrayal that left one suspicious of those who claim to be eager to be your friend.

The power of these accumulated experiences is to create two realities. One is a cognitive map for guiding behavior, making choices, and predicting outcomes. The other is an unarticulated emotional realm of hopes, fears, threats, aspirations, and confidence (or the lack of it). The emotional legacy of previous experiences is probably less open to revision in light of new experiences than is the cognitive framework one uses to guide behavior. Contemporary adult attachment theory, for example, has shown that cognitive "working models" of close interpersonal relationships, and the affective concomitant aspect of feeling "secure" or "insecure" with others (especially strangers), can predict which incoming freshmen, both of traditional age and older, may be at heightened risk for poor adjustment to college. Howard, Morey, and Briancesco (2003) found that freshmen with an insecure "fearful" attachment status, measured in the first weeks of the semester, showed significantly poorer adjustment than the more "secure" freshmen. Individuals who are categorized as fearful have expectations that others are not trustworthy and may even be dangerous. Moreover, they evaluate their own capacities to function successfully as inadequate. By October of their first semester, the fearful students had significantly more visits to both the campus counseling center and the health center, had a greater number of psychological and health symptoms, and rated themselves as significantly lower on the Physical/Emotional Adjustment Subscale of the Student Adaptation to College Questionnaire. Three years later, 75% to 90% of the more secure freshmen groups were still enrolled, but only half of the fearful students persisted to the fall of their senior year.

Clearly, the cognitive and affective expectations one brings to college have an impact on how college life is perceived and experienced, both in the classroom and beyond. What do we know about the consequences of incongruence between expectations and reality?

Psychological Contract Theory

A novel perspective on student expectations can be acquired from psychological contract theory (PCT), an emerging line of inquiry in the field of work psychology (Patterson, 2001). Rousseau (1995) defines the psychological contract as an individual's subjective beliefs regarding the terms and conditions of an exchange agreement with another party. The exchanges are contracts because they entail paid-for promises and reciprocal obligations, as in the terms and conditions of a job (for example, a company pays wages in exchange for productive work). However, unlike a written contract, the psychological contract is composed of beliefs and perceptions. Both sides hold implicit understandings of the terms and conditions, and may not share a common understanding.

Psychological contracts are built upon the formation of mental models or schemas, which help people, through interpretation and inference, to fill in the blanks created from missing information. A *schema* is the cognitive organization of conceptually related elements (Rousseau, 2001). Through schemas it is possible to make good guesses in the absence of all requisite information. Schemas are both culturally and situationally determined, thus some elements may be widely shared by people who work in the same setting or occupation or by members of a particular societal culture. Others may be idiosyncratic, tied to particular individual experiences with their current employer throughout their career. For example, what it means to be a "professor" is a schema developed by experience (Rousseau, 2001). Most people, educators and non-educators alike, have an idea of what a professor is. But to the layperson, the most recognizable aspect of the professorship is that of teaching and perhaps stereotypes that involve older men with beards and corduroy jackets with elbow patches. Yet, professors themselves have a more elaborate understanding of the role, which includes teaching, research, writing, dissertation committees, and service to the institution.

Psychological contracts are dynamic; they change throughout the tenure of the formal relationship and coincide with changes in the individual's perceptions. In order to influence the psychological contract, one must find a way to affect the individual's schema. This is done by stimulating individuals to more deeply consider information inconsistent with their schema. Changing a psychological contract, then, requires people to be motivated to process discrepant information more deeply than they would do otherwise.

Psychological Contract Theory and Higher Education

It is interesting to consider the application of psychological contract theory to higher education, and precedents already exist. For example, Sims (1992) uses the theory to build effective learning environments in employee training programs, and Danielson (1995) applies the theory to an examination of the role of course syllabi. Perhaps more relevant was Arnold and Kuh's (1999) use of mental models to describe differences among various stakeholders in higher education. They identified several diverse schemas at play in undergraduate learning and personal development that guide faculty, student affairs professionals, and different types of students (for example, traditional-age, commuter, and older students). Arnold and

Kuh argue that the perspectives of faculty, administrative staff, and various groups of students can differ widely and have the potential to create faulty communication and misunderstanding. Psychological contracts are thus a logical extension of their treatise.

It appears that three conditions must exist for PCT to be applicable in a particular setting: (1) an explicit formal, written, or contractual relationship; (2) a reciprocal exchange of things of value; and (3) subjective interpretations of the terms and conditions of the arrangement. The relationship between a student and higher education institution certainly qualifies. First, without question, the student and institution enter into a formal relationship through the admissions and matriculation process, during which many terms and conditions of the arrangement are communicated both verbally and in writing (for example, tuition cost, course requirements and grading system, campus housing policies, and student conduct codes). Many of these details are documented in campus policies and legal documents that comprise the formal contractual relationship between student and institution. In addition, this formal relationship is refreshed each time the student enrolls in another course or returns for another year.

Second, the student is expected to pay tuition and fees to the institution and in return expects to receive access to degree programs, grades and credit hours, interaction with faculty members, academic and social services, and so on. Also implicit in this agreement is the exchange of future benefits. Students expect that receiving a diploma will afford them greater career opportunities and earning power, while the institution desires lifelong contributions by its alumni.

Yet, third, not all expectations between student and institution are shared with clarity so as to ensure full mutual understanding. This is the realm of the psychological contract. Thus, the college experience is founded on an exchange of beliefs and expectations about the actions of the student in relation to the institution, and vice versa. For example, psychological contracts held by entering students involve expectations about learning conditions, course requirements, and the level of effort (participation) to be expended in courses and degree programs. These important aspects of the relationship are not always agreed upon.

Students develop psychological contracts with their college or university during the recruitment process. The psychological contract of the entering student may involve beliefs about the purpose of college (for example, finding a purpose in life? training for a specific career? being able to make more money?), the role of faculty members (for example, lecturer? career counselor? researcher? mentor? friend?), the role of the institution (for example, guardian? room and board provider? academic service provider?). It is likely that no two students enter college with exactly the same mental models and psychological contracts. Internalized past experiences produce a diversity of mental models as unique as each individual student. Still, because schemas are culturally and situationally determined, one might generalize that, for example, first-generation students from a rural background share some portion of their psychological contracts in common. The same might be true of the various racial and ethnic groups, older nontraditional students, or students whose parents have both earned doctoral degrees.

Whereas we often think of student expectations in precollege terms, psychological contracts are ongoing and dynamic throughout the student's relationship with the institution. Contracts are not cashed in on the first day of classes, but are filtered through experiences, shaped and continually refined as the institution either meets or violates them. Because of this, the institution has an ongoing opportunity to work with students to communicate and clarify mutual expectations.

Breach of Contract

Much of the research regarding psychological contract theory has to do with the meaning and consequences of violations of the contract (Robinson & Rousseau, 1994; Rousseau, 1995). A violation occurs when one party in a relationship perceives another to have failed to fulfill promised obligations. In employment settings, violations result in turnover, loss of trust, dissatisfaction, and attrition (Robinson & Rousseau, 1994). In higher education, one may speculate the same range of responses when the student believes the institution has failed to fulfill its obligations. It may be, for example, that the student perceives the institution is not challenging enough, that faculty members are unapproachable, or that academic and social support systems are not meeting the student's needs. At any rate, the student who perceives a violation is at risk of disengagement, lack of trust in the institution, or attrition (drop out or transfer). Accepting that motivation and trust are vital in a healthy learning environment, such violations can impede academic performance.

Outcomes Resulting from Incongruence of Expectations and Reality

The incongruence between the expectations of the freshmen and the reality of their actual experiences requires an adjustment. The failure of the cognitive map to match the territory, and the potency of emotional needs and sensitivities, can lead to the potential for overwhelming stress and anxiety. Like an immigrant coming to America, the new students' past experiences may or may not serve them well as they try to create new lives for themselves. They will misjudge situations. They will make mistakes. They will find that there are things that they didn't expect. As we consider the transition to becoming a college student, both traditional-age and non-traditional students face the same situation, and a major life change. Transitions like going away to start college are, by definition, stressors. Stress is usually associated with major life transitions (Selye, 1956), but it can also be the cumulative result of many little things, as in the straw that broke the camel's back (Holmes & Rahe, 1967). With his classic work in the 1950s, Selye launched the contemporary field of psychoneuroimmunology, the study of how psychological stresses negatively impact specific components of the immune system and affect resistance to disease. When threatened, the body responds with an effort to defeat the offending germs (or stressor) by mobilizing defensive resources. If the stressor continues, the body's resources are exhausted, leaving the body in a weakened and much more vulnerable state. Such is the case with college students who are constantly exposed to germs from their dorm mates but don't succumb to illness until midterm exams time, when the workload becomes overwhelming, that is, stressful. As long as one still expects to be able to get the work done, there is little stress. When the deadlines loom large and ominous, and one realizes the impossibility of completing all of the assigned tasks, the toll is obvious.

Transitions, assignments, and the multiple tasks of daily life present challenges. They require coping. If one is confident that one's coping resources are adequate, these things will be seen as a challenge but not impossible. The key is to understand how the situation is perceived through a cognitive appraisal process. Lazarus (1966) provided a useful model of this process presented schematically in his General Model of Reactions to Stressors (see Figure 2.1). Fundamental to this appraisal process is the assessment of one's abilities relative to the demands of the situation. The cognitive appraisal process begins with expectations and compares an assessment of the "threat" or challenge, on the one hand, to an assessment of one's capacity to successfully deal with the challenge on the other. How "threatening" is the challenge? If the decision is that "I can't do this," and it is subjectively and explicitly important that I do it, then I'm in trouble. I get nervous, then anxious, and then stressed, and then . . . I will pull out all of my coping strategies. Taking a nap is a primitive defense mechanism (denial), but it may work for the moment. Of course, no work is getting done, and the chronic nature of living with stressors is apparent. A more adaptive strategy, like working harder, may be used, but I may get frustrated by failed attempts and the slowness of progress and react physiologically with arousal (triggering a fight-or-flight response) or with some other strategy designed to blow off steam (arousal). Drinking, drugs, vandalism, or just playing video games can distract one from facing the reality of the threat, and one may feel better in the short term. Clearly there is a need for healthy and positive coping strategies. This is not a trivial goal, since the emotional impact of these stressors results in rampant depression on college campuses, "acting out," self-medicating, and risk for suicide.

The point here is to shine a bright light on the role of expectancies in the appraisal process. For example, if the student expects to be able to write well, based on high school success, and college writing assignments receive failing grades, there is a mismatch. Many high schools require little writing, and those assignments are often possible with a "night before it is due" strategy. Students may sincerely believe that they do their best work under pressure. Of course, that may be because they don't do any work until they are under pressure, convinced that they will be, once again, able to pull it off. These expectations will be tested in various ways. Understanding these and other expectations enables us to comprehend the way that the students perceive their world and behaviors. It also helps us to understand their (not always rational) responses to their experiences.

Figure 2.1 Lazarus's General Model of Reactions to Stressors

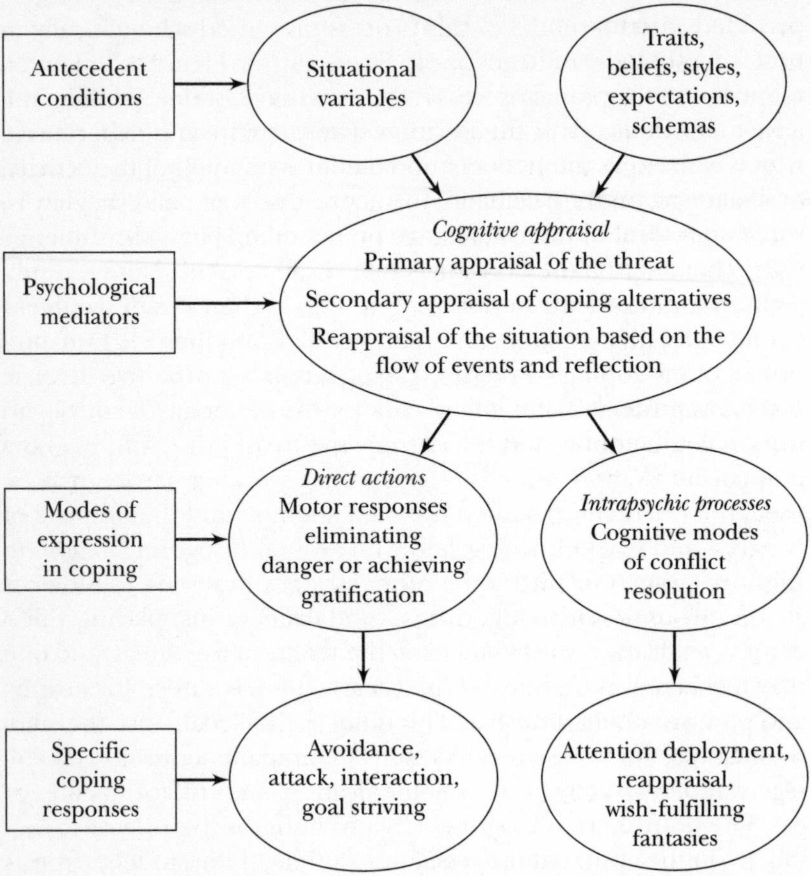

Antecedent conditions	Situational variables	Traits, beliefs, styles, expectations, schemas

Cognitive appraisal
Primary appraisal of the threat
Secondary appraisal of coping alternatives
Reappraisal of the situation based on the flow of events and reflection

Psychological mediators

Modes of expression in coping

Direct actions
Motor responses eliminating danger or achieving gratification

Intrapsychic processes
Cognitive modes of conflict resolution

Specific coping responses

Avoidance, attack, interaction, goal striving

Attention deployment, reappraisal, wish-fulfilling fantasies

Source: Lazarus (1966).

Not all college students are stressed out and unhappy, of course. Some are fine, and are thriving. They are able to find what they need to be successful and soon feel that their college world is their new "home." There is another group that we should remember. Some students report being chronically bored with their classes and the whole college scene. Csikszentmihalyi (1977) launched a movement that has provided a more comprehensive view of the relationship between one's abilities and the challenges one faces. If the challenges are too great for the student's skill level, then anxiety and stress result. If the student perceives the challenge level as below the skill level, then boredom and anxiety of a different sort result. These students may become chronically disengaged as well, and may begin to entertain thoughts of transferring to one of the other schools that attempted to recruit them. Ideally, the correct balancing of challenge and skills results in an intrinsically motivating experience, which empowers the person and facilitates creativity, productivity, and learning. As we have seen, the actual challenge and skill levels, while important in themselves, are perceived through the student's expectations and past experiences. This model has been used in a variety of educational contexts, most recently in a number of Web-based interactive programs. The very first step to designing an educational experience is to assess student expectations of both their own capabilities and the challenges or demands that would match those expectations.

Conclusion

The transition to college is an opportunity to reinvent one's "self" and form a new identity. For those with the psychological and personal resources, it can be an exciting time of growth. For all new students, it will be a time of coping with new challenges, sizing up their skills and abilities, and searching for an appropriate and exciting educational trajectory that will take them to their professional goals. Given their thinking abilities, which can imagine new worlds but also create anxieties of apocalyptic proportions, it is likely that the transition to college will be a dynamic experience filled with discovery and excitement, with confirmation of some expectations and surprise when other expectations are disabused. There will be inevitable stressors and coping, as well as successes, confidence, and at times, boredom.

The student's responsibility to understand just what he or she is jumping into is clear. The student needs to "get with the program" quickly and make the required adjustments in expectations and behaviors. The sooner that the student adapts to the college environment, the less likely he or she is to be frustrated.

From the perspective of higher education, the need to discover the student's beliefs and expectations should be foremost in our minds as we design the educational environment and activities that will engage the student and produce the outcomes that are important to us, as well as our students. If students expect certain things to be true, they will operate in a manner consistent with those expectations. If we don't know what those expectations are, we will certainly be less effective in the goals that we have set for ourselves as educators. And it's not just market research. Every aspect of the students' behavior is the result of past learning, which has become a part of their mental framework of schemas, in combination with their (not always skillful) cognitive processing of their new experiences. Not only do people see things from their own point of view, research on perception has demonstrated that people often see what they expect to see. What do they expect? As they work on their new identities as educated persons, the unique filters of personal relevance that militate against irrelevant cognitions may guide students to see aspects of college life very differently than do their professors and university leaders. The task of trying to understand their college experience from the students' perspective must begin with gathering expectations data. Without that data, how can informed decisions be made? If an important goal is to avoid having so many guests leave the party early, we need to find out (in some detail) what they were expecting when they came.

References
Arnold, K., & Kuh, G. D. (1999). What matters in undergraduate education? Mental models, student learning, and student affairs. In E. J. Whitt (Ed.), *Student learning as student affairs work: Responding to our imperative.* Washington, DC: National Association of Student Personnel Administrators.

Bandura, A., & Schunk, D. H. (1981). Cultivating competence, self-efficacy, and intrinsic interest through proximal self-motivation. *Journal of Personality and Social Psychology, 41,* 586–598.

Berzonsky, M. D. (1992). Identity style and coping strategies. *Journal of Personality, 60*(4), 771–788.

Covey, S. (1989). *The seven habits of highly effective people.* New York: Simon & Schuster.

Csikszentmihalyi, M. (1977). *Beyond boredom and anxiety.* San Francisco: Jossey-Bass.

Danielson, M. A. (1995, April 19–23). *The role of the course syllabi in classroom socialization.* Paper presented at the Annual Meeting of the Central States Communication Association, Indianapolis, IN.

Elkind, D. (1979). *The child and society.* New York: Oxford University Press.

Erikson, E. H. (1968). *Identity: Youth and crisis.* New York: Norton.

Holmes, T. H., & Rahe, R. H. (1967). The social readjustment scale. *Journal of Psychosomatic Research, 11,* 213–218.

Howard, J. A., Morey, K. M., & Briancesco, L. A. (2003). Roots and wings: The role of attachment theory in adjustment to college. *Journal of College Orientation and Transition, 10,* 42–51.

Keating, D. (1990). Adolescent thinking. In S. S. Feldman & G. R. Elliott (Eds.), *At the threshold: The developing adolescent* (pp. 54–89). Cambridge, MA: Harvard University Press.

Kelly, G. (1955). *The psychology of personal constructs.* New York: Norton.

Lazarus, R. S. (1966). *Psychological stress and the coping process.* New York: McGraw-Hill.

Marcia, J. E. (1980). Identity in adolescence. In J. Adelson (Ed.), *Handbook of adolescent psychology* (pp. 159–187). New York: Wiley.

McAdams, D. P. (2001). *The person: An integrated introduction to personality psychology* (3rd ed.). Fort Worth, TX: Harcourt College.

Mischel, W. (1979). On the interface of cognition and personality: Beyond the person-situation debate. *American Psychologist, 34,* 740–754.

Patterson, F. (2001). Developments in work psychology: Emerging issues and future trends. *Journal of Occupational and Organizational Psychology, 74,* 381–390.

Perry, W. G., Jr. (1970). *Forms of intellectual and ethical development in the college years: A scheme.* New York: Holt, Rinehart, & Winston.

Robinson, S. L., & Rousseau, D. M. (1994). Violating the psychological contract: Not the exception but the norm. *Journal of Organizational Behavior, 15,* 245–259.

Rousseau, D. M. (1995). *Psychological contracts in organizations.* Thousand Oaks, CA: Sage.

Rousseau, D. M. (2001). Schema, promise and mutuality: The building blocks of the psychological contract. *Journal of Occupational and Organizational Psychology, 74,* 511–541.

Selye, H. (1956). *The stress of life.* New York: McGraw-Hill.

Sims, R. R. (1992). Developing the learning climate in public sector training programs. *Public Personnel Management, 21*(3), 335–346.

Chapter Three

What Students Expect from College and What They Get

George D. Kuh, Robert M. Gonyea,
and Julie M. Williams

What do today's college students expect from their college experience? How do they think they will spend their time? What do they think the campus environment will be like? More important, how do student expectations affect what they subsequently do in college and what they get from the experience?

Knowing the answers to these questions has always been important for institutions to establish appropriate academic standards and social norms that will make it possible for both the school and students to accomplish their objectives. Given the dramatic changes over time in various aspects of college cohorts, a systematic examination of student expectations is essential, as subsequent chapters make plain.

Recent reports, for example, suggest that today's students are more diverse than ever in virtually every way and want to acquire job skills more than general knowledge (Levine & Cureton, 1998). At the same time, record numbers of students are less prepared for college than their predecessors and are thought to be very different in some ways from previous cohorts of students. According to Diana Oblinger (2004), Executive Director of Higher Education at the Microsoft Corporation, today's undergraduates are highly digitally literate. "By age 21, the average student will have spent 10,000 hours playing video games, 20,000 hours watching TV, and 10,000 hours on the cell phone, but only 5,000 hours reading. . . . Their learning preferences are team-oriented, technological, structured, engaged, and experiential." It's not clear how shifting demographics, less-than-adequate academic preparation, and the technological orientation of today's students affect what they think college will be like and what they will do, at least in the first year of college.

In addition to these major shifts in attitudes and predilections, students attending the same college may differ in what they expect of and from college. These varying expectations are a function of previous academic achievement, family socioeconomic and educational backgrounds, previous educational opportunities, and exposure to information regarding college. Students also come to college with expectations for the nature of the campus community. The extent to which student expectations for campus life are congruent with what they experience early on appears to be an important factor for determining their subsequent satisfaction and overall success (Braxton, Hossler, & Vesper, 1995). Moreover, setting academic performance expectations and educational and career aspirations at appropriately high, challenging levels is necessary to maximize student learning and personal development (Ewell & Jones, 1993; Kuh, 1999, 2001).

In this chapter we briefly review some pertinent literature related to studying the expectations for college of the current cohort of undergraduate students and whether their experiences during the first year of college live up to their expectations. After summarizing some of the key studies on this topic, we examine the expectations and experiences of first-year college students using information from a national database. We conclude with some thoughts about what these findings suggest for first-year programs and related institutional policies and practices.

What the Research Says About Student Expectations for College

Though the published research linking student expectations, learning, and their overall satisfaction with the collegiate experience is limited (Kuh, 1999), there are at least two ways in which student expectations appear to influence what students do when they get to college (Olsen et al., 1998). First, expectations serve as a filter, or screening mechanism, through which students evaluate and make sense of the information they are presented and their experiences inside and outside the classroom. If one does not expect to do research with a faculty member, take part in cultural events, or study abroad, for example, chances are that opportunities to pursue these activities will be overlooked or dismissed out of hand. Expectations, therefore, shape subsequent behaviors and experiences (Feldman, 1981).

A second way expectations affect experiences is to be either a psychological catalyst or deterrent to certain types of behavior. According to some frameworks, such as expectancy theory, self-efficacy theory, and motivational theory, expectations predispose students to seek certain kinds of activities (Kuh, 1999; Olsen et al., 1998). This view suggests that expectations not only shape students' decisions, including how they spend their time in college, but also that these decisions ultimately influence students' overall performance inside and outside the classroom (Bandura, 1982; Dweck & Leggett, 1988; Lawler, 1981). Together, these two perspectives indicate that expectations influence the types of opportunities students pursue and thus are an important factor in shaping student success in the first year and beyond (Kuh, 2005).

As Howard discussed in Chapter 2, psychological contract theory (Rousseau, 1995) is another perspective with which to understand how expectations may influence the college experience. A psychological contract represents a student's tacit beliefs about the institution, specifically what the nature of one's relationship is with the college and its agents of socialization, such as faculty members, student life professionals, and peers. As part of the psychological contract, the individual student assumes there is agreement on the part of the individual and the institution that binds the parties involved to a particular set of behaviors (Rousseau, 1995). Of course, these understandings are almost always implicit; rarely are they made explicit or orally articulated by the student, though the institution may set forth expectations in catalogs and other materials, such as a code of conduct. When the student perceives the contract is breached, the student may lose trust in the institution as represented by peers or faculty, which may further result in such negative consequences as the student dropping out of school, transferring to a different institution, or otherwise becoming disengaged.

Research on Expectations and Experiences

Over the past several decades, studies suggest that students have a fair understanding of many of the aspects of what they will experience in the first year of college. Students appear to be reasonably accurate in terms of how they will manage the transition to college (Baker, McNeil, & Siryk, 1985; Berdie, 1966, 1968; Stern, 1970; Whitely, 1982), though some of this may be a function of self-fulfilling prophecy (Merton, 1948). One area where student expectations are less accurate has to do with estimating the nature of the campus environment. Braxton, Hossler, and Vesper (1995) found that first-generation student expectations about the college environment were less congruent with what they actually experienced. Learning more about this potentially deleterious mismatch between expectations and experience is especially important, because an increasing number of first-generation students are pursuing higher education and have less tacit knowledge about what college is like. As a result, if their perceptions and expectations are off the mark, they will be less well prepared to respond to the challenges inherent in the college experience, which will reduce the likelihood they will succeed academically, adjust socially, and persist to graduation.

In addition to the difficulties many students have in accurately describing and predicting what the college environment will be like, the extensity and intensity of the expectations many students hold for college often outstrip what they subsequently experience (Berdie, 1966; King & Walsh, 1972; Pate, 1970). This phenomenon, known as the "freshman myth," refers to the situation wherein student expectations surpass what they actually do or encounter when they get to college. First-time college students expect to study more, write more, and attend a wider range of cultural events than they subsequently do. In addition, they often find that college coursework is less intellectually challenging than they expected. Studies of the freshman myth phenomenon underscore some of the complexities of understanding the college student experience and suggest that mismatches between expectations and experiences can have a deleterious effect on student performance (Berdie, 1966; King & Walsh, 1972; Pate, 1970). This is confirmed by Braxton, Hossler, and Vesper (1995), who found that when expectations and experiences were relatively well aligned, students were more likely to be satisfied with their college experience and to persist to graduation. That is, when expectations closely match the reality they encounter, students appear to "fit" better with their college environment, which is a happy outcome for both students and institutions.

Olsen et al. (1998) examined the expectations and experiences of more than 900 first-year students at a large residential public Research I university, using the College Student Expectations Questionnaire administered to the same first-year students before fall classes started and the College Student Experiences Questionnaire just before the end of the following spring semester. The results suggested five tentative conclusions about the relationships between students' college expectations and subsequent experiences. First, the findings confirmed the freshman myth phenomenon, or the tendency for students to expect that they would do more of a wide range of activities and overstate the academic challenges college presented. Second, precollege academic characteristics and experiences influenced to some degree what students expected to do in college and what they subsequently did. Students with strong high school records of academic achievement were more likely to get involved in a range of activities during college. Third, student demographic and background characteristics had small, almost negligible effects on their collegiate experiences and outcomes, which was mildly surprising given that other research suggested a reasonably strong relationship among background, expectations, and experiences. Fourth, students whose expectations for college were relatively low were more likely to report college experiences that were congruent with their expectations starting college, compared with students with relatively high expectations. Finally, those students who indicated a desire to participate in a wide range of intellectual, social, and cultural activities during the first year of college were more likely to do so, compared with others whose expectations were more narrowly defined. As a result of their somewhat broader range of interests, these students also were more likely to subsequently participate in activities that are predictors of academic success and persistence.

On balance, the literature related to student expectations for college suggests that students' precollege characteristics and experiences shape their expectations to varying degrees. At the same time, student background characteristics fall well short of determining what students actually do during the first year. Additionally, expectations and experiences individually and together affect key outcomes of college, including academic performance, persistence, and self-reported gains.

Another Empirical Look at Expectation and Experiences

While the literature provides some instructive insights into the relationships between college expectations and experiences, a more comprehensive understanding is needed of how expectations affect experiences and outcomes, especially as colleges and universities attract more diverse, technologically savvy students, many of whom are the first in their families to go to college. More specifically, it would be helpful to have answers to the following questions:

1. What are the expectations first-year students have for college?
2. What factors account for differing levels of expectations among first-year students?
3. What role do student expectations play in shaping their actual experiences and perceptions of the campus environment? Of particular interest are the relationships between expectations and experiences of students from historically underrepresented groups, such as racial and ethnic minorities, students first in their families to go to college, and students from low-income families.
4. What patterns of expectations and experiences are associated with students' self-reports of making substantial progress toward desired outcomes after the first year of college?

To answer these questions, we turn to the national database of the College Student Expectations Questionnaire (CSXQ) and the College Student Experiences Questionnaire (CSEQ), instruments that are intentionally designed for such a task. In the next section, we describe the study and briefly summarize the key findings.

Comparison of College Expectations with College Experiences

The second edition of the CSXQ (Kuh & Pace, 1999) is a shortened version of the fourth edition of the CSEQ (Pace & Kuh, 1998), and was developed in 1997 for use in a Fund for the Improvement of Postsecondary Education (FIPSE) project (Schilling & Schilling,

1999). The CSXQ measures student expectations for college, including their attitudes and beliefs about how they will spend their time during their first year. It is typically administered prior to the start of fall classes to new students. The CSEQ assesses the quality of effort students devote to educationally purposeful activities. Quality of effort is the single best predictor of what students gain from college; this measure can also be used to estimate the effectiveness of an institution or its component organizations in promoting student learning. Generally, the CSEQ is administered in the spring of the academic year, so that students respond taking into account the range of activities in which they have taken part during that year.

In addition to student background questions, the CSXQ and CSEQ have 87 items in common that represent educationally purposeful college activities and perceptions of the campus environment. The CSXQ college activities items are organized into eleven categories that mirror those on the CSEQ: Library and Information Technology, Student Interactions with Faculty Members, Course Learning Activities, Writing Experiences, Campus Programs and Facilities, Clubs and Organizations, Student Acquaintances, Scientific and Quantitative Experiences, Topics of Conversation, Information in Conversations, Amount of Reading and Writing. The campus environment items represent expectations for how much emphasis the school gives to scholarly or intellectual qualities and the quality of the personal and social climate of the campus. This section also asks students what they anticipate relationships will be like with other students, faculty members, and administrative personnel and offices on the campus.

Taken together, the Course Learning and Information in Conversation CSEQ scales represent "integrative learning." Chickering (1974) argued that, in addition to involvement in academic and social experiences, learning requires integration of those experiences in efforts to apply what is learned to different settings (Davis & Murrell, 1993; Pike, 1995). Integration also is akin to learning for understanding, or what some call "deep learning," as contrasted with superficial learning (Miller, Imrie, & Cox, 1998). The latter emphasizes memorizing facts and ideas or completing discrete tasks, while the former emphasizes holistic understanding of ideas, reflection on the relationships among concepts, and how ideas can be used. Integration experiences may include students being asked to apply what they have learned to a different setting, bringing ideas from various sources together in a paper or project, or explaining material to another person such as a family member or in a tutoring relationship. Recent studies (Pike, 1999, 2000; Pike & Killian, 2001; Pike, Kuh, & Gonyea, 2003) using the integration construct offer additional evidence for the validity and utility of this concept in studies of the undergraduate experience, including the causal ordering of engagement, integration, and learning.

Data Sources

To answer the first two research questions about what accounts for differences in student expectations, we drew upon the CSXQ second edition national norms dataset, which contains more than 38,000 student records from 43 different colleges and universities. For the remaining research questions, we used data from eight institutions where we could match student responses to both the CSXQ and CSEQ. This produced a CSXQ-CSEQ panel data file with 970 complete cases. The demographic characteristics for each of these student samples are provided in Table 3.1.

We used factor analysis (principal axis) to create two measures of expectations that serve as dependent variables in the subsequent analyses. The first dependent variable is a single-factor score of 7 of the 11 CSXQ scales that measure student expectations for participating in various educationally purposeful activities, inside and outside the classroom (see Table 3.2). This factor, "Expectations of College Activities," has an alpha reliability coefficient of .82 and factor loadings that range from .53 to .70. The second expectation measure, "Campus Environment Expectations," is a factor score of seven scales measuring student perceptions of the campus environment (Table 3.2). It has an alpha reliability of .83 and factor loadings between .61 and .75.

The independent variables tested included institutional characteristics, student background variables, and estimates of student ability, motivation, and expected effort. Institution-level variables were the Barron's selectivity rating (*Barron's Profiles of American Colleges,* 2002), Carnegie classification (dummy-coded with "Master's" institutions as the reference group), and institutional control. Student-level predictors included gender, race (dummy-coded with "Caucasian

Table 3.1 Student Demographics of Samples

Student Demographics of Samples	CSXQ Norms Data	CSEQ-CSXQ Matched Sample
Total students in sample	38,013	970
Number of institutions represented	43	8
Gender		
Percentage female	56%	63%
Percentage male	44%	37%
Age		
Traditional-age (19 or younger)	96%	95%
First-generation	33%	26%
Race/Ethnicity		
White/Caucasian	81%	85%
Black	6%	2%
Latino	4%	2%
Asian	3%	2%
Expected/Enrolled in 12+ credit hours	92%	96%

other than Hispanic" as the reference group), expected major (collapsed into six categories: pre-professional, math and science, business, social sciences, humanities, and undecided, and dummy-coded with "pre-professional" as the reference group), amount of college expenses paid for by parents or family, first-generation status, commuting (driving) to campus, expected number of hours working on campus, expected number of hours working off campus, and positive orientation to college (how well the student expects to like college). We then used OLS regression to fit the best possible model using all available institution and student characteristics.

Structural equation modeling[1] (SEM) (Bentler, 1992) was the primary analytical approach to answer the remaining research questions. SEM permits testing of causal relationships among multiple variables based on a preconceived theoretical framework (Byrne, 1994). A structural equation model is a set of simultaneous, interrelated regression equations and is commonly represented in flow-type diagrams as shown in Figure 3.1.

Table 3.2 Expectation Factors

Expectation Factor	Alpha Reliability
Expectations for participating in educationally purposeful college activities	
Information in conversations	
Course learning	.82
Experiences with faculty	
Conversation topics	
Student acquaintances	
Clubs, organizations, service projects	
Writing experiences	
Campus environment expectations	
Emphasis on critical, evaluative, and analytical qualities	
Emphasis on developing aesthetic, expressive, and creative qualities	.83
Emphasis on developing academic, scholarly, and intellectual qualities	
Emphasis on the personal relevance and practical value of your courses	
Emphasis on developing vocational and occupational competence	
Emphasis on developing an understanding and appreciation of human diversity	
Emphasis on developing information literacy skills (using computers, other information resources)	

Confirmatory factor analysis of the activity and environment scales produced nine corresponding pairs of expectation and experience factors[2] (Table 3.3). The measurement models that appear in Table 3.3 represent only those items that had corresponding matches between the CSXQ and CSEQ surveys with strong factor loadings (that is, greater than .58). The reliability coefficients were acceptable, ranging from .60 to .86 for the "experience" factors and between .70 and .89 for the "expectation" factors.

**Figure 3.1   Conceptual Model for Testing Relationships
Among Expectations, Experiences, and Self-Reported
Gains in the First Year of College**

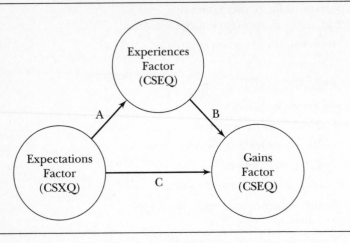

We also used confirmatory factor analysis to create the two additional dependent variables from the "Estimate of Gains" questions that ask students about how much progress they have made in a variety of learning and development outcomes since starting college (Table 3.4). The first dependent variable is called "Gains in General Education" (GENED), which is based on six Estimate of Gains items. We selected this outcome domain because most colleges and universities typically encourage or require enrollment in general education courses in the first year of college to help students acquire the knowledge, skills, and competencies that will prepare them for concentrated study in the major. Thus, we assume that student learning outcomes assigned to the first year of college have more to do with general education rather than learning within a major or acquisition of specific vocational skills.

The second dependent variable, "Gains in Intellectual Skill Development" (INTSKILL), is also based on six Estimate of Gains items (Table 3.4). Arguably, the acquisition and honing of intellectual skills is a key outcome of general education courses and becomes the building blocks on which rest subsequent learning in the major and self-directed learning beyond college. Engagement measures are

Table 3.3 Measurement Models
for CSEQ and CSXQ Factors

		Scale Reliability CSEQ a	CSXQ a

Course Learning

COURSE5	Tried to see how different facts and ideas fit together		
COURSE6	Summarized major points and information from your class notes or readings	.80	.76
COURSE8	Applied material learned in a class to other areas (your job or internship, other courses, relationships with friends, family, coworkers, and others)		
COURSE9	Used information or experience from other areas of your life (job, internship, interactions with others) in class discussions or assignments		
COURSE10	Tried to explain material from a course to someone else (another student, friend, coworker, family member)		
COURSE11	Worked on a paper or project for which you had to integrate ideas from various sources		

Writing Experiences

WRITE3	Asked other people to read something you wrote to see if it was clear to them		
WRITE4	Referred to a book or manual about writing style, grammar, and so on	.77	.72
WRITE5	Revised a paper or composition two or more times before you were satisfied with it		
WRITE6	Asked an instructor or staff member for advice and help to improve your writing		

(continued on the next page)

Table 3.3 *continued*

| | | Scale Reliability | |
		CSEQ a	CSXQ a

Experiences with Faculty

FAC1 — Talked with your instructor about information related to a course you were taking (grades, make-up work, assignments)

FAC2 — Discussed your academic program or course selection with a faculty member   .82   .84

FAC3 — Discussed ideas for a term paper or other class project with a faculty member

FAC4 — Discussed your career plans and ambitions with a faculty member

FAC6 — Socialized with a faculty member outside of class (had a snack or soft drink, or similar)

FAC8 — Asked your instructor for comments and criticisms about your academic performance

FAC10 — Worked with a faculty member on a research project

Experiences with Diversity

STACQ1 — Became acquainted with students whose interests were different from yours

STACQ2 — Became acquainted with students whose family background (economic, social) was different from yours   .86   .89

STACQ3 — Became acquainted with students whose age was different from yours

STACQ6 — Had serious discussions with students whose philosophy of life or personal values were very different from yours

STACQ7 — Had serious discussions with students whose political opinions were very different from yours

(continued on the next page)

Table 3.3 *continued*

	Scale Reliability	
	CSEQ a	*CSXQ a*

Experiences with Diversity *(continued)*

STACQ8	Had serious discussions with students whose religious beliefs were very different from yours	
STACQ9	Had serious discussions with students whose race or ethnic backgrounds were different from yours	

Topics of Conversation

CONTPS2	Social issues such as peace, justice, human rights, equality, race relations		
CONTPS3	Different lifestyles, customs, and religions	.85	.85
CONTPS4	The ideas and views of other people such as writers, philosophers, historians		
CONTPS8	Social and ethical issues related to science and technology such as energy, pollution, chemicals, genetics, military use		
CONTPS9	The economy (employment, wealth, poverty, debt, trade, and so on)		
CONTPS10	International relations (human rights, free trade, military activities, political differences, and so on)		

Information in Conversations

CONINF1	Referred to knowledge you acquired in your reading or classes		
CONINF2	Explored different ways of thinking about the topic	.85	.82
CONINF3	Referred to something one of your instructors said about the topic		
CONINF4	Subsequently read something that was related to the topic		

(continued on the next page)

Table 3.3 *continued*

| | Scale Reliability | |
	CSEQ *a*	CSXQ *a*

Reading and Writing

READTEXT   During this current year, about how many textbooks or assigned books have you read?

READPAK*   During this current year, about how many assigned packs of course readings have you read?   .60   .70

WRITESS   During this current school year, about how many essay exams have you written for your courses?

WRITTERM   During this current school year, about how many term papers or other written reports have you written?

Perceptions of the Intellectual Environment

ENVSCH   Emphasis on academic, scholarly, and intellectual qualities

ENVESTH   Emphasis on aesthetic, expressive, and creative qualities   .74   .76

ENVCRIT   Emphasis on critical, evaluative, and analytical qualities

* READPAK appears on the CSEQ, but not on the CSXQ. Thus, the expectation version of this factor is composed of three items.

known to correlate positively with intellectual skills, such as the ability to think critically (Astin, 1993; Pascarella & Terenzini, 1991).

The second step in SEM analysis involves specifying the structural model; that is, explicating the theorized set of relationships between factors and other measured variables in the model. These influences may be correlational, represented by a bidirectional arrow to show mutual effects, or causal, represented by a one-way arrow.[3]

Figure 3.1 shows the conceptual model guiding the structural equation analysis. Consistent with Pace's (1984) quality of effort concept, Astin's (1984) involvement theory, and Kuh's (1981, 2001) engagement framework, this model assumes that student expectations will directly influence subsequent corresponding college experiences in a particular area (path A), and that those experiences will directly influence the magnitude of gains that students report (path B). The model also assumes that student expectations will directly influence self-reported gains (path C). Separate and parallel

Table 3.4 Measurement Models for CSEQ Gains Factors

Gains in General Education (GENED)		*Alpha Reliability* a
GNGENLED	Gaining a broad general education about different fields of knowledge	
GNARTS	Developing an understanding and enjoyment of art, music, and drama	.76
GNLIT	Broadening your acquaintance with and enjoyment of literature	
GNHIST	Seeing the importance of history for understanding the present as well as the past	
GNWORLD	Gaining knowledge about other parts of the world and other people (Asia, Africa, South America)	
GNPHILS	Becoming aware of different philosophies, cultures, and ways of life	

Gains in Intellectual Skill Development (INTSKILL)		
GNWRITE	Writing clearly and effectively	
GNSPEAK	Presenting ideas and information effectively when speaking to others	.80
GNCMPTS	Using computers and other information technologies	
GNANALY	Thinking analytically and logically	
GNSYNTH	Putting ideas together, seeing relationships, similarities, and differences between ideas	
GNINQ	Learning on your own, pursuing ideas, and finding information you need	

structural models were analyzed for each pair of corresponding expectation and experience factors listed in Table 3.4.[4]

Results

Table 3.5 presents the results from the regression analysis, which answers in part the first research question. In this analysis, the standardized beta coefficient can be interpreted as an effect size, which allows us to compare the relative influence of each variable on the dependent variable. Because regression analysis is highly sensitive to sample size, only those coefficients with p values less than .01 and .001 are noted. The third and fourth columns in Table 3.5 show the effect of each independent variable in the Expectations of College Activities and Expectations of Campus Environment models respectively.

While most variables in the college activities model are statistically significant, the standardized beta coefficients indicate they have small, mostly trivial effects and do not explain much of the variance in student expectations for college. The total amount of variance explained is about 21%, so much of what affects student expectations is unexplained. The set of institutional variables (institutional type, selectivity, percentage minority, sector, and enrollment size) does not tell us much about student expectations for participating in educationally purposeful activities in college. As expected, students entering the more selective, private institutions have slightly higher expectations, as do students entering doctoral-extensive, doctoral-intensive, and baccalaureate liberal arts colleges. At the student level, gender seems to make the largest single contribution, meaning that women expect to more frequently participate in a range of educationally purposeful activities. Race also makes a small contribution, indicating that students of color expect to take part more frequently in a wider range of activities than white students. Perhaps this is because students of color attending predominantly white institutions believe college will be far more challenging academically and socially than their high school experience and that they will need to devote more effort to various college activities in order to succeed, as contrasted with their white counterparts.

Of the five items in the model that are proxies for student socioeconomic status, only the number of hours students expected to work on or off campus influenced college experiences. Despite some evidence to the contrary, first-generation status and family financial support did not have significant effects. In addition, expected major also made some contributions, with math and science majors and undecided students having somewhat lower expectations than the reference group of pre-professional majors. The four variables with the strongest influence on expectations are student ability (represented by expected grades), educational aspirations (plan to seek an advanced degree), motivation (number of hours expected to devote to class preparation), and positive orientation to college (how well the student expects to like college).

The fourth column in Table 3.5 shows the results of the effects of institutional and student background characteristics on expectations of the campus environment. Overall, the pattern of effects of the independent variables in this model is similar, though somewhat weaker, explaining only about 11% of the variance. Again, institutional characteristics have a significant but almost negligible influence on what students expect the campus environment will be like. It's worth noting that students attending doctoral- or research-extensive institutions, which in this dataset are large state universities, were less inclined (compared with students attending master's colleges and universities) to expect their campus to have an engaging campus environment (that is, one that emphasizes scholarly, aesthetic, diversity-oriented, and analytical work, as well as practical and vocational efforts). Similarly, gender, race, and other variables that were significant in the college activities model were less potent in the quality of campus environment model.

Although first-generation status had a significant effect, it was inconsequential in that the proxies for socioeconomic status had virtually no influence on student expectations for the campus environment. Again, the same four items accounted for most of the explained variance: student ability, educational aspirations, motivation, and positive orientation to college, with the latter having a particularly large impact.

The results in Tables 3.6 and 3.7 begin to answer the last two research questions. The data are presented to correspond to the conceptual model portrayed in Figure 3.1. The columns represent magnitude of each of the three direct effects (paths A, B, and C) between latent factors in the structural models. Table 3.6 also lists the

Table 3.5 Regression Models Explaining Expectations of College Activities and Campus Environment

		Standardized Beta Coefficient	
Variable Name	Dummy Categories	Expectations of College Activities	Expectations of Campus Environment
Institution characteristics			
Barron's selectivity rating		.05 **	.02 *
Private institution (0 = public, 1 = private)		.04 **	.06 **
Percentage minority		−.03 **	—
Carnegie Classification (*Reference = Master's*)	*Doctoral/research extensive*	.04 **	−.04 **
	Doctoral/research intensive	.09 **	.02 *
	Baccalaureate liberal arts	.03 **	.01
	Baccalaureate general	−.04 **	−.02 *
Enrollment size		−.05 **	—
Student background characteristics			
Gender (0 = male, 1 = female)		.09 **	.07 **
Race (*Reference = Caucasian, other than Hispanic*)	*Asian or Pacific Islander*	.01	.00
	Black or African American	.08 **	.05 **
	Mexican American, Puerto Rican, other Hispanic	.05 **	.02 **
	Other/Multiple	.04 **	.00
First-generation status (0 = no, 1 = yes)		−.01	.02 **

Table 3.5 *continued*

		Standardized Beta Coefficient	
Variable Name	Dummy Categories	Expectations of College Activities	Expectations of Campus Environment
Student background characteristics (continued)			
Expenses provided by family		—	—
Commuter: driving to campus		.00	.01
Expected hours working on campus for pay		.05 **	.01
Expected hours working off campus for pay		.04 **	—
Expected major (*Reference = Pre-professional*)	*Math and science major*	−.07 **	−.03 **
	Humanities major	.03 **	.01
	Social major	.04 **	.01
	Business major	−.03 **	.01
	Undecided major	−.04 **	−.02 *
Expected number of term credit hours		−.02 *	—
Expects to enroll for a post-baccalaureate degree		.10 **	.04 **
Expected grades at this college		.12 **	.09 **
Expected hours on out-of-class academic preparation		.18 **	.11 **
How well will you like college?		.23 **	.22 **
	R^2	.21	.11

$*p < .01, **p < .001$

Table 3.6 Effects of Student Expectations on Experiences and Gains in General Education

Outcome Factor	Model	A Direct Effect of Expectation on Experience	B Direct Effect of Experience on Gain	A * B Indirect Effect of Expectation on Gain	C Direct Effect of Expectation on Gain	(A * B) + C Total Effect of Expectation on Gain	Goodness-of-fit CFI	RMSEA
Gains in general education	Writing experiences	.46	.20	.10	.10	.20	.97	.04
	Course learning experiences	.46	.55	.25	.05	.30	.95	.04
	Student-faculty interactions	.40	.32	.13	.04	.17	.95	.04
	Experiences with diversity	.42	.42	.18	.03	.21	.95	.05
	Topics of conversation	.53	.43	.23	.10	.33	.95	.05
	Information in conversations	.43	.54	.23	.11	.34	.98	.03
	Amount of reading and writing	.37	.42	.15	.08	.23	.95	.04
	Time spent preparing for class	.34	.09	.03	.12	.15	.97	.05
	Perceptions of the intellectual environment	.37	.32	.12	.23	.35	.96	.05

Table 3.7 Effects of Student Expectations on Experiences and Gains in Intellectual Skill Development

Outcome Factor	Model	A Direct Effect of Expectation on Experience	B Direct Effect of Experience on Gain	A * B Indirect Effect of Expectation on Gain	C Direct Effect of Expectation on Gain	(A * B) + C Total Effect of Expectation on Gain	Goodness-of-fit CFI	RMSEA
Gains in intellectual skill development	Writing experiences	.46	.32	.15	.11	.25	.96	.04
	Course learning experiences	.46	.55	.25	.08	.33	.95	.04
	Student-faculty interactions	.40	.42	.17	.09	.26	.94	.05
	Experiences with diversity	.42	.30	.13	.05	.18	.95	.05
	Topics of conversation	.53	.40	.21	.03	.24	.95	.05
	Information in conversations	.43	.54	.23	.09	.32	.98	.04
	Amount of reading and writing	.36	.37	.13	.05	.18	.96	.04
	Time spent preparing for class	.34	.17	.06	.13	.18	.97	.05
	Perceptions of the intellectual environment	.37	.41	.15	.15	.30	.96	.05

indirect effect of the expectations factor on the gains factor, mathematically represented as path A times path B, and the total effects (direct plus indirect) of expectations on gains. To illustrate, Figure 3.2 diagrams the results for the first Writing Experiences model with Gains in General Education as the dependent variable. This model shows that students who expect to write a great deal in college are more likely to do so (that is, writing expectations have a substantial direct effect of .46 on subsequent writing experiences), which in turn influences how much students report gaining in general education (a direct effect of writing of .20 on gains in general education). Multiplying these numbers (path A times path B) yields an indirect effect of .10 for expectations on gains. Path C shows a direct effect of .10 from writing expectations to gains in general education, and thus, the sum of the indirect and direct effects is .20.

As we predicted, student expectations directly affect the corresponding experiences, showing fairly strong influences, ranging from .34 to .53. The largest effects are for student expectations for topics of conversations and their actual experiences in that area. In part, this may represent academic self-esteem, whereby students who have a high degree of academic success in high school are more interested in and confident in their ability to engage in intellectually

Figure 3.2 Relationships Among Writing Expectations, Writing Experiences, and Self-Reported Gains in General Education Learning in the First Year of College

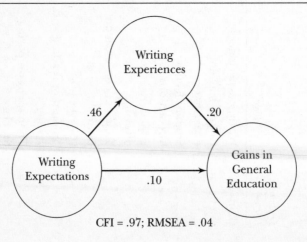

CFI = .97; RMSEA = .04

oriented discussions. The lowest direct correlation between expectations and experiences is the amount of time devoted to preparing for class. The .34 correlation, however, is still fairly strong, indicating that those students who expect to study more hours do so compared with their peers who expect to study fewer hours.

The direct effects of experiences on self-reported gains at the end of the first year of college (Column B) vary considerably more than the direct relationships between expectations and experience. Again, the factor with the weakest direct influence on gains is the amount of time spent preparing for class. Initially, this is somewhat puzzling. It may be a function of inefficient or ineffective study habits. That is, weaker students may spend more time studying but realize lower returns on their investment compared with stronger students who do not have to study as much in order to reap the intended benefits. In any case, this area warrants additional examination.

Strong direct paths from "experiences" also exist with "course learning experiences and information in conversations." These two scales suggest that integration and processing of course material is especially important for learning and development. The strongest indirect effects are related to expectations for course learning and engaging with peers on substantive matters (topics of conversations), and sharing information in conversations. Consequently, these also translate into the strongest total effects. Weak indirect effects are seen in expectations for writing and time spent in preparing for class. Finally, the factor representing student perceptions of the intellectual environment shows a modest direct effect on gains in general education, and on gains in intellectual skills to a lesser extent. Therefore, the environment factor has the greatest overall effect of any variable in any of the models.

What We Have Learned About Expectations and Experiences

The multiple regression models explain only a small amount of the variance in the relationships between student and institutional characteristics and expectations for college. As a result, we can only provide, at best, an equivocal, speculative answer to the first research question, "What factors account for differing levels of expectations among first-year undergraduate students?" It appears that student cognitive and psychological factors (ability, aspirations, motivation, and positive orientation to college) have more influence on college expectations than other student background characteristics measured in this study. Also, institutional characteristics have such weak influences that they are largely irrelevant. Consequently, colleges and universities of virtually any size and type have an equal chance of shaping student expectations, after taking into account student ability, aspirations, and motivation. Indeed, these student characteristics require additional study in terms of how they shape expectations. For example, student life professionals along with institutional researchers should consider as much precollege information about students as possible, such as their high school courses, placement test scores, grades, and class rank, to better understand expectations. It may also be the case that key agents in the students' academic development and college choice experiences are strong influences on the student's expectations. Certainly, parents, siblings, close relatives, high school teachers, peers, and employers may have a significant role in shaping a student's college expectations. Also, it is possible that high school guidance counselors, college admission administrators, various admission materials (college viewbooks, Web sites), campus tours, and orientation programs could also influence student expectations to some degree. Such questions are not currently asked on the CSXQ instrument, but may be fruitful in explaining more of the sources of expectations.

The parsimonious structural models were more effective at identifying meaningful relationships among the student expectations, engagement, and outcomes measures. In general, students who enter college with relatively high expectations are more likely to follow through on these expectations in terms of the activities they report after the first year of college. This pattern of behavior seems to hold across institutional types and student background characteristics. That is, whether a student is attending a selective liberal arts college or a large public university, or happens to be white, a student of color, or a first-generation student, expectations have much the same effect on subsequent experiences. The implication is that colleges and universities need to be as effective and persuasive as possible in explaining to students what is required to succeed in college and then holding students accountable to those expectations once they arrive.

As with other important dimensions of student learning and personal development in college, the relationship between expectations and experiences appears to be mediated to some degree by peers. That is, among the stronger direct and indirect relationships between expectations and experience and experiences and gains are activities such as diversity experiences, conversations with peers and others about academic and substantive matters, and the information peers exchange with one another about their studies and larger world events. It would seem that efforts to involve influential upper-division peers to work with new students on how to take advantage of the institutions educational resources would be a good investment on the part of the institution. Programs such as freshmen interest groups and living learning centers, and learning communities that bring small groups of new students together to focus on academic and educationally purposeful topics, would help reinforce and/or enhance expectations through experiences.

As with other studies about the influence of the institutional characteristics on student development, students' perceptions of the institutional environment also seemed to have substantial effects on what students do with their time as well as what they gain from college. Student affairs professionals working in concert with faculty colleagues and academic administrators can be especially helpful in establishing such environments. The most desirable impact will likely come from working together to (1) prepare students for what the college environment is actually like through providing anticipatory socialization efforts such as accurate admissions materials, summer orientation, and fall welcome week; (2) help students adjust their expectations so that they are appropriately realistic; and (3) make certain the environment provides the necessary academic and social support. To do this well will require assessment and feedback protocols to be certain programmatic initiatives are having the desired effects.

The relatively low conversion ratio of time spent preparing for class on gains in general education and intellectual skills is somewhat puzzling. As mentioned earlier, this may be in part a function of first-year students being unable to study as efficiently as necessary to maximize the learning benefits, as Kuh and Hu (2001) speculated. Higher-ability or academically well-prepared students may need less study time in order to realize the same degree of benefit as do lower-ability or academically less well-prepared students, even though the latter group spends more hours studying. Pace's (1984) concept of quality of effort provides a similar interpretation, namely that all effort is not the same; some students concentrate more effectively than others and get more out of participating in an activity.

A confounding factor in interpreting the relationships among expectations, experiences, and gains is that students may not use the same baseline when estimating progress toward desired outcomes of college (Pascarella, 2001). That is, students at different institutions or even within the same institution may enter college with different levels of intellectual skills or general knowledge. Because of possible ceiling effects, those who start at higher levels may report gaining less but may still be at an absolute higher level of functioning than their peers who started college at much lower levels in the respective areas.

The question remains as to why class preparation does not have a larger effect on gains. Perhaps it is a function of the developmental level of many first-year students who are not yet well prepared to make gains in these areas of general education and general intellectual skills. It's also worth exploring further why students with low expectations are able to more accurately predict their college experiences. Is this a by-product of the freshman myth, whereby students with "great" expectations simply cannot accomplish all the things they believe are attractive and possible during college? Or are institutions in part co-conspirators, especially in the academic arena, where faculty members largely determine through course assignments, feedback, and other curricular devices (seminars, internships, capstone experiences) how much reading, writing, and group work students do. In other words, are faculty members and student affairs professionals expecting too little of students, despite protestations that students are unwilling to perform at the levels expected? A review of average college grades would suggest that students are receiving B or better grades, and it is the faculty who are assigning those high grades.

Finally, student expectations are a moving target. Although developed less than a decade ago, the CSXQ contains few technology items. In these few short years, the cohort of entering college students has become increasingly technologically savvy; some argue that their precollege experiences have wired their brains in such a way that solitary library time and tasks requiring single-minded concentration for extended periods of time are boring. While this paper provides a glimpse of the college expectations and experiences of currently enrolled students, it is far short of an exhaustive treatment. Much more needs to be discovered about how technology and contemporary issues shape precollege expectations and the extent to which college experiences match these expectations. For example:

- Can measures be developed to explain a larger portion of the variance in student expectations?
- What forms of anticipatory socialization are most effective in helping establish high expectations for college on the part of new students?
- Why are students with low expectations able to more accurately predict what they will do in college?

These are but a few of the questions that need to be answered in order to more effectively shape student expectations for college in ways that will enable them to make the most of the college experience and gain the skills and competencies they will need to succeed after college.

References

Astin, A. W. (1984). Student involvement: A developmental theory for higher education. *Journal of College Student Personnel, 25,* 297–308.

Astin, A. W. (1993). *What matters in college? Four critical years revisited.* San Francisco: Jossey-Bass.

Baker, R. W., McNeil, O. V., & Siryk, B. (1985). Expectation and reality in freshman adjustment to college. *Journal of Counseling Psychology, 32,* 94–103.

Bandura, A. (1982). Self efficacy mechanisms in human agency. *American Psychologist, 37,* 122–147.

Barron's Profiles of American colleges. (2002). (23rd ed.). Hauppauge, NY: Barron's Educational Series.

Bentler, P. M. (1990). Fit indexes, Lagrange multipliers, constraint changes, and incomplete data in structural models. *Multivariate Behavioral Research, 25,* 163–172.

Bentler, P. M. (1992). *EQS: Structural equations program manual.* Los Angeles: BMDP Statistical Software.

Berdie, R. F. (1966). College expectations, experiences, and perceptions. *Journal of College Student Personnel, 7,* 336–344.

Berdie, R. F. (1968). Changes in university perceptions during the first two college years. *Journal of College Student Personnel, 9,* 85–89.

Boomsma, A. (2000). Reporting analysis of covariance structures. *Structural Equation Modeling, 7*(3), 461–482.

Braxton, J., Hossler, D., & Vesper, N. (1995). Incorporating college choice constructs into Tinto's model of student departure: Fulfillment of expectations for institutional traits and student withdrawal plans. *Research in Higher Education, 36*(5), 595–612.

Byrne, B. M. (1994). *Structural equation modeling with EQS and EQS/windows.* Thousand Oaks, CA: Sage.

Chickering, A. W. (1974). *Commuting versus resident students: Overcoming the educational inequities of living off campus.* San Francisco: Jossey-Bass.

Davis, T. M., & Murrell, P. H. (1993). A structural model of perceived academic, personal, and vocational gains related to college student responsibility. *Research in Higher Education, 34*(3), 267–289.

Dweck, C. S., & Leggett, E. L. (1988). A social-cognitive approach to motivation and personality. *Psychological Review, 95*(2), 256–273.

Ewell, P. T., & Jones, D. P. (1993). Actions matter: The case for indirect measures in assessing higher education's progress on the national education goals. *Journal of General Education, 42*(2), 123–148.

Feldman, D. C. (1981). The multiple socialization of organization members. *Academy of Management Review, 6,* 308–318.

King, H., & Walsh, W. B. (1972). Change in environmental expectations and perceptions. *Journal of College Student Personnel, 13,* 331–337.

Kuh, G. D. (1981). *Indices of quality in the undergraduate experience.* AAHE-ERIC/Higher Education Research Report, no. 4. Washington, DC: American Association for Higher Education.

Kuh, G. D. (1999). Setting the bar high to promote student learning. In G. S. Blimling, E. J. Whitt, & Associates, *Good practice in student affairs: Principles to foster student learning* (pp. 67–89). San Francisco: Jossey-Bass.

Kuh, G. D. (2001). Assessing what really matters to student learning: Inside the National Survey of Student Engagement. *Change, 33*(3), 10–17, 66.

Kuh, G. D. (2005). Student engagement in the first year of college. In L. M. Upcraft, J. N. Gardner, & B. O. Barefoot (Eds.), *Challenging and supporting the first-year student: A handbook for improving the first year of college.* San Francisco: Jossey-Bass.

Kuh, G. D., & Hu, S. (2001). Learning productivity at research universities. *Journal of Higher Education, 72,* 1–28.

Kuh, G. D., & Pace, C. R. (1999). *College student expectations questionnaire* (2nd ed.). Bloomington: Indiana University, Center for Postsecondary Research.

Lawler, E. E. (1981). *Pay and organization development.* Reading, MA: Addison Wesley.

Levine, A., & Cureton, J. S. (1998, May/June). Collegiate life: An obituary. *Change,* 12–17, 51.

Merton, R. K. (1948). The self-fulfilling prophecy. *Antioch Review* (Summer), 193–210.

Miller, A. H., Imrie, B. W., & Cox, K. (1998). *Student assessment in higher education: A handbook for assessing performance.* London: Kogan Page.

Oblinger, D. G. (2004, January). *A changing world: Technology and student success.* Address to the Council of Independent Council's Presidents Institute, San Diego.

Olsen, D., Kuh, G. D., Schilling, K. M., Schilling, K., Connolly, M., Simmons, A., et al. (November, 1998). *Great expectations: What students expect from college and what they get.* Paper presented at the annual meeting of the Association for the Study of Higher Education, Miami, FL.

Pace, C. R. (1984). *Measuring the quality of college student experiences: An account of the development and use of the college student experiences questionnaire.* Los Angeles: Higher Education Research Institute.

Pace, C. R., & Kuh, G. D. (1998). *College student experiences questionnaire* (4th ed.). Bloomington: Indiana University, Center for Postsecondary Research.

Pascarella, E. T. (2001). Using student self-reported gains to estimate college impact: A cautionary tale. *Journal of College Student Development, 42*(5), 488–492.

Pascarella, E. T., & Terenzini, P. T. (1991). *How college affects students.* San Francisco: Jossey-Bass.

Pate, R. H., Jr. (1970). Student expectations and later expectations of a university enrollment. *Journal of College Student Personnel, 11*, 458–462.

Pike, G. R. (1995). The relationship between self reports of college experiences and achievement test scores. *Research in Higher Education, 36*, 1–21.

Pike, G. R. (1999). The effects of residential learning communities and traditional residential living arrangements on educational gains during the first year of college. *Journal of College Student Development, 40*(3), 609–621.

Pike, G. R. (2000). The influence of fraternity or sorority membership on students' college experiences and cognitive development. *Research in Higher Education, 41*, 117–139.

Pike, G. R., & Killian, T. (2001). Reported gains in student learning: Do academic disciplines make a difference? *Research in Higher Education, 42*, 429–454.

Pike, G. R., Kuh, G. D., & Gonyea, R. M. (2003). The relationship between institutional mission and students' involvement and educational outcomes. *Research in Higher Education, 44*(2), 241–261.

Rousseau, D. M. (1995). *Psychological contracts in organizations.* Thousand Oaks, CA: Sage.

Schilling, K. M., & Schilling, K. L. (1999). Increasing expectation for student effort. *About Campus, 4*(2), 4–10.

Stern, G. G. (1970). *People in context.* New York: Wiley.

Whiteley, J. H. (1982). Effects on the freshman year. In J. M. Whiteley, B. D. Bertin, J. S. Jennings, L. Lee, H. A. Magana, & A. Resnikoff (Eds.), *Character development in college students: Volume I. The freshman year* (pp. 129–172). Schenectady, NY: Character Research Press.

Notes

1. SEM entails a two-step process for data analysis: (1) a measurement model is tested using confirmatory factor analysis, and (2) a series of structural equations is specified and tested. In the first step, the measurement model defines which observed variables are used to represent latent constructs, or factors. Confirmatory factor analysis (CFA) provides evidence that a set of survey questions, chosen a priori to represent a particular phenomenon, does in fact do a good job identifying the factor. CFA shows the relative strength of correlation between the underlying factor and each observed item.

2. The CSXQ was intentionally designed to be much shorter than the CSEQ, so not every CSEQ item appears on the CSXQ. Moreover, a handful of items that have equivalent counterparts on both surveys did not fit well into the single-factor structures within the measured scales, and thus were not included in the factor with one exception. The item "During this current year, about how many assigned packs of course readings have you read?" does not have an equivalent on the CSXQ form, but was included in the CSEQ factor for reading and writing because of its obvious fit, and because it doesn't change the meaning or the comparability of the expectations and experience factors for reading and writing.

3. The recommended goodness-of-fit measure for analyzing structural models is the Comparative Fit Index (CFI) (Bentler, 1990; Byrne, 1994) because it takes sample size into account. Values of the CFI range from .00 to 1.00, and current standards for acceptable fit suggest that it should exceed .90 for an acceptable fit, and .95 for models considered to fit very well. In addition to the CFI, Boomsma (2000) recommends a misfit index known as the Root Mean Square Error of Approximation (RMSEA). The RMSEA score should be equal to or below .05 for the models considered to fit well.

4. All latent factors in the model were controlled for the influence of gender due to its effects on expectations of college activities and the campus environment in the results of the first research question.

Chapter Four

When Expectations and Realities Collide

Environmental Influences on Student Expectations and Student Experiences

Larry Moneta and George D. Kuh

Most entering students generally have a good idea of what many aspects of the college experience will be like. As Kuh, Gonyea, and Williams explained in Chapter 3, the one area where student expectations are often off the mark is with regard to aspects of the college environment. This discrepancy between what students expect and subsequently experience can have a significant influence on student success and desired college outcomes. Indeed, studies that include measures of the college environment, broadly defined, show that the environment both directly affects student satisfaction and persistence and indirectly affects learning outcomes (Baird, 1988; Pascarella & Terenzini, 1991). This suggests that an institution's contextual conditions are as important in encouraging student engagement in learning opportunities as any particular set of organizational or programmatic features (Kuh, 2000).

In this chapter we examine the role of the campus environment in both shaping and responding to the expectations that contemporary students bring with them to college. First, we summarize the ecological perspective that is a foundational frame of reference for understanding the impact of college on students. Then, we review some characteristics of the external environment that shape the expectations of what college will be like for the current cohort of college students. We close with some implications for student affairs professionals and others committed to promoting higher levels of student success, learning, and personal development by improving the fit between students and the college environment.

Student Expectations and Campus Ecology

According to Strange and Banning (2001), "Campus environments set conditions that affect student learning and, in turn, students influence the shape of campus environments" (p. 200). In the broadest sense, the campus environment includes the physical component, a social component, an institutional component, and an "ecological-climate dimension" derived from the interaction of the other three (Conyne & Clack, 1981).

The physical or built environment can shape—for better or worse—students' behavioral patterns and social choices. For example, the amount, locations, and arrangement of physical spaces shape behavior by facilitating or discouraging social interaction. The proximity of academic buildings to student residences can promote or inhibit interactions between students from different majors (Kuh, 2000). Thus, "the actual features of the physical environment can encourage or discourage the processes of learning and development" (Strange & Banning, 2001, p. 12). At the same time, the physical environment is relatively expensive to modify, though the proliferation of construction cranes on many campuses belie that observation.

The social component represents students' demographic characteristics as well as the dominant personality orientations that can be seen in the availability of major fields and the proportions of students pursuing various majors. That is, institutions with large numbers of engineering and science majors differ in their environmental press from schools that have large numbers of business and performing arts students, as the personalities of the former tend to be realistic and conventional while the latter are enterprising and artistic (Holland, 1973).

Institutional components reflect the norms, informal practices, rituals, and traditions of the campus community that are established and reinforced over time. These elements of institutional culture are rooted in enduring social systems that often are impervious to attempts to intentionally alter them (Kuh & Whitt, 1988). Some of the more debilitating aspects of undergraduate student cultures, such as binge drinking, are grounded in these normative practices.

The "ecological perspective" (Banning, 1978, 1989) underscores the mutually shaping relationship between students and the college campus. It also provides a vocabulary and template to examine and understand the nature of the multiple ecosystems that comprise the college environment that must be managed effectively in order to encourage student interactions with faculty, peers, and others and students' use of the institution's other resources for learning.

Another way to think about the campus as an ecosystem is to examine its various subsystems. According to Blocher (1974, 1978), three subsystems operate simultaneously in an optimal learning environment: opportunity, support, and reward. The *opportunity* subsystem includes the availability, frequency, and intensity of ways students take advantage of an institution's human and physical learning resources. Opportunities range from the availability of formally recognized clubs to participating in curricular innovations such as freshman interest groups and other forms of learning communities to a climate that encourages spontaneous interaction between students and their teachers. The *support* subsystem can take the form of formal programs and services such as advising, counseling, and other services to meet the needs of various groups of students, to invisible safety nets and an ethic of care that is stitched into the institution's culture and operating philosophy (Kuh, Schuh, Whitt, & Associates, 1991). The *reward* subsystem represents the nature and quality of the feedback students receive, including recognition for performance inside and outside the classroom. What an institution chooses to reward is a manifestation of its values and sends strong signals to students and others as to the kinds of behaviors that are expected. Understanding the relationship among these subsystems is important, because it helps explain how an institutional environment can promote or discourage student involvement in educationally purposeful activities and their learning and personal development (Kuh, 2000).

We now turn to several of the more important characteristics of today's undergraduates and the implications for managing campus environments.

Guess Who's Already on Campus?

By now, everyone knows that college students in the early 21st century are more diverse in every possible way than any previous generation. Demographic changes in the past couple of decades have resulted in complex shifts in the ages of various cohorts, especially those attending community colleges and proprietary institutions. Women now outnumber men by an increasing margin, and more students from historically underrepresented groups are attending college (Woodard, Love, & Komives, 2000). On some campuses, such as the University of Texas at El Paso, Hispanics who were once "minority" students are now the majority. Often overlooked are changes in the American family that also may be influencing students' "levels of preparation, identity development, shifts in attitudes, and increased levels of psychological and emotional damage" (Woodard et al., 2000, p. 40). Today's college-going cohort brings with them to campus a myriad of psychological challenges that, if left unattended, can have a debilitating effect on their academic performance and social adjustment.

A substantial fraction of traditional-age students are being "bred" for America's elite colleges and universities. David Brooks (2001) profiled the attitudes, desires, and expectations of a recent cohort of Princeton students, describing them as "professional" students whose job is to attend college and obtain a degree. Today's elite college students are further described as "super accomplished," "goal oriented," and "workaholics." He concluded, "College is just one step on the continual stairway of advancement, and they are always aware that they must get to the next step (law school, medical school, whatever) so that they can progress up the steps after that" (Brooks, 2001, p. 46).

Another characteristic of the current cohort of undergraduates that extends well beyond those at elite colleges is an unmistakable consumerism that colors virtually all aspects of the college experience. As Fallows (2003) pointed out, many colleges and universities are willing co-conspirators, feeding this mentality with "marketized" admissions approaches focused on recruiting the right "customers."

Among the antecedents of the commercialization of higher education are the growing competition for top-achieving high school graduates, recruiting efforts that segment national and international markets, the availability of a common application, and changing financial aid strategies.

While it is tempting to dismiss the observations of *Atlantic Monthly* contributors such as Brooks and Fallows as irrelevant to the largest segment of the college-going population, other arguably more representative data sources corroborate similar tendencies. The 2003 report from UCLA's Cooperative Institutional Research Program (CIRP) portrays a college student population increasingly disengaged from their academic activities, though generally satisfied with their collegiate experiences. They seek and use support services, though many prefer their own peers over formal advising personnel. They have rich social lives and are less involved in community service than their predecessors, despite expressed concern with the welfare of others (The Nation, 2003). They also work more, presumably to cover ever-escalating college costs, but also to enjoy the amenities to which they've become accustomed (Kuh, 2001). Data from the College Student Experiences Questionnaire (CSEQ) database at the Indiana University Center for Postsecondary Research indicate that the proportion of seniors attending residential campuses who work more than 30 hours per week today has more than doubled, from less than 10% in the early 1980s to about one-fifth today. The proportions of students at urban and commuter campuses who work this much are even higher.

There are other indications that, in the eyes of students, college is a decidedly different type of learning environment than it was even just a couple of decades ago. Schwartz (2004, p. B6) notes that "the modern university has become a kind of intellectual shopping mall." Universities offer a wide array of different "goods" and allow, even encourage, students—the "customers"—to shop around until they find what they like.

Once they arrive on campus, students spend as much time doing other things as going to class and studying. Table 4.1 shows the approximate amount of time full-time students devote to various activities over the course of an academic year. The information comes from about 91,000 randomly sampled first-year and senior students who responded to the National Survey of Student Engagement in spring 2003. The majority of all students (with the exception of those at liberal arts colleges) spend fewer hours studying than attending class; the latter number assumes that students attend *all* their classes, which is a convenient fiction for creating a common metric for comparison across different types of schools. The standard rule of thumb among faculty members is that students should spend at least two hours outside of class preparing for every one hour in class. Clearly, few students come even close to this academic mantra. A fifth of all students "frequently" come to class unprepared. Less than three-fifths of first-year students (53%) and seniors (58%) say they've had to work harder than they thought they could to meet an instructor's standards. Moreover, just as the percentage of high school seniors with A– or better average grades is at an all-time high (CIRP, 2003), so are average college grades at many institutions (Kuh & Hu, 1999).

These measures of the student experience fall well short of what might be considered a strong academic press in place in many col-

Table 4.1 How College Students Spend Time
(Hours per Semester)

	Research Universities	Master's Colleges and Universities	Liberal Arts Colleges	Urban Universities
In class	450	450	450	450
Preparing for class	420	390	480	390
Working on or off campus	300	420	240	480
Participating in co-curricular activities	150	120	210	90
Relaxing or socializing	390	360	360	360
Providing care for dependents	60	150	30	180
Commuting to class	120	150	90	150

Source: National Survey of Student Engagement (2003).

leges and universities. It also appears that many students in addition to those attending elite colleges who go directly from high school to college have been groomed for success—at least on their terms. They are focused on the material and ephemeral rewards associated with what is ideally a not-too-rigorous academic experience at their college or university of choice.

At the same time, today's students don't necessarily want to defer their material gains until after college. Spending more than $200 billion annually (Harris Interactive, n.d.), college students exhibit an almost insatiable demand for an expanding array of products and services (Table 4.2). Emboldened by such substantial spending potential, efforts to understand student consumer preferences and processes are proliferating with data collected by research firms such as Student Monitor, 360 Youth, and Campus Client. These data, offering spending analysis on everything from travel to computers, with a particular focus on electronics and food, fuel corporate America's hunger for access to college students' wallets and pocketbooks.

Student spending patterns transcend institutional types, though actual expenditure amounts vary substantially from campus to campus, depending upon the relative affluence of the corresponding student body. Most students at community colleges, for example, have far fewer discretionary funds, and thus spend less on nonacademic activities, than many of their counterparts at selective, private four-year college and universities. Nonetheless, all are viewed by marketers as desirable consumers and, for their part, the vast majority of students appear to appreciate the attention as evidenced by their purchases and increasing debt levels.

Implications for Managing Campus Environments

Given this admittedly incomplete description of today's students and campuses, what are those charged with creating and maintaining student success-oriented collegiate environments to do? What can be done to ensure that colleges and universities are providing the types of physical, social, and interactive environments where optimal learning, both formal and informal, can occur?

Table 4.2 The "10 Best Tips"
for Marketers to College Students

1. "Recognize Their Potential": Students are serious shoppers who represent a unique and lucrative segment of the consumer population:
   - Two-thirds (67%) have paid jobs
   - They represent $53.9 billion in discretionary spending annually
   - They were responsible for more than $210 billion in sales last year alone

2. "Make Them Laugh": When asked what they want in advertisements, students named the following:
   - Humor (36%)
   - Affordable product cost (44%)
   - Everyday people (33%)

3. "Don't Forget the 'Rents": Appealing to students is important, but parental approval shouldn't be underestimated. More than half of college students brand loyal in these categories reported they were introduced to the brand by their parents:
   - Laundry detergent (60%)
   - Bar soap (55%)
   - Toothpaste (54%)

4. "Have a Heart": Young adults care about global and community issues. Students are most concerned with:
   - Environmental causes (56%)
   - The potential for war (53%)
   - Unemployment and lack of job opportunities (51%)
   - The rise in poverty (51%)

5. "Give Them Credit": College students are well versed in credit usage:
   - 65% have loan payments
   - 65% have a major credit card
   - 41% of freshman have a credit card; 79% of seniors have one

6. "Think Active": Don't assume that today's youth are just in class or in front of the TV. In the past year, students have been on the move, spending their money on the following:
   - Nearly $5 billion on travel
   - $790 million at the movies
   - $390 million on attending music concerts
   - $318 million at amusement parks
   - $272 million at professional sporting events

7. "Be Connected": College students represent one of the most connected groups:
   - 93% access the Internet in a given month
   - 56% of online students have broadband connections
   - One in eight (12%) consider themselves tech leaders—they're the first to buy new electronic devices and gadgets
   - Two-thirds (67%) own cell phones, and 36% use them to access the Internet

8. "Give Them What They Want": Students are price conscious and look for a good selection:
   - 93% cite low prices as important when shopping
   - 94% cite having a good selection as important when shopping
   - College students are more than twice as likely to look for sales than to want certain brands (66% versus 27%)
   - 80% shop at general purpose retailers like Wal-Mart and K-Mart
   - 54% shop at clothing retailers such as Gap or Abercrombie & Fitch

9. "Plug In": Students want the latest technology:
   - 88% of college students own a computer
   - 85% own a television
   - 58% own a DVD player
   - 45% own a video game system
   - 24% own a digital camera
   - 20% of college students *intend* to purchase digital cameras, DVD players (18%), and cell phones (18%) within the next year

10. "Figure Them Out": College students are not all the same—*know* their differences:
    - Freshman (28%) are more likely than seniors (12%) to use totally new and different brands
    - Freshman (35%) are more likely than seniors (13%) to use the same brands as their friends
    - Males are more interested than females in trying a product in a store (57% versus 48%) and in having salespeople be knowledgeable about what's cutting edge (30% versus 13%)
    - College students' favorite snack foods are candy bars, salty snacks, and chewing gum, but females are more likely than males to purchase salty snacks (71% versus 55%), chewing gum (68% versus 49%), and packaged cookies or brownies (53% versus 40%).

Source: Alloy's 360 Youth College Explorer™ Study, conducted by Harris Interactive® (2003).

In our view, significant gaps exist on many campuses between the expectations that students have for the campus environment and what institutions committed to student success are trying to provide. We describe several domains where the gaps are increasingly obvious and worrisome, including residential experiences, the role of the student's family, experiences with diversity, contact with faculty, peer relations, and some physical features of the campus.

Campus Residences

Among the more disconcerting disconnects between what institutions expect and students' predilections and expectations is at residential campuses. Despite decades of experience and research, many institutions still fall well short of providing optimal living-learning environments for the majority of their students. Some campuses have one or two "gemstone" living settings—a language house, theme hall, or the like. But on too many campuses the residential experience is not organized around educational purposes. Even "best practices" are in dispute. That is, as one campus redevelops a first-year experience (for example, Cornell and Duke), another chooses to abandon that approach in favor of an intergenerational approach (for example, Penn). Different living space configurations abound, with new undergraduate housing designs varying from traditional double-room, common-bath models to kitchenless suites to motel-style, high-rise, and luxury apartments. Residential colleges in the tradition of Harvard and Yale are becoming more popular, with institutions using various means to cobble together the needed resources to offer communal dining and spaces to hold seminars and discussions.

But even if an institution's campus housing philosophy is coherent, widely shared, and rooted in theory and research findings, student preferences can trump educational purpose, as evidenced by the amenities "arms race" (Winter, 2003). Campuses seem to be competing to see who can provide the most comfortable quarters, replete with abundant recreation elements such as pools, fitness centers, multimedia options, expansive culinary choices, and oversized rooms to accommodate the ever-expanding arsenal of electronic devices, all of which appear to have little to do with creating an intellectually vibrant living-learning experience and which in many instances are antithetical to the goals of higher education.

Students and Their Families:
Breaking Away or Connected Forever

Picture this in your mind's eye: Hordes of students milling about the campus quad as if no one else were present, seemingly at once talking to themselves while distracted by an aural presence that encapsulates them from any form of contact with passersby. Is this a scene from the latest horror film? Are these students pondering the implications of the last class lecture? What is so compelling and consuming of their attention? Welcome to cell phone conversations with friends and families!

Parent connections with their sons and daughters as well as with their institution are at an all-time high. Student problems become parent problems, and institutions increasingly are asked to inform and consult with parents, the Family Educational Rights and Privacy Act regulations notwithstanding. Examples include parents who expect to participate in campus judicial proceedings or have been known to attend a class lecture on behalf of a son or daughter too busy to do so! Much of this flies in the face of the student development philosophy that promotes encouraging and supporting students taking more responsibility for their own behavior and self-mediated management of associated age- and stage-related developmental challenges. But many current students, with a strong family-of-origin support system, seem less willing and interested in being on their own. Thus, student life professionals, bursars, and increasingly faculty members find themselves negotiating with Mom and Dad about various matters, including grades, housing assignments, and judicial sanctions.

Experiences with Diversity

The historic Civil Rights Act of 1964 set the stage for the diversifying campuses. While ensuring access to qualified students—especially those from low-income backgrounds—continues to be a challenge, most institutions have made considerable progress in increasing the numbers of students from historically underrepresented groups. But simply altering student profiles does not produce the nature, frequency, and quality of intergroup interactions that enrich the learning environment (Hurtado, Milem, Clayton-Pedersen, & Allen, 1999;

Umbach & Kuh, 2003). In fact, some observers believe that institutions are now more "Balkanized" than ever, as students claiming membership in various groups representing racial, religious, and sexual orientation backgrounds focus more on interacting with people who belong to their group than people who have other characteristics. Such self-segregation is not unique to campus environments, of course, as David Brooks (2003, p. 29) explains: "Maybe somewhere in this country there is a truly diverse neighborhood in which a black Pentecostal minister lives next to a white anti-globalization activist, who lives next to an Asian short-order cook, who lives next to a professional golfer, who lives next to a postmodern-literature professor and a cardiovascular surgeon. But I have never been to or heard of that neighborhood. Instead, what I have seen all around the country is people making strenuous efforts to group themselves with people who are basically like themselves."

To the extent Brooks's description accurately captures college campuses, it is a modern educational tragedy. College is, for better or worse, the last best opportunity to bring people from different backgrounds together in a setting where they can learn firsthand about human differences and practice new ways of interacting with others who look, think, and act in novel ways. More specifically, this opportunity seems to be concentrated in the critical first year of college, when students report experiences with diversity to be at the highest level (Kuh, 2003). By the senior year, students—like most of their parents—avoid "the road less traveled" and move off campus to live with people who are more (not less) like themselves. All this underscores why institutions must design campus environments and complementary policies and programs to encourage diversity experiences.

Student-Faculty Contact

Despite occasional lamentations by career center professionals that students cannot secure letters of recommendation from faculty, the nature and frequency of student-faculty contact has not declined over the past two decades. If anything, it has increased slightly, perhaps because of the increased attention brought to this important educational practice by a constant stream of reform reports since *Involvement in Learning* (National Institute of Education Study Group, 1984). For example, the College Student Experiences Questionnaire (CSEQ) database indicates that the proportions of students in recent years who say they at least "occasionally" socialize with faculty members outside the classroom is about the same as it was in the early 1980s.

Also, the percentages of students who do research with a faculty member, seek feedback about their performance, and discuss career plans are comparable or slightly larger. Even so, the perception lingers that few students frequently come into contact with their professors outside the classroom, as research and writing pressures grow not only at the research institutions, but also at the small colleges, as they, too, reward faculty inquiry over teaching (Fairweather, 2004).

One disconcerting theme in these data is that students who have the most contact with faculty members do not necessarily benefit as much in terms of desired outcomes from these interactions or from college in general as do their peers who have less contact. This may be due more to what transpires during the interactions than anything inherently problematic in the exchanges. As Kuh and Hu (2001, p. 328) explained, this may be because the nature of such interactions are not focused on things that matter to desired learning outcomes. For example, talking with faculty members about writing has a negative effect on student satisfaction, perhaps because many students—especially in the first year—interpret faculty feedback on their writing as overwhelmingly critical, while faculty members may intend their critique as a challenge to spur students on to higher levels of performance. Such criticisms may come as a shock to many new students who earned relatively high grades in high school.

The aforementioned residential college movement represents one attempt to boost opportunities to enhance the quality of student-faculty interactions. However, faculty live further away from home campuses, interact more often with discipline-based colleagues throughout the world, and do not necessarily identify with the undergraduate experience other than through mandated teaching, often with direct student contact relegated to a graduate student teaching assistant.

Expansion of Campus Boundaries to Enrich Student Learning

With the advent of the technological revolution, some have prophesied the end of the "bricks and mortar" campus in American higher education (Levine, 2000). The massive investments in the current physical plants plus the amount of new construction of academic, residential, and recreational facilities suggest otherwise. Indeed, traditional campuses continue to expand and renew facilities, assuming historically consistent patterns of student engagement with the physical campus.

At the same time, the physical campus is no longer the exclusive locus for student learning. For example, there is dramatic growth in the numbers of students who study abroad and participate in cooperative work programs and internships, service learning courses and projects, and various spring break community service activities. The latter are fueled by strong state and local Campus Compact chapters and institutionally sponsored volunteer services offices. Indeed, as the data from the National Survey of Student Engagement (2003) in Table 4.3 show, large numbers of students are pursuing learning opportunities off campus in nearby neighborhoods and internship sites that may be in a different state.

Table 4.3 Percentage of Seniors Participating in Educationally Enriching Activities

	DR-Ext	DR-Int	Master's	B-LA	B-Gen	Total
Practicum, internship, field experience	72%	72%	72%	74%	71%	72%
Community service/ volunteer work	66%	60%	64%	77%	67%	66%
Research with faculty member	29%	26%	23%	39%	24%	27%
Learning community	25%	25%	27%	25%	28%	27%
Foreign language	44%	35%	35%	65%	36%	41%
Study abroad	18%	14%	14%	35%	15%	18%
Independent study/ self-designed	24%	26%	26%	43%	30%	29%
Culminating senior experience	49%	58%	55%	73%	66%	60%

Source: National Survey of Student Engagement (2003).

These are but a few of the challenges to maintaining developmental powerful learning environments that are posed by the changing expectations and characteristics of the contemporary student cohort. The cell phone example is but one of many technological innovations that have permanently altered student communications, peer interactions, and learning approaches. Student health issues—especially the mental health challenges and student alcohol issues we briefly mentioned—deserve more attention. Other changes on campus, such as the internationalization of our campuses, must also be considered when estimating how the campus learning environment is changing.

Management of Tomorrow's Campus Environment

It is incumbent on college administrators and policy makers to design and modify as necessary the physical and social features of the campus environment to respond to the characteristics of contemporary student cohorts. Student affairs staff, in particular, are obliged to develop novel approaches to "manage" the campus environment to promote student learning. To be effective, these approaches must address but not accede to student expectations and preferences that are counter to the institution's academic purposes. A key tactic will be to attempt to teach students what college can and should be like, in ways that are consistent with holistic student development and the aims of a liberal education, while at the same time being sensitive to the diversity of needs and interests students bring with them. These efforts and others we undertake to reconcile differences in student and institutional expectations must be grounded in relevant theory and research and compatible with the institutional mission and values.

Our first suggestion deals with the "un-packaging" of student expectations. Given what appears to be efforts to "breed" a class of students for elite institutions, some attention must be paid to helping students develop realistic expectations for the college environment as well as assisting them in examining the preconceived notions they may have about themselves and their peers. For some, this will take place through academic advising, career counseling, or psychological support. For others, the residence halls, student clubs and organizations, and all parts of the "extended campus" must work in concert with curricular opportunities to "disturb the comfortable."

Some controversial options are worth considering. Simply scheduling a discussion on racial difference may not be as effective as adjusting residence hall assignment policies to ensure diversification of floors and halls. But, balancing the free market preferences of students (and their parents) with institutional desires for cross-identity interaction is difficult and leaves staff open to challenges from both liberal and conservative viewpoints. Nonetheless, the more challenging approaches will likely be the most successful if we truly aspire to see students choosing less comfortable and more interesting paths. This is especially important as students' experiences with diversity decrease as they move through college. Institutions should consider incentives that would encourage students to live on campus beyond the first year of college (Kuh, 1994). Of course, this requires making certain that attractive living spaces are available to compete with, but not necessarily trump, what is available off campus. There are many advantages to living on campus, and these advantages must be marketed more convincingly.

Second, student affairs staff must develop new, productive partnerships with their faculty colleagues. Whether as advisors to student organizations, live-in members of residence hall communities, or members of advisory boards consulting on student services and needs, meaningful faculty contact directly with students continues to be important to an intellectually vibrant learning environment. The extended campus offers novel opportunity to expand the service learning curriculum, to have faculty travel abroad with students, and to sustain the educational relationship through electronic communications of varying sorts. Student affairs personnel must take the lead in identifying those options and serving as intermediaries in building bridges between available faculty and interested students.

Third, student affairs staff will require new competencies to be effective in managing the campus living and learning environments of the future. Current staff will require on-the-job training through the work of the National Association of Student Personnel Administrators, the American College Personnel Association, and the many function-specific associations that represent this profession. Graduate preparation programs have the opportunity now to develop new curricular and internship programs that will prepare the next generation of practitioners for service to this rapidly evolving population of learners. The new curriculum must offer exposure to both consumer and learner data such as those presented in this chapter, with opportunity for students to discuss the student as learner as well as the student as customer. Graduate courses and experiences must include expanded focus on environmental theories and practices, engagement influences, and values education.

Further, this new curriculum and the professional development offerings of our associations must provide guidance on the development of partnerships—partnerships with faculty and administrative counterparts, with the consumer sector seeking to penetrate higher education and with the parents and families of our students. Understanding the interconnectivity of all these players and the environmental ramifications of the role each plays individually and collectively will be critical to effective environmental management by the coming cohort of student affairs practitioners.

Finally, we must better understand how students benefit from learning beyond the campus to more effectively leverage student exposure to local neighborhoods, to other parts of our country, and to the world at large to help students dispel their myths and uncover new passions. For in this age of intergroup enmity and global influences, an enlightened citizenry emerging from our diverse campuses will be essential if we are to enrich the undergraduate experiences of all students and prepare them for a life of economic independence and civic responsibility.

References

Baird, L. L. (1988). The college environment revisited: A review of research and theory. In J. C. Smart (Ed.), *Higher education: Handbook of theory and research* (Vol. 4; pp. 1–52). New York: Agathon.

Banning, J. H. (Ed.). (1978). *Campus ecology: A perspective for student affairs.* Cincinnati, OH: National Association of Student Personnel Administrators.

Banning, J. H. (1989). Creating a climate for successful student development: The campus ecology manager role. In U. Delworth & G. Hanson (Eds.), *Student services: A handbook for the profession* (pp. 304–322). San Francisco: Jossey-Bass.

Blocher, D. H. (1974). Toward an ecology of student development. *Personnel and Guidance Journal, 52,* 360–365.

Blocher, D. H. (1978). Campus learning environments and the ecology of student development. In J. Banning (Ed.), *Campus ecology: A perspective for student affairs* (pp. 17–23). Cincinnati, OH: National Association of Student Personnel Administrators.

Brooks, D. (2001, April). The organization kid. *Atlantic Monthly, 287*(4), 46–54.

Brooks, D. (2003, November). People like us. *Atlantic Monthly, 292*(2), 128–130.

College students spend $200 billion per year. (n.d.). Retrieved August 24, 2004, from http://www.harrisinteractive.com/news/allnewsbydate. asp?NewsID=480.

Conyne, R. K., & Clack, R. J. (1981). *Environmental assessment and design.* New York: Praeger.

Fairweather, J. S. (2004). The relative values of teaching and research—revisited. In H. Wechsler (Ed.), *The NEA 2004 almanac of higher education* (pp. 39–60). Washington, DC: National Education Association.

Fallows, J. (2003, November). The new college chaos. *Atlantic Monthly, 292*(4), 106, 108–110, 112–114.

Holland, J. L. (1973). *Making vocational choices: A theory of careers.* Englewood Cliffs, NJ: Prentice-Hall.

Hurtado, S., Milem, J., Clayton-Pedersen, A., & Allen, W. (1999). *Enacting diverse learning environments: Improving the climate for racial/ethnic diversity in higher education.* Washington, DC: George Washington University.

Kuh, G. D. (1994). Creating campus climates that foster learning. In C. C. Schroeder, P. Mable, & Associates, *Realizing the educational potential of residence halls* (pp. 109–132). San Francisco: Jossey-Bass.

Kuh, G. D. (2000). Understanding campus environments. In M. J. Barr & M. Desler (Eds.), *Handbook of student affairs administration* (2nd ed.; pp. 50–72). San Francisco: Jossey-Bass.

Kuh, G. D. (2001). College students today: Why we can't leave serendipity to chance. In P. Altbach, P. Gumport, & B. Johnstone (Eds.), *In defense of American higher education* (pp. 277–303). Baltimore: Johns Hopkins University Press.

Kuh, G. D. (2003). What we're learning about student engagement from NSSE. *Change, 35*(2), 24–32.

Kuh, G. D., & Hu, S. (1999). Unraveling the complexity of the increase in college grades from the mid-1980s to the mid-1990s. *Educational Evaluation and Policy Analysis, 21,* 297–320.

Kuh, G. D., & Hu, S. (2001). Learning productivity at research universities. *Journal of Higher Education, 72,* 1–28.

Kuh, G. D., Schuh, J. H., Whitt, E. J., & Associates. (1991). *Involving colleges: Successful approaches to fostering student learning and personal development outside the classroom.* San Francisco: Jossey-Bass.

Kuh, G. D., & Whitt, E. J. (1988). *The invisible tapestry: Culture in American colleges and universities.* ASHE-ERIC Higher Education Report, no. 1. Washington, DC: Association for the Study of Higher Education.

Levine, A. (2000, March 13). The soul of a new university. *New York Times* editorial, p. A21.

The nation: Students, their attitudes and characteristics. (2003, August 29). *Chronicle of Higher Education,* p. 17.

National Institute of Education Study Group. (1984). *Involvement in learning: Realizing the potential of American higher education.* Washington, DC: National Institute of Education.

National Survey of Student Engagement. (2003). *Converting data into action: Expanding the boundaries of institutional improvement.* Bloomington: Indiana University, Center for Postsecondary Research.

Pascarella, E. T., & Terenzini, P. T. (1991). *How college affects students: Findings and insights from twenty years of research.* San Francisco: Jossey-Bass.

Schwartz, B. (2004). *The paradox of choice: Why more is less.* New York: Harper Collins.

Strange, C. C., & Banning, J. H. (2001). *Creating campus living environments that work.* San Francisco: Jossey-Bass.

Umbach, P., & Kuh, G. D. (2003, May). *Student experiences with diversity at liberal arts colleges: Another claim for distinctiveness.* Paper presented at the annual meeting of the Association for Institutional Research, Tampa, FL.

Winter, G. (2003, October 5). Jacuzzi U.? A battle of perks to lure students. *New York Times,* p. 1.

Woodard, D. B., Love, P., & Komives, S. R. (2000). *Leadership and management issues for a new century.* New Directions for Student Services, no. 92. San Francisco: Jossey-Bass.

Chapter Five

Campus Services

What Do Students Expect?

*Frank P. Ardaiolo, Barbara E. Bender,
and Gregory Roberts*

In Chapter 4, Moneta and Kuh described how student expectations
for the campus environment and the culture of the community differ from their real experiences. This chapter addresses another aspect of the campus experience, the services that institutions provide
to students to support their learning. Of course, there are services
recognized by all as such, career services, health care, counseling
services, and the like. Some other aspects of campus life, such as
residence halls, affect and are imbued with the culture of the campus, while they also include aspects of services that students expect.
Student expectations of the services that will be provided by their
colleges and universities are developed in myriad ways, resulting in
various degrees of congruence with what actually is available. Some
students develop expectations based on the experiences of their
parents, siblings, or friends, while others rely on the popular press
or television and movies to form impressions about what they can
expect when they attend an institution of higher education. The extent to which student expectations are accurate has an enormous
influence on both student satisfaction and persistence.

While there are variations in student expectations and per-ceptions of their colleges, as consumers, they are consistent in their wish to have their institutions offer high-quality services in a pro-fessional manner. Beginning with the recruitment and admissions process through graduation, students expect to be treated as pay-ing customers who receive accurate and timely information from their collegiate service providers and have access, through the in-stitutions, to a broad spectrum of social and recreational oppor-tunities. At the same time, students expect to be more marketable as a result of attending their colleges, able to find a job upon grad-uation, and eligible to be admitted to a graduate or professional school and have the appropriate academic background to succeed.

As colleges and universities grapple with enormous financial dif-ficulties, the increasing costs of technological support, and dilapi-dated infrastructures, maintaining quality and "personal" student services operations is an increasing challenge. At the same time, parents are forming local and national associations to ensure that they have a strong and collective voice in their children's college experience. The Associated Press (2003) reported in newspapers throughout the country that one organization, College Parents of America (2003), has formed to serve as an advocacy group to in-fluence the manner in which colleges and universities develop their priorities and serve their children. Much like stockholders in a cor-poration, the parents view their payment of a term bill as an act of declaring their right to influence the direction of their children's education. College Parents of America (2003) states to parents via its Web site that it is "the only national membership association ded-icated to advocating on your behalf and to serving as your resource as you prepare for and put your children through college."

The financial pressures of the continually escalating costs of college attendance have "raised the bar" for colleges and universi-ties; students and their families expect more programs and better services. Families who have been saving for years or have assumed loans and rearranged their home budgets to pay for college ex-penses expect to see tangible results for their efforts. In return for the financial sacrifices that they make, students and their families expect that colleges and universities will (1) provide what they say that they will provide in promotional materials, (2) offer services and programs to make the college experience valuable and useful,

(3) create opportunities to ease the transition to the world of work or graduate school, (4) and create and implement a collegiate environment that meets their perceptions of what the college experience should entail. They also expect that students will learn while in college, although it is unclear, in many sectors, what they are expected to learn.

The purpose of this chapter is to examine student expectations of the services provided for them at their colleges and universities, identify where and how there may be either misperceptions or inaccuracies, and discuss how colleges and universities can enhance the quality of the services that they provide. The authors discuss the developmental compact that colleges and universities have with their students and focus on aspects of the educational components associated with institutional service operations. In addition, the authors identify approaches for institutions to consider for developing more accurate expectations regarding student services for students and their families.

Student Expectations

The fall 2002 *Chronicle of Higher Education Almanac*, "The Nation: Students, Their Attitudes and Characteristics" (The Nation, 2002), provided data gathered from incoming students at four-year colleges across the nation regarding their expectations and hopes for their college experience. Nearly 50% of first-year students reported that they applied for admission to fewer than two other institutions, and 69% of the respondents attended the institution that was their first choice. The students surveyed in this report expected to be admitted and succeed in the college that they selected.

The first-year student data included the following reasons as "very important" for students making their college selection (The Nation, 2002, p. A37):

- College has very good academic reputation (56%).
- Graduates get good jobs (51%).
- College offered financial assistance (33%).
- Graduates gain admission to top graduate and professional schools (30%).

- College has a good reputation for its social activities (27%).
- College offered merit-based scholarship (21%).
- College offered a need-based scholarship (12%).

The report (The Nation, 2002) also indicates that 57% of the respondents plan to earn at least a B average, and 20% expect to graduate with honors.

The 2002 *Chronicle* report indicated that only 49% of the respondents expected to be satisfied with college even though 76% anticipated earning a bachelor's degree. With three-quarters of the respondents having high hopes for earning a degree, but fewer than half expecting to be satisfied, could it be that those who do not persist had initial low expectations that were realized upon matriculation? Or, could it be that there is a dissonance between what students expect and what institutions provide that results in student dissatisfaction?

The nature of the relationship of students with their institutions is quite complex. Students pay the bills, but institutions set the policies. Institutions enforce their regulations, while students question and sometimes complain about institutional practices and the quality of services and programs. The nexus of the contractual relationship between students and their institutions and students' rights as consumers (Ardaiolo, 1978) presents a fascinating dynamic that continues to shape the creative tensions on campuses across the country. Certainly students should be able to enjoy quality service and programs, but the nature of these services must be defined and offered within the context of the institution's overall mission. The reality is that very few colleges and universities, if any, have the depth and resources to provide everything students expect.

What Should Colleges and Universities Provide for Students?

Contemporary students have high expectations regarding the breadth and quality of services provided by their colleges. In addition to the formal curricular offerings, and with some variations likely as a result of an institution's location, mission, or resources, most students expect their colleges to provide services and co-curricular programs including career planning and placement, recreation and athletics, student activities and social programming, services for students with disabilities, veterans affairs, financial aid, health services, international services, day care, residence life and housing, multicultural and community affairs, academic advising, registration, computer assistance, tutoring, public safety, parking and transportation, campus ministries, and psychological counseling.

In many instances, commercial guidebooks add to the increased expectations that prospective students and their families hold, even if the books are little more than advertising tools focusing on amenities rather than on academic offerings. Still, almost in self-defense, institutions have placed increasing emphasis on providing popular amenities both to "keep up with the competition" and to ensure their admission yields and student satisfaction levels. Formerly stark residence halls have been transformed to hotel-like facilities with private bedrooms, cable TV, Internet connections, appliances, and beautifully constructed recreation centers. "In general, colleges and universities have altered the ways they provide programs and services to recruit and retain students, often in response to the 'consumer sovereignty' which categorizes student-institutional relationships" (Low, 2000, p. 4).

Colleges and universities generally have well-defined mission statements delineating their missions and goals that serve as the guide for determining what academic offerings, programs, and services they offer. Registration services, for example, interpret and communicate institutional academic policies to students, faculty, staff, and the general public and serve as custodians of student records within the context of the institution's mission. The quality of service that the registrar provides subsequently affects students and almost all institutional constituencies. Similarly, financial aid offices, charged with providing access and disbursement of all forms of governmental and private aid to students, have an enormous responsibility for implementing their work in an effective and efficient manner.

The extensive lists of other services enumerated are standard operations at most contemporary colleges and universities. This does not mean, however, that all institutions must provide all services. In an urban community with multiple hospitals and easy access to physicians, for example, administrators should ask whether they should maintain a costly health services program. Similarly, prudent administrators should ask whether a university located near public mental health facilities should provide comprehensive psychiatric and psychological services. The response to these issues will depend on the information institutions glean from the assessment of their programs combined with their goals enumerated in their mission statements.

Assessment and Expectations

In addition to institutionally based research and self-study practices, national studies have been undertaken to discern student expectations and institutional performance in meeting them. One comprehensive study (Low, 2000) focused on changes in student expectations and institutional performance observed in student satisfaction data over a four-year period including 1994 through 1998. The inventory used assessed student perceptions of campus experiences at 745 community, junior, and four-year public and four-year private institutions in North America and included data collected from 423,003 students. Insights gleaned from this study suggested that two-year institutions are outperforming their four-year counterparts in meeting student expectations. Four-year public and private colleges and universities exhibited stable performance, while the public institutions were maintaining a slight edge over those in the private sector. The four-year private colleges, typically the most expensive, seemed to be losing ground in meeting student expectations.

All students, regardless of the type of institution in which they were enrolled, expressed concern about the quality of academic advising offered. Students' basic personal needs, like safety and security, predominated throughout the study, offsetting concerns about more academic and institutional issues. The data suggest also that institutional responsiveness to diversity issues varies widely among institutions and for ethnic groups. There also appeared to be a mismatch between student and institutional values.

Low's study also included focus groups to gain a more complete understanding of the underlying factors affecting student expectations and satisfaction. The major factors that emerged included the following (Low, 2000, p. 10):

- *Cost.* The higher the cost for attending an institution, the higher the expectations of its students, whether the student is paying for tuition and other costs or the institution is paying through scholarships and other forms of financial aid.
- *Reputation.* The more selective the institution, the higher the expectations of its students and the higher levels of satisfaction. Selective institutions tend to know who they are; they have figured out what students want, need, and expect; and they have continued to receive positive feedback for their performance.
- *Value.* Students tend to value much of what the institution says it values. Thus, the greater the value articulated by the institution, the higher the expectations of its current and future students.
- *Overpromising and underdelivering.* An inability to deliver on promises made, especially those made during the recruitment process, results in inflated student expectations and lowered satisfaction.
- *Basic personal needs.* Student expectations rise accordingly when basic personal needs are not acknowledged and addressed by the institution.

These data demonstrate the role that consumerism has on student expectations of their colleges and universities. The importance of student expectations cannot be underestimated, but institutional mission must be the driving force in determining what services are provided and in what fashion.

Expectations, Services, and Learning

Providing efficient and effective services for students is essential, but equally important, we must also strive to provide services in a fashion that complements our educational missions. Service provision, in other words, must consider the learner as the focus, as well as the learning outcomes that will occur as a function of participating in the programs. Cross (2001) suggests that colleges are the "units" in which learning resides and that learning should occur across the institution, not just in the classroom. In other words, it is not as important what teachers teach; it is more important what students learn.

In recent years, the perceived disconnect between the educational and financial benefits of earning a degree has grown. In other words, many students fail to recognize the value of learning for learning's sake (Tagg, 2003). Tagg observes that students, while physically present on our campuses, are simultaneously psychologically absent. He further suggests that the fundamental challenge facing colleges today is to change the expectations of incoming students, their attitudes, and their beliefs about how they think about their school setting, academic work, and their own relationship to their academic institutions. "What we can say with fair confidence at this point is that most students who leave high school and enter college bring with them a set of attitudes and beliefs about schooling and their interaction with educational institutions that tend to insulate them against learning rather than to prepare them for it" (Tagg, 2003, p. 47). Chapter 3 of this volume explores student engagement and the reality that many students are not learning and developing because they are not involved with their institutions or their own education.

Clearly there is much more involved in purchasing an education than buying any other product or service. Failure by students to grasp this can lead to great frustration and, more sadly, an unexamined life. The confluence of educational consumerism, assessment, business practices, and even state funding plans may be contributing to college students' reduced emphasis on the importance of real learning. Students fail to engage fully not only with faculty but with the out-of-class learning opportunities available on campuses today. Students need to embrace the ethos that a college education is more than just attending classes, and institutional practices need to stimulate that understanding. Through developing an appreciation of the totality of the educational experience and the types of engagement that lead to learning, the dissonance between institutions' expectations for students and student expectations for institutions can diminish.

As one enters any train in the London Underground, there are constant reminders to be personally responsible to "Mind the gap!" between the station platform and train doors because the gap varies with each station and passengers cannot take the distance for granted as the same at every station. Indeed, false expectations brought on by habit or inattention can result in personal physical disaster. Students too must mind the gap between the new rising expectations for learning at colleges and universities and their own preconceived consumer mentality of their expectations. Above all, students must be willing to change, for college makes students different—learning is the result of change. Equally important is that students must take responsibility for their own development and learning.

Although Londoners can expect the trains to be safe and efficient, students who come into a university or college should not expect first-class service delivery. A residence hall is not a hotel and cannot be run like one unless students are willing to pay at least $100 a night every night of the semester.

Enlightened colleges and universities expect their residence halls to be integral components of the educational process, where learning occurs and the personal development of students is a primary goal. In residence halls, organizations that are an intentional and integral part of an institution's educational mission, staff members, including student resident assistants, are responsible for creating educational programs that help residents to engage their fellow residents in applying the knowledge gained in the classroom. This engagement outside the classroom leads to appreciating oneself as well as others of different backgrounds and beliefs while building a collegiate community. Students living together in an intentional educational community can learn to express their own beliefs and to be exposed to new ways of doing things while reinforcing or expanding their own values—they learn to negotiate, to compromise, and to lead.

A positive residence hall experience should extend a student's expectation beyond the consumer approach of a good overnight accommodation; certainly all students should expect and be provided with residence halls that are safe, clean, and comfortable. Various reports in the popular press, however, suggest that students are now expecting residence facilities that compete with some of the best hotels in the world, and, as suggested earlier, some schools are attempting to meet this demand to keep the occupancy rates at optimum levels.

At the same time that students seek luxurious accommodations, they often thwart an institution's efforts to maximize learning opportunities through interactions with other students. Students who expect to live in private rooms, for example, often are seeking comfort zones that will protect them from the possibility of living with a roommate of a different racial or cultural background. Such students are failing to embrace the collegiate experience as an extraordinary opportunity to learn about other human beings. Engaging in higher education is a challenge and forces students to cross the gap of comfort that they seek.

The dissonance in expectations can be exemplified when students get frustrated when they have an argument with their new roommate and expect a resident assistant to immediately resolve the issue. The resolution to vacate a room rather than try to address the interpersonal problem is, in the view of many students, the better solution. Parents also will insert themselves into situations and are even encouraged to do so by their children while also failing to see the learning opportunities that can arise in such situations.

The dissonance between the harried student development educator in the residence hall and the involved parents and students can be palpable, because each party brings different expectations—the student affairs educator hopes for learning to occur, and the parents and students want immediate customer satisfaction. This dissonance can be resolved most productively if all involved parties focus on the root causes of problems and take personal responsibility for their actions while being willing to work to change behaviors or attitudes that are more respectful of all involved. We must remind parents and students continually in nonprovocative ways that student development and learning occurs in many ways, including the interactions that occur between students outside of the classroom.

Davis and Murrell (1993) noted that research during the past two decades has demonstrated that the more energy that students direct into their academic lives, including becoming engaged with their studies and campus programs, the greater the likelihood of their having a positive college experience. Assuming that students are willing to learn, total student development can occur that gives meaning through students' newfound knowledge and understanding.

An additional example of the dissonance between expectations and reality can be found in financial aid operations across America. Every institution has an office of financial aid that disburses varying forms of federal, state, private, and institutional monies.

Funding agencies rigorously hold institutions to strict standards that ensure eligible students are provided all possible help within governmental financial aid guidelines.

Institutions also must also provide counseling for those with new loans and those who are exiting, so students fully understand their future fiscal obligations when their loans come due. Students and their families need information and expect high-quality service. Institutions, however, are continually frustrated in their quest to process aid forms for eligible students when many undergraduate and graduate students fail to provide accurate documentation in a timely fashion. Not surprisingly, students who fail to receive a financial aid award invariably blame their colleges, even when they, themselves, are responsible for the problem. Given the complexity of the financial aid process, students' unwillingness to tackle the required details properly is understandable, but managing one's own financial aid application is an important learning experience. Indeed, for many students, signing a promissory note is the first time they enter into a legal contract for which they will be responsible. The most successful student aid administrators are those who continually evaluate their operations and engage students in the process, making even this basic consumer activity a learning experience for students.

Of all administrative areas, career services operations can provide one of the best examples of dissonance when it comes to student expectations and campus realities. Administrators working in career services can speak volumes about the challenges of dealing with students who expect their career counselors to find jobs for them, even on a moment's notice. Without fail, as commencement approaches, students find their way to career services offices for the first time, despite the fact that they have been asked to participate in career seminars from their first semester of enrollment.

Career services professionals rightfully view themselves as educators who want to match students' aspirations and career opportunities with their capabilities. They want students to understand that the most satisfying positions come to those students who are cognizant of their own aspirations and abilities, and who are willing to work to overcome the gaps in their preparation. Regrettably, students, as consumers, can become dissatisfied quickly if they view their career services operation as an employment agency rather than an educational service linked to the institution's mission.

What Institutions Can Do: Strategies for Action

Make Student Expectations a Priority

We have examined the expectations that students have for the services and programs provided by their colleges and universities and considered the fact that, in many cases, what students expect is not the reality of what their institutions provide. This dissonance may be a result of an institution's failure to provide a promised service, or the quality of service is not what students expected. In other instances, however, the expectations that students hold are based on their incorrect or inaccurate assumptions—students expected a certain service or program that the college does not offer. In the case of incorrect and inaccurate assumptions by students, colleges and universities may share part of the blame with the students. Too often, colleges fail to provide enough accurate and accessible information to enable students to know precisely what the institution provides and in what fashion.

The consequences of "expectations dissonance" can be very challenging for students as well for as their colleges and universities. Students expecting smoothly functioning financial aid services, for example, who find a mismanaged and inefficient campus system will be disgruntled and can feel mistreated by their institutions. Rather than speaking well of their alma maters, they can become negative ambassadors very quickly. Administrators, now more than ever, must recognize that the encounters and experiences that students have with campus program and service operations and the manner in which they are treated often are remembered for years beyond graduation.

Institutions can no longer afford to disregard the expectations of their students. If students feel they are receiving less than what they contracted for by enrolling at their colleges, they will make their voices heard collectively on campus, in state legislatures (especially for public institutions), in the media, and, not surprisingly, in the courts. Beyond the potential fallout from failing to provide quality programs, colleges and universities should want to maintain excellence in all aspects of their programs as a source of institutional pride. A college's ethos is perhaps best exemplified in the manner in which it serves students; institutional values are evidenced through the daily fashion in which the college conducts its business. On the one hand, if students are treated with dignity and respect, they recognize that they are a priority. On the other, when students are not treated appropriately or served adequately, the reverse message is received.

To make student's expectations a priority, colleges and universities need to create accurate expectations for students; routinely assess the quality of service programs and adapt services as needed; ensure that effective communications channels are in place and working; and create an institutional ethos that makes student expectations and student learning core institutional values. The remainder of this chapter addresses each of these strategies.

Create Accurate Expectations

In David Lipsky's *Absolutely American: Four Years at West Point* (2003), the author describes the extraordinary experience and transformation that members of the Corps of Cadets undergo at the United States Military Academy (USMA). From their initial treatment at "Beast Barracks," to marching to meals, the first-year student experience is an extraordinary one. What is so critical in helping the cadets to succeed under harsh and extremely stressful conditions is that the USMA makes its expectations extremely clear in their recruitment and admissions materials, in their interviews with prospective students, and through the media. Even casual observers who have never had any direct contact with the USMA have a notion of what is expected of students at West Point and the rigorous demands that will be placed on them.

Conveying the reality of the USMA experience enables potential applicants to know what to expect when they enter West Point. The mission is clear and the expectations for students are clear. All must pass the same tests, clear the same hurdles, and embrace the ethic of a professional soldier committed to duty, honor, and country. In return, the cadets, based on their accurate expectations of USMA, anticipate what they will receive, including professional skills, compensation, character development, monthly compensation, and eventually, a commission as an officer in the U.S. Army.

While there are only a handful of institutions that have missions similar to the USMA, most colleges and universities could benefit from applying the same rigor as West Point does in providing more accurate information about what enrollment in the institution means in the classroom, in out-of-class activities, and in the services that are provided. Utilizing carefully crafted Web sites, recruitment literature, admissions representatives, and alumni ambassadors, colleges and universities need to be more proactive in highlighting their mission and then conveying to prospective and current students how that mission is accomplished through various programs and services. Students need to comprehend the institution's methods for achieving its goals and how those methods will influence students' lives. How, for example, will the institution help the student find a job after graduation, if at all? Does the institution bring prospective employers to campus for student interviews? Are career fairs convened on a regular basis? The answers to these questions should be based on the mission and goals of the institution and how the organization implements those goals.

The need for focusing on institutional mission is critical when developing institutional information for prospective students. While the adage that families do more research when buying a $25,000 automobile than they do when considering a $120,000 investment in a college education may hold true, administrators should still work vigorously to bring clarity to prospective students on what it means to attend their institution. A college's admissions materials must enumerate how attendance at the institution will make a difference—how matriculation will affect the student's life. To do so, of course, means that the institution itself needs to know how students change as a result of their enrollment at the college.

An institution's mission must be at the forefront when making decisions regarding student services and programs and the integration of those activities with the academic experience. The mission statement is the glue that guides all decisions regarding what a college offers and in what fashion. If students then understand and embrace the mission, they will be able to develop a more accurate set of expectations regarding their college experience. This is particularly true in the area of services and programs. Students who attend a professional school with a narrow focus geared to providing a specific credential should not expect broad opportunities for enrolling in courses that diverge greatly from the fields offered by the institution. Similarly, the programs and services provided by that school, and the nature in which the services are provided, should complement and support the academic program.

The mission-specific information that is prepared to help students must be comprehensive to prepare students for their college experience. Without such information, how can administrators think that students will understand what to expect, let alone what the institution expects of them? Why, for example, does an institution provide residence halls, career services, or student activities? What role does the distribution of financial aid play in the mission of the institution? How does the delivery of service in these operations support the mission of the institution? Are these realistic questions asked by senior administrators? Or, if the questions are asked, how are the answers conveyed to students so they know what to expect? Without information from the college, how would a first-year student know that living in a residence hall is considered an integral part of the developmental experience for undergraduates as much as it is a place to plug in their computers and DVD players?

Assess, Adapt, and Anticipate

Institutional assessment efforts should be geared, in part, toward identifying student expectations as they entered the institution, whether they are being met, and, if not, what can be done to address student concerns. Without such efforts, colleges cannot know whether they are meeting their goals and the expectations of their students. Simultaneously, when trends appear in the data that suggest a widely perceived problem, efforts can be undertaken to address the concerns. "To plan effectively and make the critical decisions that affect our student affairs divisions and institutions, we must have the ability to gather information in a rational, planned, financially feasible, and believable fashion" (Bender, 1995).

Comprehensive national research on student expectations has, for example, highlighted "academic advising" as an endless source of frustration for students at countless institutions (Low, 2000). Perhaps from expectations developed through watching Mr. Chips' films, or promises made in recruitment literature, college students expect to have routine and sustained interactions with a faculty member who will guide them through the collegiate experience. The reality of how academic advising works, however, varies greatly. Some factors that influence how academic advising is conceptualized and delivered include the nature and size of an institution, a student's major, whether or not faculty signatures are required when registering or dropping courses, and whether advising undergraduate or graduate students is even considered a part of a faculty member's job description. These institutional realities, however, are not necessarily understood or embraced by students who expect individual attention. Academic advising is just one aspect of the college experience that must be portrayed accurately prior to enrollment. Students need to know what to expect, so that disappointment will not influence their overall satisfaction with their colleges and universities.

Monitoring student utilization of services and programs and the reasons students may not be engaging in them will also help to identify whether resources are directed or delivered appropriately and whether the students consider the service or program beneficial. As suggested by Schuh and Upcraft, "If our intended clientele do not use what we offer, then our intended purposes cannot be achieved" (Upcraft & Schuh, 1996, p. 113). Gathering, maintaining, and using comprehensive evaluative data regarding programs and services will enable institutions to make informed decisions about the allocation of resources (Upcraft & Schuh, 1996, p. 114).

Anticipating student expectations can be difficult, but using sound benchmarking practices, as suggested earlier, can help considerably throughout the process. Benchmarking can enable colleges and universities to compare their programs with the best practices of other comparable operations to identify new ways of doing things. Especially important in the Internet age, if one college has instituted an innovative and successful practice that engages students, administrators can be sure that students across the country will know about the innovation and ask why the new program or service is not available on their campus.

Of particular importance in this process is the need to keep institutional mission in the forefront. Are the new programs or services for which students are clamoring appropriate for another institution? Do they complement the institutional mission? Do they appropriately engage students in activities that foster learning? These questions must always be asked when trying to meet student expectations.

Provide Communication Channels

In addition to formal assessments of services, the creation and use of easily accessible communications methods can provide students with opportunities to raise questions and voice their concerns before problems become crises. Minor problems with service delivery can escalate to major student dissatisfaction with the institution when deficiencies are not addressed. Electronic and paper suggestion boxes, telephone surveys, and advertising widely the names and contact information for administrators and faculty to whom concerns should be voiced can make a big difference in resolving problems with campus services. Some institutions have also appointed people to serve as ombudspersons, or independent advocates, to help research and resolve complaints for all campus constituencies.

Maintain Institutional Integrity

When describing our institutional missions and the services we provide, our primary concern must be to do so with accuracy and integrity. Much like the question asked during accreditation processes, "Are we doing what we say we are doing?" institutional leaders must ensure that their colleges and universities follow through on what they promise their students. If an institution promises in its literature that students will receive routine academic advising and learn in small class settings, for example, then such expectations must be met. The most significant indicator of a higher education institution's values is the manner in which it conducts its business and provides its services to its multiple publics, especially its students. It is incumbent on institutional leaders to ensure that the services that are provided are those that are promised.

References

Ardaiolo, F. P. (1978). *Educational consumer protection at Indiana University.* Unpublished dissertation, Indiana University, Bloomington.

Associated Press. (2003, November 29). Advocate helps parents adjust to college demands. *Home News Tribune,* A2.

Bender, B. (1995, March). *NASPA symposium on institutional research, assessment, and evaluation: An examination of contemporary practice in student affairs.* Program presentation, National Association of Student Personnel Administrators National Conference, San Diego.

College Parents of America. (2003). Retrieved December 2, 2003, from http://www.collegeparents.org/advocacy.html.

Cross, K. P. (2001, July–Aug.). Leading-edge efforts to improve—the Hesburgh Awards. *Change*, 31–37.

Davis, T. M., & Murrell, P. H. (1993). *Turning learning into teaching: The role of student responsibility in the collegiate experience.* ASHE-ERIC Higher Education Report, no. 8. Washington, DC: George Washington University, School of Education and Human Development.

Low, L. (2000). *Are college students satisfied? A national analysis of changing expectations.* New Agenda Series. Indianapolis: USA Group.

Lipsky, D. (2003). *Absolutely American: Four years at West Point.* New York: Houghton Mifflin.

The nation: Students, their attitudes and characteristics. (2002, August 30). *Chronicle of Higher Education*, pp. 26–31.

Tagg, J. (2003). *The learning paradigm college.* Bolton, MA: Anker.

Upcraft, M. L., & Schuh, J. H. (1996). *Assessment in student affairs: A guide for practitioners.* San Francisco: Jossey-Bass.

Chapter Six

Student Expectations About Paying for College

Are They Reasonable?

John H. Schuh and Leah Ewing Ross

Stories about the cost of attending college are pervasive in the popular press and higher education publications. In Iowa, for example, commercials air regularly on radio stations inviting students to contract with various companies to help them resolve their questions about how they will pay for college. The *Chronicle of Higher Education* publishes frequent columns that focus on the cost of attending college, as well as how institutions of higher education are coping with reduced budgets and increased costs. At the time of this writing, a recent issue of the *Chronicle* (Pulley, 2003) featured a series of stories under the banner "The Big Squeeze," all of which focused on the relatively precarious financial positions of many colleges and universities. Despite the enormous financial pressures, in fall 2001, 14,120,740 undergraduate students (U.S. Department of Education, 2003a) enrolled in colleges and universities across the country. In addition to the inevitable academic pressures that they will face, in order to succeed, these students will have to manage an increasingly complex financial aid system, consider how much debt to incur, and determine how many hours they can work at a job to help pay for their educations.

This chapter describes selected aspects of student expectations pertaining to the costs of college attendance. Specifically, we examine the following four questions:

1. What does it cost to go to college?
2. What do students and their parents expect a college education to cost?
3. How do students finance their educations?
4. How do students manage their debt after they graduate?

In exploring these questions, we focus primarily on dependent students—those who are claimed as exemptions by their parents or guardians for the purposes of federal tax requirements in the United States. We have chosen this population because the financial backgrounds of independent students are unique and even more complex than those of dependent students, making attempts to generalize or categorize their experiences prohibitive.

When it comes to financing college, student experiences vary widely. For those who are fortunate, whose parents or other benefactors assume the expenses, financing their educations is not much of an issue. On the other end of the continuum are those students who depend solely on their personal resources to pay for tuition, fees, room and board, and ancillary expenses. These students face tremendous pressures to pay their bills and not acquire significant debt. Then there are those in the middle, who have some resources but not enough to cover the entire cost of attendance. For these students and their parents, financing an education can evolve into a patchwork quilt of spending one's savings, borrowing, working at various jobs, and personal ingenuity.

What Does It Cost to Go to College?

The answer to this question is complex, because it depends on myriad factors and variables. Particularly significant among these factors is the type of institution that students choose to attend. Public institutions cost less than private colleges, and two-year colleges tend to be less expensive than four-year institutions. Institutional costs also vary greatly depending on their locations. As we consider an overview of how institutional type is related to the cost of college attendance, it is important to note that a school's advertised costs, or "sticker price," are not necessarily the bill actually paid by its students. Similar to buying an automobile, the advertised cost for college is the highest amount that might be charged, but, in reality, the net price, what the students actually pay, may be less. Hill, Winston, and Boyd (2003) suggest that a discussion of sticker prices for colleges and universities can be misleading, because such conversations center on the "average" student when, in fact, a student from a median family income "won't pay the sticker price at a school with need-based financial aid" (p. 4).

To keep the cost comparisons simple, we consider the basic charges that students incur when they enroll. While the costs of books and supplies, transportation, and personal items are not inconsequential, they can vary widely from student to student. To avoid confounding this discussion with those costs, therefore, we focus on the required costs of attendance—tuition, fees, and room and board.

The range of the cost of attendance can be dramatic, as we suggested. The College Board (2003a) conducts periodic surveys of attendance costs, and recently published its analysis of the costs of attendance for the 2003–04 academic year. Two-year public institutions (also known as community colleges) charged, on average, $1,905 for tuition and fees, an increase of 13.8% over the previous year. Room and board costs were not computed for these schools, since community college students generally live at home and commute to campus.

Four-year public institutions charged an average of $10,636 for tuition and fees and room and board, an increase of 9.8% from 2002–03. This included a 14.1% increase in tuition and fees, up from $4,115 in 2002–03 to $4,694. Four-year private institutions, not surprisingly, were the most expensive. On average they charged $26,854 for tuition and fees and room and board, an increase of 5.7% over the $25,403 they charged in 2002–03. Tuition alone increased 6%, from $18,596 in 2002–03 to $19,710 in 2003–04. The College Board's (2003a) analysis of the distribution of tuition and fees at public and private institutions revealed the wide range of differences within institutional types. The cost of tuition and fees at public four-year institutions, for example, ranged from less than $2,000 (1.2% of all students attending public four-year institutions paid that amount) to more than $8,000 (3.6% paid that amount). The majority of students paid between $3,000 and $5,999 for tuition and fees (more than 65%), and many students paid between $3,000 and $3,999 (24.3%).

The range in the cost of tuition and fees for students attending private institutions was similarly striking. A few students (2.4%) paid less than $4,000, while 14.1% paid more than $28,000 in tuition and fees. On average, students paid $16,000 to $19,999 to attend private colleges. More than 44% paid more than $20,000 in tuition and fees to attend private colleges in 2003–04, as reported by the College Board (2003a).

Particularly significant are the differences between sticker prices and the net prices charged at private colleges. In a recent study of affordability at selective private colleges and universities, Hill, Winston, and Boyd (2003) found that in 2001–02, "low income students . . . [paid] a net price of $7552 while aided high income students [paid] $23,690—a difference of 214%" (p. 14). This does not necessarily mean, however, that the cost of attending these colleges represented a lower portion of the students' family incomes than the portions paid by other students. Rather, it provides an example of how much costs can vary for students attending the same institution, particularly private colleges and universities. Yet regardless of the types of institutions students attend and the amounts they pay, nearly all have experienced annual increases in tuition and fees in recent years.

The effects of reduced purchasing power have also had an influence on the increase in the cost of college attendance, but that represents only a portion of the increase. According to the College Board (2003a), if one were to look at the rise in the cost of attendance using constant 2003 dollars, going to college has become more expensive over time. The average cost of tuition and fees at a private four-year college, for example, was $7,940 (using constant 2003 dollars) in 1976–77, but had risen to $19,710 in 2003–04. At a public four-year institution, the cost in 1976–77 was $1,933 but had risen to $4,694 in 2003, again using constant 2003 dollars. Community college attendance has not been immune from these increases. In 1976–77 the average cost of attendance was $887 using 2003 dollars. By the

2003–04 academic year, the cost of attendance at a community college had grown to $1,905. Similarly, when the cost of room and board is added to the total cost of attendance, the sticker price had exceeded the rate of inflation (College Board, 2003a).

The rates described are gross costs that do not take into account the increasing income of families. Davis (2000) examined the net cost (after subtracting institutionally funded financial aid) as a percentage of median family income. He found that in 1980 the cost of attendance at public institutions as a percentage of median family income was 8.8%, and that by 1997 it had grown to 11.2%. For a private college, the cost of attendance had risen from 18.0% of the median family income in 1980 to 25.2% of the median family income in 1997. These increases, to be sure, represent growth in the costs to families, but as Davis puts it, "the 'affordability' crisis may for many relatively affluent families be a crisis of *willingness to pay* rather than a crisis of *ability to pay* for rising college charges" (2000, p. 53; author's emphasis).

Davis (2000) also examined the number of days of median earnings for the average worker, by state, required to cover net average costs of attendance at four-year public colleges in 1997. He found a great range in the number of days required, from 45, 38, and 35 in Vermont, Rhode Island, and Pennsylvania, respectively, to 21 in Alaska, North Carolina, Utah, and Wisconsin. If one were to think of this analysis as a measure of effort, people have to work more than twice as hard to pay for a year of college in some states as compared to others. Presumably, the challenge of paying for a college education at a public institution has a different meaning to citizens depending on the state in which they reside.

Finally, the College Board (2003a) reported the cost of attendance by region. In general, it indicated that the cost of attendance consistently is more expensive in some regions of the country than others. Two- and four-year public institutions and four-year private colleges, for example, have a higher cost of attendance in New England and the Middle Atlantic states than the rest of the country. Institutions in the South, West, and Southwest have lower costs of attendance. Consistent with their geographic location, colleges and universities in the Midwest rank in the middle, regardless of institutional type.

What Do Students and Their Parents Expect a College Education to Cost?

Hartle (1998) reported on a study conducted by the American Council on Education that examined "the public's knowledge and attitudes about financing higher education" (p. 20). A number of conclusions were reached from this study:

- In spite of the high cost, the respondents thought that higher education represents a good value.
- The public thinks college is too expensive and that costs can be brought down without affecting academic quality.
- While members of the public believe that they have a good knowledge about the cost of college, they greatly overestimate costs.
- The public has no idea why the price of college continues to increase.
- The public is not aware of how much financial aid is available to help pay college costs.
- Members of the public think colleges are indifferent to concerns about college costs. (Hartle, 1998)

Among the overarching conclusions that might be drawn from this study is that in spite of the perceived costs of college attendance, the respondents still agree that the cost of attending college is a price worth paying. Equally important, however, is the reported perception that those who determine and set college costs are seemingly indifferent to the plight of those who have to pay the bills. Finally, while the respondents think that the cost of attending college is too high, they do not seem to be aware of the net costs.

In another study reported by the *Chronicle of Higher Education* (Chronicle Survey of Public Opinion on Higher Education, 2004), the majority of the respondents (68%) strongly agreed or agreed that they thought colleges could cut costs without reducing the quality of their institutions. Of these same respondents, 93% indicated that colleges and universities are among the most valuable resources in the United States.

It's All Relative

Stringer, Cunningham, O'Brien, and Merisotis (1998) produced a comprehensive report (*It's All Relative*) on the role of parents in financing their children's college educations. The report examined such issues as saving and borrowing for college, and how selected characteristics of parents related to their approaches to preparing for helping to finance their child's education. Parents who possess the following characteristics are more likely to save and contribute more to the students' educations than those who do not possess these attributes:

- Parents who have higher income or wealth
- Parents who are older
- Parents who have fewer dependents
- Parents who are married
- Parents who have higher education levels

Student characteristics also related to parental contributions to their educational expenses. The following factors seem to relate to larger parental contributions:

- Students who are in their first or second years of college
- Students who attend college full time
- Students who are women
- Students who are white
- Students who have aspirations for advanced degrees
- Students who do not have access to non-family resources such as work or financial aid

Finally, they found that students who attend comparatively expensive institutions or live away from home can expect more in the way of parental contributions.

Stringer et al. concluded the following in their report: "Parents are contributing slightly increasing amounts of money to their children for higher education, primarily in the form of gifts. It is common for them to provide non-cash assistance, such as clothing, food and medical care. Their levels of financial support vary depending on the unique circumstances of each family. It is clear that

parent income and the price of attendance are the two predomi-
nant factors influencing the levels of parents' financial assistance
to their children" (1998, p. 30).

Additional conclusions related to this discussion include the
following:

- The dollar amounts that parents contribute to their children's
  educations cover an increasingly diminished proportion of the
  average price of attendance.
- Current income is the most common source of funds for parents who assist their students.
- Parents generally do not go into debt to provide assistance to
  their children.
- Parents are not realistic about the cost of attendance. On average, according to the study, parents saved about $9,956 to assist
  their children with college costs.

The conclusions from this report mirror, to a great extent, the
conclusions from Hartle's analysis. Once again, parents do not seem
prepared to assume the costs of college, and even though parents
perceive the costs as higher than they are, they are not adjusting
their behaviors (saving more money) to meet these expenses.

Getting Ready to Pay for College

The U.S. Department of Education (2003b) published a comprehensive report on what students and their parents know about paying for college in 2003 (*Getting Ready to Pay for College*). This report
was produced using the Youth Survey of the 1999 National Household Education Survey. The basic goal was to identify and report
what 6th to 12th grade students and their parents knew about the
cost of higher education tuition.

The respondents who participated in the survey reported that
they had obtained information about college costs, already knew
the cost of attendance, or that they had not obtained such information, or could not estimate the cost of attendance. This summary reports just on those who reported that they had obtained
information about the cost of attendance or were confident that
they could estimate the cost. Several patterns emerged based on

the responses of those students and their parents who felt they were informed about college costs. They include the following:

- High school students in grades 11 and 12 and their parents were more likely to have obtained information about the cost of tuition and fees than families with students in 6th–8th grade.
- Female students and their parents were more likely than male students to have obtained information about costs.
- Other, non-Hispanic (as categorized specifically in the report) students and white students and their parents more commonly had obtained cost information than African American or Hispanic students or their parents.
- Students with higher grade point averages and their parents more likely had obtained cost information than those students with lower grades and their parents.
- Students who attended private schools and their parents had obtained cost information more often than those who attended public schools by a narrow margin, and more commonly than students who were home schooled by a wide margin (U.S. Department of Education, 2003b).
- Parents with more education and higher incomes had obtained cost information more often than parents with less education and lower incomes (U.S. Department of Education, 2003b, pp. 18–19).

These patterns typically repeated themselves for respondents who indicated they could estimate the cost of tuition and fees at the institutions their children planned to attend. Exceptions were male students and their parents who reported more often that they could estimate college costs, and that 6th-8th grade students and their parents reported being able to estimate costs more often than 11th and 12th grade students and their parents.

Students and their parents' reporting that they had obtained information or could estimate the cost of attendance, and actually being able to do so, are two different issues. In actuality, this study found that students and their parents typically overestimated the cost of tuition and fees, regardless of institutional type. Summarizing the responses of 11th and 12th grade students and their parents who were the most informed according to their self-report, Table 6.1 indicates the estimates of the students and their parents and the actual costs of the institutions about which the students reported having information. As the table illustrates, typically students and parents overestimated the cost of tuition and fees. This is particularly the case for those students (and their parents) who planned to attend a two- or four-year public institution. Students also overestimated the cost of tuition and fees at private four-year colleges, although their parents underestimated the cost by only $200.

The U.S. Department of Higher Education (2003b) report also reported the extent to which students and parents could accurately estimate the cost of tuition, defining accuracy as being within 25% of the actual average cost for the types of institutions the students planned to attend. Parents were more accurate in their estimates than students. Of the total sample, 26% of the parents and 16.3% of the students met the accuracy test. Family income, parental education, private schooling, higher student grades, ethnicity, and being closer to college in age (11th and 12th graders) all affected the ability of the respondents to estimate cost accurately. For those who estimated incorrectly, students and parents were more likely to overestimate the cost of tuition and fees.

Such factors as plans to attend a private college, having talked with someone or read materials about financial aid, and higher parental educational attainment were related to having more information about college costs for both students and parents. Parents who were more involved in their children's schooling tended to know more about college costs than parents who were less involved,

Table 6.1 Costs of Tuition and Fees Reported by 11th and 12th Grade Students and Parents (1998–1999 Academic Year)

| Institutional Type | Tuition and Fee Estimates | | |
	By Students	By Parents	Actual Cost
Four-year public	$5,366	$5,799	$3,247
Four-year private	$16,539	$14,506	$14,709
Two-year public	$5,276	$3,933	$1,554

Source: U.S. Department of Education (2003b).

and higher household income was also related to more parental knowledge about college costs. Several characteristics were related to student self-reported knowledge about college costs. These included male students who reported having more information than female students, and black students who reported having more information than white students.

Several factors were related to accurate cost estimates, according to the report. While parental education was related to knowledge about costs, it was not related to being able to predict them accurately. On the other hand, higher household income was not related to knowledge about costs, but it was related to being able to predict them. Parents with higher incomes and higher levels of education were able to predict costs more accurately. The study also indicated that if parents had sought information about financial aid or other methods of offsetting costs, they were able to predict expenses with greater precision. Similarly, if students had talked to their parents or their teachers or counselors about college costs, they, too, more accurately estimated the tuition and fees at the colleges in which they planned to enroll (U.S. Department of Education, 2003b).

Several conclusions emerge from these studies. While students and their parents consistently overestimate the cost of tuition and fees, parents have not changed their saving behaviors to meet these increasing costs. Additionally, parents, taken in the aggregate, did not appear to be interested in going into debt to help their children pay for their educations. As a result, students have to find other sources to pay for their college educations. In the next section we examine how students actually pay for their educations.

How Do Students Finance Their Educations?

The U.S. Department of Education (2003c) prepared a lengthy report on how dependent low- and middle-income students financed their college educations during the 1999–2000 academic year. This report is the primary reference source for this portion of the chapter. As mentioned previously in this chapter, every student's story is somewhat different, so inferences should not be made about the experiences of individual students when examining these data in the aggregate.

Low-Income Students

Low-income students were defined as those students whose family income was below $30,000. Typically, they were eligible for Pell Grants (U.S. Department of Education, 2003c). The approaches they took to financing their educations are summarized in Table 6.2. The key components of Table 6.2 are the net price and expected family contribution (EFC). When the EFC is less than the net price, students have to make up the difference through work and borrowing (represented by loans on Table 6.2). One can conclude from Table 6.2 that the larger the net price, the more students have to rely on loans and work to cover their expenses. This is particularly true if they attend private not-for-profit doctoral or liberal arts institutions. The net price of these institutions is $9,100 with an EFC of $1,400. The difference, $7,700, needs to be made up through loans and work.

Middle-Income Students

Middle-income students were defined as coming from families with incomes ranging from $45,000 to $74,999. Typically, they were not eligible for Pell Grants, but they did qualify for subsidized loans.

Table 6.2 How Low-Income Students Financed Their Educations (1999–2000; in dollars)

Institutional Type	Budget	Net Price	Grant Aid	Loans	Work	EFC
Public two-year	8,400	5,400	2,900	500	5,000	1,000
Public nondoctoral	10,300	4,600	5,600	2,200	3,600	1,100
Public doctoral	12,900	5,500	7,400	2,900	3,800	1,500
Private nondoctoral except liberal arts	18,100	6,000	11,900	4,100	2,700	1,200
Private doctoral and liberal arts	27,300	9,100	18,200	5,600	2,800	1,400

Source: U.S. Department of Education (2003c), Fig. 8.

Among the differences these students faced is that they received less aid money than their low-income counterparts, resulting in a larger net price with a considerably larger EFC. In fact, the EFC was large enough to cover the costs of attendance at all of the public institutions. Loans became particularly important for these students if they chose to attend private institutions. On average, they borrowed more than $5,000 to cover their costs for the 1999–2000 academic year. A summary of their approaches to financing is illustrated in Table 6.3.

Table 6.3 How Middle-Income Students Financed Their Educations (1999–2000; in dollars)

Institutional Type	Budget	Net Price	Grant Aid	Loans	Work	EFC
Public two-year	8,600	7,700	1,000	400	6,000	8,800
Public nondoctoral	11,000	7,500	3,600	2,500	4,200	8,300
Public doctoral	13,300	8,700	4,600	2,900	3,700	9,000
Private nondoctoral except liberal arts	22,100	9,400	12,800	5,800	2,800	8,400
Private doctoral and liberal arts	28,700	14,600	14,100	5,100	2,700	8,600

Source: U.S. Department of Education (2003c), Fig. 8.

Borrowing

The use of loans has become an increasingly important way to pay for college. The College Board (2003b) reported that for the 2002–03 academic year, loans constituted 54% of all financial aid, grants represented 40% of total assistance, and work income and education tax credits comprised the remainder of all student aid. Using constant 2002 dollars, the College Board noted that total aid that financed college expenses had grown by 137% from academic year 1992–93 through academic year 2002–03 (2003b, p. 7). Federal loans and nonfederal loans grew the most rapidly, followed by institutional grants, state grant programs, and federal grant programs. Since loans are the most common form of financial aid as measured by student participation, it is particularly important to study the growth of loan programs to understand how students finance their college educations.

Taking all loans into consideration, the number of student borrowers has grown from 3,845,000 in 1993–94 to 6,174,000 in 2002–03. The average loan, measured in constant dollars, had grown from $3,672 to $4,124 from 1992–94 to 2002–03, according to the College Board (2003b). More students are borrowing, and those who borrow are borrowing more money over time.

Undergraduate participants in the subsidized Stafford loan program exhibit a number of common characteristics. They include the following:

- Female students are more likely to borrow than males.
- Students 23 years of age or younger borrow more commonly than older students.
- Proportionally, black students are more likely to borrow than white students, Hispanic students, or Asian Pacific Islander students.
- Dependent students are more likely to borrow than independent students.
- Dependent students from lower- or middle-quartile family incomes are more likely to borrow. Students from the highest quartile family income are less likely to borrow.
- Students with parents who have less than a bachelor's degree are more likely to borrow. Students whose parents have bachelor's degrees or education beyond a bachelor's degree are less likely to borrow.
- Students who attend full time are more likely to borrow than students who attend part time.
- Third- and fourth-year students are more likely to borrow than students who are in their first or second years of college.
- Students who work between 1 and 34 hours per week are more likely to borrow than students who work more than 35 hours per week, or do not work at all.
- Students who attend public two-year colleges are less likely to borrow than students who attend public four-year colleges, private not-for-profit four-year colleges or private for-profit institutions.

- Students in bachelor's degree programs are more likely to borrow than students who are pursuing two-year degrees or are enrolled in certificate programs.
- Undergraduate students who aspire to master's or professional degrees are more likely to borrow than those who aspire to bachelor's or associate's degrees, or who seek to complete certificate programs.
- Students with an unmet family need of $3,000 or more are more likely to borrow than those with an unmet need of $2,999 or less.
- Students who attend institutions with an estimated price of attendance of less than $5,000 are less likely to borrow than those who attend institutions with higher estimated prices of attendance.

Private Loans

Private loans are an important source of financial aid when all other forms of aid, combined, do not provide the necessary resources for students to enroll in their chosen colleges. Private loans grew in volume from approximately $1.1 billion in 1995–96 to $5 billion in 2001–02. This amount compares with $27.6 billion in federal loan volume in 1995–96 and $41.3 billion in 2001–02 (Wegmann, Cunningham, & Merisotis, 2003). While federal loans dwarf private loans in terms of the total award amount, the 346% increase in private loans over this time period indicates that these loans are becoming increasingly important to a growing portion of the borrowing population.

Wegmann, Cunningham, and Merisotis (2003) identified several characteristics of undergraduate private loan borrowers. These include the following:

- The majority attended private not-for-profit institutions or private for-profit institutions.
- They enrolled in institutions located in the plains or the mideast regions of the country.
- They are 23 years of age or younger.
- They are single, never married, dependent students.
- The family income of dependent students was in the middle quartile.

- They attended college full time and worked part time.
- They were enrolled in bachelor's degree programs.
- They lived on campus.
- They enrolled in institutions with tuition and fees ranging from $10,000 to $19,999.
- Their estimated family contribution (EFC) was $1,000 to $4,999.
- Their financial need was $20,000 or more.
- They had borrowed the maximum total allowable under the Stafford loan program.

Wegmann, Cunningham, and Merisotis (2003) concluded that "the characteristics of students who receive private loans—especially their attendance at relatively high priced institutions or programs—suggest that many private loan borrowers prefer to borrow the additional funds to enroll at the institution or program of their choice, rather than attending lower-priced schools because of inadequate financial resources" (p. 53). They add that "private loans help students go to schools they *want* to attend, rather than schools they might *have* to attend because of inadequate financial resources" (p. 70; italics in original).

Once students develop and implement plans to finance college, which may include borrowing, they will also need to identify a plan to manage and repay their debt. Debt management is examined in the final section of this chapter.

How Do Students Manage Their Debt After They Graduate?

Various studies have been conducted to determine the amount of debt that students incur as a result of borrowing to finance college and the extent to which they have repaid the debt. In general, the number of borrowers in default has declined over time. A recent report from the Inspector General of the U.S. Department of Education concluded that the cohort default rate had declined from 9.6% in 1996 to 5.7% in 1999. The third-year default rate for years studied had ranged from 4.1% in 1996 to 3.5% in 1999 (Office of the Inspector General, 2003).

The U.S. Department of Education examined the experiences of students who received bachelor's degrees during 1992–93 and found that half of the students had taken out loans to pay for college (U.S. Department of Education, 2000). On average, they had borrowed $10,100. By 1997, of the students who did not borrow additional money to support pursuit of a graduate or professional degree, 18% had retired their loans. Thirty-three percent (33%) of bachelor's degree recipients still owed, on average, $7,100 and were repaying an average of $151 per month. As might be expected, the more that had been borrowed as students, the more they had to pay each month to retire their loans, ranging from $64 if they had borrowed less than $5,000 to $241 if they had borrowed $15,000 or more (U.S. Department of Education, 2000).

Scherschel (2000) examined changes in borrowing patterns from 1995 to 1999. She found that the compounded average annual percentage change from 1995 to 1999 for those who had Stafford loans was 3.7% for undergraduate students. Their average Stafford debt was $9,805 in 1999. Scherschel also found that the percentage of undergraduates who borrowed more than $10,000 had grown from 33.7% in 1995 to 40.1% in 1999. She concluded, "The majority of community college, proprietary school and undergraduate students owe less than $10,000 when they leave school. Still, this group is shrinking" (p. 5).

Do increasing debt loads affect students' decisions to attend graduate school? According to Heller (2001), it does not. He concluded that "undergraduate borrowing appears to have little impact on whether students attend graduate school" (p. 32). Concomitant with the effect of loans on attending graduate school is the relationship between borrowing and occupational choice. Heller noted that "there were no significant differences in the undergraduate borrowing rates and loan levels in April 1994. All had borrowing rates with three percentage points of the average rate of 50 percent, and the range of borrowing was within 2 percent of the average for all students ($10,210)" (2001, p. 17). These calculations may be different for more recent college graduates who have higher levels of borrowing than their predecessors from the early to mid-1990s.

Finally, Volkwein and Cabrera (1998) reported on characteristics of those who default on student loans. They found that people who were married without dependents and who earned bachelor's degrees were far less likely to default on their loans than single parents without degrees or certificates. "Degree completion, marital status, and dependent children—are the great equalizers among the races. Borrowers in similar circumstances, especially with respect to earned degrees, marital status, and family size, exhibit generally similar levels of income and loan default, regardless of race or ethnic group" (pp. 114–115).

Conclusion

From the previous discussion, several conclusions emerge. First, the cost of a college education varies widely. Students who are particularly interested in managing their cost of attendance can start at a two-year college, transfer to a public four-year college, and spend considerably less than students who attend a private four-year college exclusively for their baccalaureate experiences. Students who attend public colleges in their states of residence spend considerably less than students who attend public colleges in other states or who enroll in private colleges. Students who live at home will spend less than those who live on campus. Should students keep their options open when applying to college, including consideration of all types of colleges? Definitely. Doing so increases the likelihood that students will have more opportunities available to them. Might students have different experiences depending on the types of colleges they attend and where they live? Of course. But in viewing the cost of college attendance exclusively through an economic lens, such differences cannot be considered, although they should not be ignored in considering the totality of a student's experience (see, for example, Pascarella, Terenzini, & Blimling, 1994).

Second, students and their parents tend to overestimate the cost of tuition and fees, even when they have sought this information or think they know it. Obviously, this disparity needs to be addressed from a variety of perspectives. Colleges and universities need to make the cost of attendance clearer to prospective students and their parents. High school counselors and others who advise applicants and their parents also need to provide clear, concise information about the cost of attendance. And while it is easy to blame the media for sensationalizing the cost of college attendance, the media could be helpful in reporting the cost from a more balanced perspective, that is, not just focusing on the most expensive colleges, or on sticker prices, and leaving the real cost of attending the local community college or state university to back pages of their publications.

Third, students increasingly are borrowing to cover college costs, and those who do borrow are borrowing at higher levels. While colleges and universities continue to contribute generously to grant programs, the fastest growing form of financial aid is loans. Parents, even though they overestimate the cost of attendance in the aggregate, are not changing their saving habits to assist their children with their college expenses.

Fourth, the best studies to date indicate that in spite of increased borrowing, no relationship has emerged between the amounts students borrow and their occupational decisions or their decisions to attend graduate school. While this may change in the future, the increasing decision to borrow has not affected these critically important areas.

Do students and their parents have reasonable expectations in terms of paying for college? The tentative answer to this question is that, if anything, they overestimate the cost of attendance, but this overestimation appears to have little or no effect on college attendance. No relationships have emerged in terms of the ever-increasing cost of attendance and students' behavior except that they borrow more. There is no way to know if such trends will continue in the future, but at the time of this writing, even though costs have continued to rise at rates exceeding the rate of inflation, students and their parents have found ways to manage the cost of attending college.

References

The Chronicle Survey of Public Opinion on Higher Education. (2004, May 7). *Chronicle of Higher Education*, pp. A12–A13.

The College Board. (2003a). *Trends in college pricing.* Washington, DC: Author.

The College Board. (2003b). *Trends in student aid.* Washington, DC: Author.

Davis, J. S. (2000). *College affordability: Overlooked long-term trends and recent 50-state patterns.* Indianapolis: USA Group Foundation.

Hartle, T. W. (1998, Spring). Clueless about college costs. *The Presidency.* Washington, DC: American Council on Education.

Heller, D. E. (2001). *Debts and decisions: Student loans and their relationship to graduate school and career choice.* Indianapolis: Lumina Foundation.

Hill, C., Winston, G., & Boyd, S. (2003). *Affordability: Family incomes and net prices at highly selective private colleges and universities* (Discussion Paper No. 66). Williamstown, MA: Williams Project on the Economics of Higher Education.

Office of the Inspector General. (2003). *Audit to determine if cohort default rates provide sufficient information on defaults in the Title IV loan programs* (ED-OIG/A03-C0017). Philadelphia: U.S. Department of Education.

Pascarella, E. T., Terenzini, P. T., & Blimling, G. S. (1994). The impact of residential life on students. In C. C. Schroeder, P. Mable, & Associates, *Realizing the educational potential of residence halls* (pp. 22–52). San Francisco: Jossey-Bass.

Pulley, J. L. (2003, December 19). The big squeeze. *Chronicle of Higher Education,* pp. A1, A8–A13.

Scherschel, P. M. (2000). *Student debt levels continue to rise.* Indianapolis: USA Group Foundation.

Stringer, W. L., Cunningham, A. F., O'Brien, C. T., & Merisotis, J. P. (1998). *It's all relative.* Indianapolis: USA Group Foundation.

U.S. Department of Education. (2000). *Debt burden after four years of college* (NCES 2000-188). Washington, DC: National Center for Education Statistics.

U.S. Department of Education. (2003a). *Enrollment in postsecondary institutions, fall, 2001 and financial statistics, fiscal year 2001* (NCES 2004-155). Washington, DC: National Center for Education Statistics.

U.S. Department of Education. (2003b). *Getting ready to pay for college: What students and their parents know about the cost of college tuition and what they are doing to find out* (NCES 2003-030). Washington, DC: National Center for Education Statistics.

U.S. Department of Education. (2003c). *How families of low and middle income undergraduates pay for college* (NCES 2003-162). Washington, DC: National Center for Education Statistics.

Volkwein, J. F., & Cabrera, A. F. (1998). Who defaults on student loans? In R. Fossey & M. Bateman (Eds.), *Condemning students to debt: College loans and public policy* (pp. 105–125). New York: Teachers College Press.

Wegmann, C. A., Cunningham, A. F., & Merisotis, J. P. (2003). *Private loans and choice in financing higher education.* Washington, DC: Institute for Higher Education Policy.

Chapter Seven

Student Persistence and Degree Attainment

Thomas E. Miller

This chapter explores the nature of student expectations regarding the likelihood of successfully completing a degree program and compares those expectations with evidence documenting the reality of the student experience. Given that expectations are developed in various ways, this chapter also explores the environmental contexts that have helped to shape student expectations. Following the presentation of expectations and the realities pertaining to persistence, the text focuses on the areas of dissonance that emerge between expectations and reality. The chapter concludes with a discussion of measures that institutions of higher education can employ to close the gaps between what students expect and what they experience. The problems associated with student degree attainment have been described as a national crisis (Smith, 2004), and much of that crisis may relate to unrealized expectations about the college experience.

Societal Expectations and Context

Students and their families are continuously reminded of the high priority that our society ascribes to the attainment of a college degree. In fact, the extent to which institutions of higher education are perceived as meeting their goals is frequently determined by analyzing the extent to which admitted students persist to graduation.

In 1992, with the passage of the Student Right to Know Act, institutions of higher education were required to provide data to the U.S. Secretary of Education regarding their rates of degree completion. Particularly important, the information that is collected is expected to be accessible to the public, suggesting that degree completion rates are one way for the general public, including prospective students, to evaluate colleges and universities. Part of the rationale for the legislation was to make prospective students knowledgeable about the educational commitments of an institution of higher education; in other words, did the institution care about undergraduate students. The act also intended to help students and their families make judgments about the educational benefits of a particular college or university. The notion that institutions of higher education can be judged on the basis of the rate at which students persist toward degrees has become widely accepted.

Even before the Right to Know Act took effect, however, regional accrediting associations required their member institutions to publish graduation and retention rates. The premise was similar: that the truth about the rate of student degree attainment is valuable information for the public and should contribute to how institutions are measured and compared.

Since the middle 1990s, the National Collegiate Athletic Association has published rates of graduation for intercollegiate athletes, separating them by sport and gender. These announcements have received significant media attention and public scrutiny and have been used to compare and contrast colleges and universities. In addition to giving the public perspective about the educational attainment of student athletes, the effect, again, has been to give prospective student athletes information to help them make judgments about their college choice.

The various popular publications that purport to scientifically rate colleges and universities also include persistence rates in their formulae. The result is that an institution with a high rate of student persistence is given a ranking higher than one with a lower persistence rate when other factors are equal, creating the public perception that the rate of student retention is an indicator of institutional quality.

As a result of these factors, the context within which students choose colleges is one where the institution has the primary responsibility for student retention. The public, including college students and their families, expect colleges to do what they must to help students succeed and persist in their educational efforts to the natural conclusion of attaining degrees.

Factors External to the Student-Institutional Relationship

In addition to the regulatory, legislative, and general information that helps form student expectations regarding persistence, there are social factors that are influential as well. Social norms and conditions associated with adaptation and change may create in the college-going population a sense of flux and an acceptance, perhaps even an expectation, of instability, movement, change, and the future being different than the present. A number of factors in the lives of students affect their sense of affiliation with their colleges and universities. The context in which contemporary students have been raised reflects more transience than at any previous time in the history of the United States. The norm used to be that young people finished high school having lived in only one or two different homes. Today, the rate at which families move has changed dramatically, and it is much more typical for students entering college to have moved quite a few times, changing neighborhoods and, as a result, schools and friends (United States Census, 2000). School busing programs, through which students may find themselves attending schools far from where they live and moving from school to school in various years, have further impacted this sense of transience.

The soaring divorce rate has also affected student perceptions of affiliation and commitment. Students who have seen the marriages of their parents, relatives, or neighbors fail may have different notions about loyalty and commitment than those students who have been part of more stable environments. Our mobile society has also been influenced, in part, by shifts in the labor force. Students have seen their parents and other adults change jobs and move from one employer to another with much more frequency than was the case 20 years ago (United States Census, 2000). Such shifts in employment have touched the lives of students in many ways, and the effect may be, again, to influence their perceptions of stability in affiliation and loyalty. Even the sports heroes of our society have been mobile, and students' favorite star athletes have moved from team to team, from city to city, to pursue more lucrative contracts. The college student of today has grown accustomed to saying good-bye to friends, neighbors, teachers, and even their parents. This may have a greater effect on the depth of commitment felt by a student to a particular institution.

In addition to what might be characterized as a lack of commitment of affiliation, there is a greater variety of choices and options for college attendance than ever before. Students have many alternatives; those who become disaffected at the institution where they start can easily find another place where they can try to fit in and feel welcome. A large portion of students do not attend their first-choice institutions, and that would seem to affect their commitment to persist.

What Students Expect

A variety of studies have been conducted that examine selected aspects of what students expect from their college experience. Summaries of these are reported following.

Cooperative Institution Research Program

The Cooperative Institutional Research Program (CIRP) annually administers a questionnaire to students enrolling at colleges and universities across the country. In existence for more than 30 years, CIPR is one of the most heavily utilized research programs for institutions interested in assessing their incoming students. It is usually administered either before the beginning of classes for new students or within a few weeks of the start of their first semester. Several items in the CIRP survey provide information about student expectations relative to persistence. This section analyzes the results published from the administration of the CIRP to the class entering college in 2002, but the results described are typical for the years immediately preceding. Although there is a small population of respondents from two-year institutions, the CIRP results are largely representative of students entering four-year colleges and universities.

A telling item in the CIRP questionnaire relates to the expectation of the respondent student regarding degree attainment.

Fewer than 1% of the respondents indicated an intention not to complete a degree at any institution, and fewer than 2% reflected an intention not to complete a degree at the institution where they initially enrolled. This is a clear statement by the group entering four-year colleges that they plan to get degrees and that the overwhelming portion of students plans to complete degrees where they started.

Another item in CIRP worthy of analysis is one where students are asked to predict the likelihood of certain outcomes and experiences while in college. Of the group enrolled in four-year colleges, nearly 80% indicated that the chances were "very good" that they would complete a bachelor's degree. Only about 7% indicated that they were likely to transfer to another college before graduating. Fewer than 1% indicated that it was likely that they would drop out of college. In the aggregate, these are clear statements of intent to remain enrolled and persist to degree attainment.

Although CIRP results are obvious indicators of student expectations to persist, there are some signals of possible disaffect. Fewer than 52% of the respondents indicated that the chances were very good that they would be satisfied with college. This seems to leave a large population of entering students unsure about whether they will connect well to their colleges, which is in juxtaposition with their expressed intentions to persist.

National Center for Education Statistics Report

The National Center for Education Statistics (NCES) published a report tracking students who entered higher education in the middle of the past decade (Berkner, He, & Cataldi, 2002). The report was generated using the results of the Beginning Postsecondary Students Longitudinal Study first administered in 1996 and then again in 2001. The NCES study provides a useful perspective about the intentions of students to persist. Of the students who entered public two-year institutions, 49% indicated an intention to complete an associate's degree, and an additional 25% expressed an intention to go on to a four-year institution and complete a bachelor's degree. Eleven percent (11%) planned to attain a vocational certificate, and about 16% indicated that they had no intention to complete a degree. Five out of six students entering two-year colleges in 1995 expected to attain some sort of specific credential, either a certificate or a degree.

Of the students entering four-year institutions in 1995–96, the overwhelming proportion of them indicated having the goal of completing a degree. Ninety percent (90%) of those starting at public institutions intended to complete bachelor's degrees, and 91% of those beginning at private four-year schools had the same goal. In each group, those at public institutions and those at private ones, small portions of respondents intended to complete associate's degrees or vocational certificates, and only 5% started with no intention to finish a degree. The NCES data reflect similar results to those of CIRP. Students entering higher education expect to complete their degrees in a successful fashion.

College Student Expectations Questionnaire

An additional source of information about expectations is the College Student Expectations Questionnaire (CSXQ), administered voluntarily at institutions seeking information about what students anticipate from their college experience. The dataset for this study is not representative of higher education in the United States, as the participating institutions are apt to be private, four-year colleges and universities. Two-year colleges and public universities are underrepresented in the data, but the results are still informative about student expectations about degree completion.

The CSXQ data show that students anticipate academic success, in that 92% expected grades of B or higher, and 74% indicated an intention to pursue an advanced degree. Ninety-three percent (93%) expect to like or even be enthusiastic about the college experience. They also anticipate friendly relationships with other students, approachable faculty, and helpful administrators, all signs of confidence in their success and persistence.

College Student Experiences Questionnaire

A final resource for perspectives about what students might anticipate as a result of their enrollment in higher education is the College Student Experiences Questionnaire (CSEQ), administered at colleges and universities to various subsets of their enrolled students.

This assessment is more broadly used than the CSXQ, but, again, two-year institutions are dramatically underrepresented.

For example, 77% of seniors indicated that they would attend the same institution again, and 82% of first-year students provided similar responses. This may reflect a more positive view of the institution by first-year students and relate to an intention to persist. Similarly, 84% of first-year students indicated either that they liked college or were enthusiastic about it, while 82% of seniors reported similar satisfaction rates. The overall opinions about college had comparable results between first-year students and senior students. In the CSEQ results, first-year students also indicated that they had more positive relationships with their peer students than did seniors, and they also reported better associations with administrators. When compared with that of seniors, the optimism and confidence of first-year students, expressed before they completed a year of enrollment, may have a positive effect on intentions to persist.

Real Experiences of Students

The careful observer of American higher education will not be surprised that students entering college expect to finish successfully and complete degrees. This traditional outcome and aspiration of students is an understandable target, and it makes sense that the vast proportion of students entering college, regardless of the type of institution, expect to receive degrees and accomplish their objectives. The truth is that, as will be demonstrated in this section, there is a much lower rate of degree completion than one would anticipate from the high aspirations that entering students express.

Higher Education Research Institute

The Higher Education Research Institute (HERI) has conducted research about degree attainment of college students. According to the HERI report (Astin & Oseguera, 2002), in 1998 only 36% of students entering four-year institutions completed bachelor's degrees within four years. Rates varied by institutional type, ranging from the 24% of students at public colleges (not including universities) graduating within four years to the 67% of students at private universities (not including private colleges) graduating in the same period. The overall graduation rate reflects a 4% decline when compared with a similar study in 1989, so fewer students are finishing degrees in four years than was previously the case.

The HERI report indicated that women students had higher degree attainment rates than men, 40% to 33%, but results for each gender reflected the 4 percentage point decline from nine years earlier, reported previously. There were substantial differences in completion rates by racial group, with Asian Americans graduating at a 39% rate, and Mexican Americans graduating at a rate of 21%.

Six-year degree completion rates also differ by institutional type. Those enrolled at private institutions have a greater rate of completion than do those at public schools. In the HERI study, the rates at which students graduated in six years were 80% at private universities and 58% at public universities. Obviously, six-year graduation rates are greater, with 21% of the starting cohort having graduated after the fourth year and by the end of the sixth. The overall completion rate at the end of six years was 58% for the cohort studied in the HERI report.

NCES Report

In 1996, the U.S. Department of Education published a report about students who were enrolled in higher education in the 1992–93 academic year (Horn & Premo, 1995). The report was generated using the results of the National Postsecondary Student Aid Study administered during the reported academic year. The report examined student enrollment patterns according to characteristics previously known to relate adversely to persistence and degree attainment.

The risk factors analyzed in the report included delaying enrollment, attending part time, being financially independent of parents, having dependents other than a spouse, and working full time while enrolled in college. Since the study only covered a one-year period, it reaches no conclusions about degree attainment or long-term persistence. The report, however, does analyze persistence within the year of study, and 81% of the subjects persisted for the entire academic year, while the remainder did not. This rate of persistence is not inconsistent with others reported elsewhere. The report had the effect of validating the known risk factors, as the subjects who demonstrated them were less likely to persist through the year.

The NCES report described earlier in this chapter, *Descriptive Summary of 1995–96 Beginning Postsecondary Students, Six Years Later* (Berkner et al., 2002), is a more powerful tool for understanding persistence patterns, because it was a longitudinal study over a six-year period. For example, of the population of students who entered two-year institutions in that academic year and who indicated a goal of completing either a bachelor's or associate's degree, 23% competed an associate's degree and 13% had completed a bachelor's degree. Of the group of students who transferred to four-year colleges and universities, 36% completed degrees within six years of starting at a two-year institution.

The NCES study reported that of those students who started at four-year institutions, 51% had completed bachelor's degrees at those same institutions within six years of their first enrollment. That establishes the institutional completion rate in a cohort reporting approach. The individual student completion rate within six years, however, is 58%, when one considers the students who attained degrees at institutions other than where they started. Another way of evaluating persistence is based upon student intentions. Considering only the population of students who entered four-year institutions with the expressed goal of bachelor's degree attainment, the rate of degree success is 55%.

Evaluating other subcategories of the population produced different results, including those students who went directly to college after graduating from high school or those students who were enrolled full time. Combining the factors had powerful results. In other words, of those students who had a goal of completing a bachelor's degree and were enrolled full time and went directly to college after high school, 69% graduated within six years. The study uncovered other distinguishing characteristics between students who persisted and those who did not, including positive predictors such as continuous (uninterrupted) enrollment, good high school grades or entrance examination scores, and the fact that women were more likely to persist.

Academic performance may have a direct relationship to persistence decisions. The study demonstrated that students with lower grade point averages (less than 2.25) were more likely to have left college than those whose grades were higher. This may relate directly to the expectations associated with academic performance as previously reported and reflected in CSXQ and CIRP. The NCES study further demonstrated that students who went directly from high school to college had a lower risk of attrition than those who delayed their enrollment. It is not clear to what extent delaying enrollment has an effect on the nature of expectations of the college experience.

Students are most likely to withdraw during the first year of college. To the extent that attrition relates to unmet expectations, the importance of persistence in the first year makes sense, since the student adjustment to the reality of the college experience would take place over time. In the NCES study, students who left during the first year were almost equally likely to transfer to another institution as they were to leave higher education altogether.

Another NCES report, *Principal Indicators of Student Academic Histories in Postsecondary Education 1972–2000* (2004), provided additional evidence about persistence, enrollment patterns, and degree attainment. For example, the report indicated that students are taking longer to complete degrees than was previously the case. For the high school graduating class of 1972, of those who earned bachelor's degrees within the eight and one-half years after graduation, their mean time to degree completion was 4.34 years. For the class of 1982, it was 4.45 years; and for the class of 1992, it was 4.56 years. That report also demonstrated that, of the students in the class of 1972 who earned more than 10 credit hours, 47% attended more than one college. In the class of 1982, it was 51%; and in 1992, it was 57%. Clearly the notion that most students can expect to graduate in four years with a bachelor's degree from where they started is one not supported by data.

Considering the entire population that entered in the 1995–96 academic year, 89% of the students had an expressed goal of attaining a bachelor's degree, an associate's degree, or a vocational certificate. Six years later, 29% had completed bachelor's degrees, 10% had associate's degrees, and 12% had completed a certificate program. Of all the beginning students, 35% had left higher education without attaining any type of degree or certificate and were no longer enrolled.

Dissonance

Clearly, a far greater portion of students who enter higher education expect to complete degrees in a timely fashion than actually do. Not surprisingly, the unmet expectation, or dissonance, presents a challenge to colleges and universities. Most students hope to attain degrees in college, and that is a logical aspiration associated with the college experience. If students make informed choices about college choice and have the expectation to persist, and if colleges make informed and educated admission decisions, then persistence to degree attainment should be the result.

There are exceptions to this, of course, and many students enroll in college, particularly in two-year institutions, with less clarity in their expectations about outcomes associated with degree completion. Students who start college to enhance their personal growth or secure a credential or skill are valued members of the college population, and exemplify the reality that not all students who do not attain degrees have failed to attain their expected goal.

There is a substantial difference between the examination of institutional persistence rates and the rates at which individual students attain degrees. Although only 43% of degree-seeking students entering postsecondary education when they started had attained them at their original institution within six years, 54% of them had earned them somewhere. Therefore, 11% had persisted to degree completion by transferring from their original institution. This is a good indication of individual commitment of the students and a reflection of higher education's success, but not necessarily a shining moment for the original colleges where students began their studies. Recalling that almost all students expect to graduate from where they first enrolled, it seems that the unmet expectations of students remain a challenge for colleges and universities across the country. In other words, did the schools prepare their incoming students adequately, through dissemination of materials or orientation programs, to enable them to form realistic expectations?

Clearly, some student attrition is expected and appropriate. Students leave college for health reasons, some decide that they are not suited for college study, and others develop new career objectives that are unattainable at the institutions in which they initially enrolled. The latter experience is actually attrition of success and may well be a function of good career counseling or academic advising.

Nonetheless, the rate at which student expectations are not met does present problems for which institutions need solutions. A premise of this work has been that when student expectations are unmet, there are several means of addressing the situation. One approach is that students need to be better informed about what they can reasonably expect. Another perspective is that institutions need to perform better and meet students' reasonable expectations. Ultimately, the responsibility is that of the higher education community. Degree attainment is a fundamental purpose, a driving force in American higher education, so those who enter college with an expectation to complete degrees should not be discouraged from realizing their goals.

Institutional Strategies for Addressing the Issues

There are strategies that institutions can employ to better understand student expectations and to meet those that are reasonable while renegotiating the ones that are not. Some such strategies are described in the following section.

Student Recruitment

It is not clear how students formulate their expectations about how they will succeed in a particular college community, but certainly a great portion of their perceptions comes from institutional recruiters and written and electronic materials about the institution. As suggested in Chapter 5 of this volume, if students are given an accurate picture of institutional characteristics and they are fully informed about the qualifications of students who succeed, they can make judgments about how they compare with those who persist. It also may be useful for prospective students to know some things about students who do not succeed. Not every college is a good match for every possible student. If students are well informed about the institutions they choose, they are better able to make intelligent and good decisions about how they will acclimate to the college environment and whether they are likely to persist until graduation.

Recruitment processes should be forthright about institutional cultures, subcultures, and the dynamics of campus life. There are college communities with cultural frameworks that are representative of institutional values that might not resonate well with all prospective students. Students need to know these values and the campus climate to be able to measure how and whether they will fit comfortably in the environment.

The nature and extent of support services, such as academic advising, counseling services, and the availability of faculty for consultation, needs to be advertised to prospective students. There are institutions that have assertive, even intrusive, support systems, for example, that challenge students who are in academic difficulty and can make certain types of students very uncomfortable and unhappy. There are other institutions with student support systems that require the individual student to seek assistance. The student who needs help in these types of colleges must be self-motivated to find and ask for help. Part of the challenge faced by admissions representatives is the difficulty associated with meeting individually with prospective students to learn the extent to which they are likely to fit into the college's undergraduate community. There are institutions that require an interview as part of the application process, and this is a good strategy in the effort to measure the student-institution fit, but given financial constraints both for applicants and colleges, this important aspect of the admissions process is often neglected.

Program Strategies

Research about student persistence has generated much useful information about programs that make a difference in the proportion of successful degree attainment within a student community. Institutions should know the characteristics of their students who do not persist and develop program responses that address the issues that point toward risk of attrition.

- *Orientation programs* should be candid and informative. They should provide genuine and honest introductions to college life, stressing the academic aspects of the experience as well as the co-curricular issues. The programs should strike a balance between those issues associated with the classroom experiences of students and those outside of class. Faculty, staff, and students should all be part of the design and production of these programs.

- *Academic advising* should be learner centered and developmental in nature, with a focus on matching honestly the interests and skills of students with the curriculum offerings of the institution.
- *Student advocacy programs* should be offered to help students navigate institutional bureaucracies. Peers helping peers or faculty mentoring programs can be effective problem-solving resources for students feeling challenged by the realities of college.
- *Academic major alternatives* can be developed for high-demand, high-attrition major fields. If popular majors have high failure rates, institutions should identify secondary disciplines with related career and professional school options.
- *Parent and family orientation programs* can provide families with access to the institution and support for their interests. The families of first-generation college students can be specifically targeted for information distribution and instructional approaches to give them insight about the college experience.
- *Commuter student services and programs* are also effective tools for engaging those students not living on campus. At many institutions with residential populations, the commuter student is more at risk of attrition. Where that is the case, institutions can set up places, programs, and advocacy organizations to give them particular support.
- *Community service and service learning programs* have been demonstrated to have a relationship to persistence. Where appropriate, institutions can use such programs to engage students and to enhance their connection to the institution and its programs.
- *First-year seminars* are used widely at institutions as strategies for new student acculturation to the environment and as extended orientation activities with form, substance, and structure.
- *Probationary students* are at risk by definition, whether their probation is a condition of entry due to an incoming academic profile or due to poor college performance. Programs that stimulate connection, enhance achievement, and establish links to subsequent enrollment periods can be very helpful to at-risk students.

Intervention Strategies

A number of intervention strategies are available to colleges and universities, and among them are responding to signals and researching risk factors.

- *Responding to signals.* Students usually find ways to signal disaffection and unhappiness with their college experience. They may miss classes, act out in residence halls, or seek personal counseling. No matter what behaviors that students exhibit, other members of the institutional community can influence their subsequent decisions. When an office staff member hears students complaining about the residence halls, for example, the right response can make a difference. A resident assistant who hears students criticizing food service or difficulties with the computer network can intercede effectively. The appropriate institutional approach to such matters is to make student persistence and educational attainment the business of all members of the institutional community. When all who interact with students assume the responsibility to help them adjust and persist and support the resolution of their problems, the culture of attainment can be enhanced.
- *Researching risk factors.* Programmatic approaches to enhance persistence can be effective, but the decisions students ultimately make are complex and highly individual. The very complicated process of individual decision making about where to enroll in college is not very different from the process of decision making about whether to persist. Therefore, the most effective interventions may be those targeted to individual students demonstrated to be at risk of attrition. There is evidence of success with this approach (Glynn, Sauer, & Miller, 2003).

The HERI report previously cited (Astin & Oseguera, 2002) suggests a set of predictive factors, including high school grades, standardized test scores, gender, and race. Institutions can supplement that information with additional studies of students, collecting individual descriptive and attitudinal information. It is possible to have a complex and institutionally specific risk prediction study that effectively anticipates the risk of an individual student leaving the institution. Knowing this in advance empowers institutional officials to prescribe remedies and interventions. Some examples follow.

The American Council on Education issued an *Issue Brief* (2003) that presented NCES data associated with, among other things, employment. Those students with jobs of more than 35 hours of work per week were substantially less likely to persist to degree attainment than those who worked fewer than 15 hours per week. Individual institutions should explore the work interests and intentions of their students and respond accordingly. If the institution determines that the significant off-campus employment of a student is a predictor of attrition, a specific intervention for all such students would be to develop an effective on-campus alternative. The student who is working in a job off campus may find that a position providing support to the research of a faculty member is more stimulating, academically relevant, and career enhancing. Institutions using their resources to develop meaningful on-campus employment opportunities for students will find that placement of students who would alternatively be working off campus may have a very good effect on persistence. The effective strategy would be to identify those students working or planning to work off campus and invite them to the on-campus alternative.

Many institutions relate financial need to persistence decisions and worry about the gap between student need and funded financial aid. The problems associated with closing the aid gap are many, as substantial expense is involved. Further, since not all students with unmet need will drop out, if the gap in aid is closed for all, there would be some wasted resources. One strategy for addressing the aid gap is to focus on those students who have a real gap in aid that is different from the apparent one. Students disenfranchised from their families or from family circumstances where there is less support than is apparent certainly are at risk of attrition, and their risk level is unique to their individual circumstances. If financial aid administrators can hold in reserve funds to address those with more need than is apparent, they may be able to make an effective difference for a special at-risk population.

There is evidence (Jacoby, 2000) that students who commute to campus have more challenge engaging with the institutional community. When family circumstances or life changes affect commuting students and the home dynamics change, enrollment consequences may follow. When the family of a commuting student moves the household or parents divorce or other life-changing experiences develop, students can be at substantial risk. In such circumstances, on-campus housing, if available, can be a cost-effective way for the student to be enabled to focus on the college experience and have a greater prospect for success.

Students who are uncertain about their major choices may benefit from an intervention associated with career planning. Strong relationships between those providing academic advising and those offering career advising are powerful partnerships in enhancing student success. The student who reflects a lack of confidence in major choice can benefit greatly from interaction with professionals in career development and acquire, as a result, a sense of direction and purpose.

There are other ways in which specific interventions can be employed to respond to the needs of students at risk of attrition. Individual institutions should explore their knowledge about their students and examine ways to identify those at risk in advance based upon characteristics at entry or shortly after enrolling. When those at risk are identified, intelligent interventions can be designed to support and assist students in their persistence to degree completion.

Conclusion

Higher education is challenged by the expectations of students and the general public regarding persistence and degree attainment. That one would enroll in college with the plan that a degree is the desired and expected end product seems logical. If the student wants a degree, surely the institution wants the student to earn it, and the school should work accordingly to facilitate the outcome. What matters most is to understand the context of student expectations and what happens between the beginning of the relationship with the college and the end to change the outcome.

It is clear that part of the dissonance between the expectation and the reality is derived from students holding other expectations that intrude on those related to persistence. Whether the matter is too substantial a commitment to employment, academic or career goals that are unreasonable, or judgments about academic effort that result in failure, the decisions that students make that have nothing to do with the institution can result in their degree expectations being unfulfilled. What institutions need to do in this respect is give counsel, information, and an orientation about the reality of the student experience and try to help students develop attitudes and behaviors that can enhance their chances of success.

At the same time that institutions should work with students to help them establish reasonable expectations of themselves and their institutions, there are ways in which institutions could perform better to increase persistence rates and the rates of degree attainment by students. Institutions should study the characteristics and the expectations of their students and determine which ones are predictors of attrition or those that lead to risk. They should intervene with students who display those characteristics and expectations and try to modify the circumstances to give the students a better chance of persisting.

References

American Council on Education. (2003). *Issue brief.* Washington, DC: American Council on Education.

Astin, A. W., & Oseguera, L. (2002). *Degree attainment rates at American colleges and universities.* Los Angeles: University of California, Higher Education Research Institute.

Berkner, L., He, S., & Cataldi, E. F. (2002). *Descriptive summary of 1995–96 beginning postsecondary students: Six years later* (NCES 2003151). Washington, DC: U.S. Department of Education, National Center for Education Statistics.

Glynn, J. G., Sauer, P. L., & Miller, T. E. (2003). Signaling student retention with prematriculation data. *NASPA Journal, 41,* 41–67.

Horn, L. J., & Premo, M. D. (1995). *Profile of undergraduates in U.S. postsecondary education institutions: 1992–93, with an essay on undergraduates at risk* (NCES 96-237). Washington, DC: U.S. Department of Education, National Center for Education Statistics.

Jacoby, B (2000). *Involving commuter students in learning.* New Directions for Higher Education, no. 109. San Francisco: Jossey-Bass.

Principal indicators of student academic histories in postsecondary education 1972–2000. (2004). Retrieved January 27, 2004, from http://www.ed.gov/rschstat/research/pubs/prinindicat/index.html.

United States Census. (2000). *Profile of selected social characteristics: 2000.* (2000). Retrieved February 25, 2004, from http://factfinder.census.gov/hom/en/datanotes/expaiansf.htm.

Smith, P. (2004). *The quiet crisis.* Bolton, MA: Anker.

Chapter Eight

Life After College

Susan R. Komives and Elizabeth M. Nuss

A convergence of attention has focused recently on college student outcomes. Previous chapters demonstrate the ways colleges of all types have examined how their mission statements relate to desirable outcomes for their graduates. Chapter 7 addresses the primary outcome on which college students are focused, the degree, but this chapter addresses other outcomes of college, other results of the college experience that occur in addition to the degree, attained or not. Accountability for outcomes has been advocated by legislatures, regional accrediting associations, and specialty associations. This accountability has fueled the assessment movement. The identification of institutionally specific outcomes is central to assessment.

The higher education community expects students to develop their intellectual ability and to become facile and proficient in science, the arts, and human culture, and to develop the ability to explore important issues from a variety of viewpoints and with a depth of understanding. State and national policymakers view college as the engine for economic growth and workforce development. The Council for the Advancement of Standards in Higher Education (2003) has included outcomes for practice in their latest standards publication. The American Association of Colleges & Universities (AACU) *Greater Expectations* panel (National Panel, 2002) asserts that society expects "graduates who can think analytically, communicate effectively, and solve problems in collaboration with diverse colleagues, clients, or customers" (p. 1). The *Greater Expectations* report indicates that for college graduates to function effectively with the future societal complexities, they must demonstrate evidence of accomplishment as an empowered learner, an informed learner, and a responsible learner. The expectations of diverse shareholders are explored in more depth in Chapter 11.

Outcomes of College

Numerous useful taxonomies of college outcomes were developed in the 1990s as part of the accountability and assessment movement (Baxter Magolda, 1999; Kuh, Douglas, Lund, & Ramin-Gyurnek, 1994). Most recently, in *Learning Reconsidered*, the National Association of Student Personnel Administrators (NASPA) and the American College Personnel Association (ACPA) (2004) have asserted a set of college outcomes synthesized from many such taxonomies. The seven outcomes clusters in *Learning Reconsidered* are (1) cognitive complexity, (2) knowledge acquisition, integration, and application, (3) humanitarianism, (4) civic engagement, (5) interpersonal and intrapersonal competence, (6) practical competence, and (7) persistence and academic achievement (pp. 22–23). Two assertions are central in understanding the clusters. One understanding is that the development of each set of outcomes includes both academic learning and personal development; cognitive complexity, for example, can no longer be viewed in isolation from identity development and other aspects of personal development that influence one's cognitions (Baxter Magolda & King, 2004). The second understanding is that the development of that outcome cluster is influenced by the student's experience in the whole environment—in and outside the classroom and on and off campus. All aspects of the college environment should be held accountable for that intentional development.

This chapter uses the set of outcome clusters presented by Hamrick, Evans, and Schuh (2002) in *Foundations of Student Affairs Practice* as a frame to examine student expectations and realities. Hamrick, Evans, and Schuh propose a succinct and useful set of five college outcome clusters that serve as a model for outcomes of graduates. These outcome clusters are described in Table 8.1.

Table 8.1 College Outcomes

Educated Persons	Mastering a selected body of knowledge generates learning opportunities that can result in great insight into oneself and one's world. Higher education fosters the pursuit of lifelong learning and demonstrates the centrality of education to life and, for the purpose of this analysis, involves postgraduate study.
Skilled Workers	Higher education has become increasingly regarded as desirable workforce preparation. In this venue, students learn about the career options available to them and develop the work skills needed to perform successfully in their chosen work setting.
Life Skills Managers	In college, students develop skills that contribute to their quality of life, such as the ability to manage their finances, maintain their health and wellness, and prioritize their leisure pursuits. Decisions in these arenas are foundational for living a purposeful and satisfying life.
Self-Aware and Interpersonally Sensitive Individuals	In light of the increasing diversity of today's society students must gain an understanding of themselves and others. They must understand how history, cultural heritage, social forces, and economic factors influence their own identity, affiliations, and allegiances as well as those of others, and affect their ability to work and communicate with individuals who are different from them.
Democratic Citizens	Higher education graduates are expected to make substantial contributions to the political and social workings of the larger society or targeted collective. Citizens involve themselves in public life through neighborhood, government, and service organizations. They also engage in principled dissent.

Source: Adapted from Hamrick, Evans, & Schuh (2002).

About This Chapter

This chapter focuses attention on student expectations for life after college. Many consider college to be the essential and necessary step for employment and career satisfaction, economic stability, community involvement and leadership, and satisfactory and enjoyable relationships with colleagues, family, friends, and neighbors—all of which are considered to be the elements of a fulfilling life. Using the Hamrick et al. (2002) categories of college outcomes, this chapter reviews existing knowledge about the expectation and reality of each outcome and explores the gaps and issues with achieving that expectation. Recommendations for action conclude the chapter. We recognize that many improvements to the quality of undergraduate education have been implemented in recent years, and the impact of these initiatives is not yet reflected in the available alumni studies. However, we believe that higher education leaders will benefit from a review of the areas of discrepancy noted to date as a way of assessing their progress.

Data Sources Examined

There are several sources of data about college student expectations for some part of their college experience. Perhaps the most well known is the annual survey of American college freshman conducted by UCLA (Astin, Oseguera, Sax, & Korn, 2002). Student expectations of their first year of college are also reported in the College Student Expectations Questionnaire (CSXQ) (Kuh & Gonyea, 2003). CSXQ data is reported by institutional classification and includes nearly 38,000 first-year students.

A few sources examine the graduating senior. The College Student Experiences Questionnaire (CSEQ) has a strong normative database divided into four class groupings (first year to senior) examining students' engagement with various college experiences ranging from academics to sports and conversations with peers. The CSEQ can be paired with the CSXQ to measure change. The *CSEQ Norms for the Fourth Edition* (Gonyea, Kish, Kuh, Muthiah, & Thomas, 2003) are calculated over nearly 88,000 students in which women comprise 61% of all respondents and nearly one-quarter were students of color (pp. 42–43).

Few studies address alumni experiences that reflect back on their college experience, and even fewer studies use a longitudinal design to track graduates into their alumni years. A major source of data is the Baccalaureate and Beyond Longitudinal Study (B & B, 93). This study tracks a random sample of students who received bachelor's degrees in 1992–93. Participants were surveyed again one year and four years after graduation (National Center for Education Statistics, 1999; National Center for Education Statistics, 2000; National Center for Education Statistics, 2001). In addition the American College Testing Service (ACT) has three surveys: the Alumni Outcomes Survey (American College Testing Service [ACT], 2003b), based on 36,596 alumni records obtained from 161 colleges that administered the survey between January 1997 and December 2002; the Alumni Survey four-year (ACT, 2003a), obtained from 28,925 alumni records administered between January 1996 and December 2002; and the Alumni Survey two-year (ACT, 2002), obtained from 17,435 alumni records from 53 two-year colleges administered between January 1993 and December 2001. The ACT alumni data are not based on random samples, and the instruments are administered in different ways to different groups. The effects on the normative data are not known.

One obvious shortcoming is that each data source asks different items for similar topics, and direct comparisons are not possible. We have drawn on these sources to illustrate the expectations and experiences of college students.

Educated Persons

There is great consensus that one of the hallmarks of a college education should be that graduates know more about themselves and their world than when they entered college (Hamrick et al., 2002). The outcome of an educated person covers issues of competence and mastery of subject matter as well as the development of skills associated with lifelong learning (Hamrick et al., 2002). Chapter 7 presented the persistence and retention rates for students completing college. This section focuses on the data about college student expectations for continuing their education and earning graduate and professional degrees.

Student Expectations

Student expectations of the level of their degree attainment have gradually increased over time. The Baccalaureate and Beyond study provides a comprehensive analysis of the 1992–93 graduates at intervals after their graduation and specifically looks at enrollment in graduate and professional school (National Center for Education Statistics, 1999). More of the 2001 freshmen expected to earn advanced degrees than did their counterparts in 1989. Forty percent (40%) of the 1989 freshmen expected to earn a master's degree, and 30% expected to earn a Ph.D. or other advanced or professional degree (Astin et al., 2002), compared with 43% and 32% in 2001 (Astin et al., 2002).

More than one-half (57%) of the entering 2001 freshman were attending college to prepare for graduate or professional school, compared with 53% of the entering freshmen in 1989 (Astin et al., 2002). The 35-year trend data on the college freshmen indicates that over time, the number of freshmen who expect to earn advanced degrees has continued to gradually increase. For example, in 1966, 35% expected to earn a master's degree, compared with 43% in 2001. In 1966, 11% expected to earn a Ph.D., compared to 17% in 2001.

Thirty percent (30%) of the entering 2001 freshman selected their college because "this college's graduates get into top graduate professional schools," compared with 26% in 1989 (Astin et al., 2002, p. 51).

A considerable number of graduates change their educational expectations over time. Table 8.2 summarizes the data on expectations for completing advanced degrees from several studies. The data presented reflect expectations for achievement at different points in time. For example, the ACT Outcomes Survey (2003b) asks alumni what was the highest lifetime educational goal you had at the time you completed high school and what is the goal now. The B & B data demonstrates how expectations changed from college graduation to four years later. "Expectations were most stable among those who initially did not plan to continue their education or who expected to complete a master's degree, while those who expected a first-professional or doctoral degree in 1993 were more likely to express a different expectation in 1997" (National Center for Education Statistics, 1999, p. 7). Data is also reported for two-year college alumni (ACT, 2002).

Female graduates in 1993 were slightly more likely than male graduates to report expectations for advanced degrees (87% versus 83%), but by 1997 their expectations were similar (73% and 71%).

Table 8.2 Expectations for Highest Degree Earned

	High School	College	Alumni			
	ACT Alumni Outcomes Survey Plan at High School Graduation	Baccalaureate & Beyond 92–93 Cohort 1993	Baccalaureate & Beyond 92–93 Cohort 1997	ACT Alumni Outcomes Survey Plans Now	ACT Alumni Survey Two-Year Schools Plan to Obtain	ACT Alumni Survey Two-Year Schools Highest Degree Earned
Associate's	4%				4%	70%
Bachelor's	49%			25%	22%	12%
Master's	17%	58%	54%	43%	21%	2%
Doctorate	6%	21%	12%	13%	7%	
Specialist or other professional	7%	6%	6%	9%		

Sources: National Center for Education Statistics (1999), pp. 2, 5; ACT (2002, 2003b).

In 1993, black (89%) and Hispanic graduates (79%) were almost as likely as white graduates (85%) to have advanced degree expectations. However, by 1997, the advanced degree expectations among blacks dropped by only 4 points, while the percentage among white graduates dropped by 15 percentage points (National Center for Education Statistics, 1999).

Student Experiences

Increasingly more Americans are earning advanced degrees. The number of master's degrees conferred in 2001 was twice the number conferred 30 years earlier. The number of doctorates earned increased by about 50% in that time period. In 2002, for persons over age 25, 17% of the population had completed some college, 8% earned an associate's degree, 18% a bachelor's degree, and 9% earned an advanced degree (U.S. Census Bureau, 2003).

Almost all of the alumni respondents felt that their college adequately prepared them for their continuing education (ACT, 2003a). Most alumni indicated their reasons for pursuing additional education were for career or job needs; to learn a new job; to increase income; for self-improvement; and to meet license/certification requirements (ACT, 2002; ACT, 2003a). One-half believed that their college education contributed to their ability to learn on their own, and one-third indicated that their education contributed to their using the library—behaviors typically associated with lifelong learning (ACT, 2003a).

College seniors assessed the extent they have gained or made progress in several key areas associated with an educated person or lifelong learner. Overwhelmingly, seniors reported quite a bit or very much gain in the following areas: broad general education, writing and speaking effectively, using computers and other information technology, thinking analytically, synthesizing ideas, learning on one's own, and adapting to change. Seniors reported less progress or gain in several other areas, including understanding the nature of science, understanding new developments in science and technology, and understanding the consequences of science and technology (Gonyea et al., 2003). Analyzing data from the ACT College Outcomes Survey from 1996–2000, Moss (2003) found that graduating seniors reported much intellectual growth and career development growth in college. Further, Moss demonstrated that "first generation college students and members of minority groups (e.g. blacks) appear to have experienced somewhat greater intellectual growth and career development than their second generation or non minority peers" (p. 4).

Application to Graduate School

The rate of application was related to the educational expectations at graduation (National Center for Education Statistics, 1999, p. 16). Those who expected to attend were more likely to apply, and those who had expected to complete a doctoral or first professional degree were more likely to attend than those who had lower expectations. By 1997, 39% of the graduates had taken at least one of the typical admissions examinations. Approximately one-half completed the Graduate Record Exam (GRE); female graduates were more likely than males to have taken the GRE, while more males took the entrance exams for business, medicine, or law (National Center for Education Statistics, 1999). Forty-one percent (41%) of the graduates applied for admission, 35% were accepted by at least one program, and 30% were enrolled. Of those who applied, 87% were admitted and 76% enrolled (National Center for Education Statistics, 1999). Women and men applied to advanced degree programs, gained admission, and were enrolled at the same rates (National Center for Education Statistics, 1999).

Not surprisingly, graduates with higher grade point averages were more likely to pursue graduate education and were also more likely to be admitted (National Center for Education Statistics, 1999).

Enrollment

Thirty percent (30%) of the B & B study's bachelor's degree recipients were enrolled in graduate school by 1997. Of those, 66% were pursuing a master's degree other than an MBA; 10% were enrolled in an MBA; 14% were enrolled in a first professional degree; and 10% were in a doctoral program (National Center for Education Statistics, 1999). Men and women were equally likely to enroll; however, there were gender differences in the types of degrees pursued. For example, 76% of the women enrolled in a master's degree other than an MBA, while men were twice as likely to enroll in an MBA program (14% versus 6%). Men were also more likely to enroll in a doctoral or first professional program (National Center for Education Statistics, 1999).

Regardless of their initial expectations, a majority of those who enrolled ended up in a master's degree program other than an MBA. Among those who expected to complete a first professional degree and who continued their education, 55% actually enrolled, and about half who had expected a doctorate had enrolled for an advanced degree. "Of this group, about one in five had enrolled in a doctoral program, and 62% has enrolled in a master's program other than an MBA" (National Center for Education Statistics, 1999, p. 21).

Doctoral students were most likely to have enrolled within one year of graduation (78%), followed by first professional students, and then those entering a master's program other than an MBA. Since many MBA programs prefer students with some post-baccalaureate experience, it was not surprising that one-third of MBA enrollees began more than three years after graduation (National Center for Education Statistics, 1999).

Graduates whose parents had earned advanced degrees were more likely to be enrolled full time in further education in 1997 than were graduates whose parents had less than a bachelor's degree ((National Center for Education Statistics, 1999).

Field of Study

About two-thirds of the alumni reported that if they had the chance they would probably select the same major. There was no difference in this assessment by gender or minority status (ACT, 2003a).

Business and education were among the fields most commonly studied by the 1992–93 graduates who enrolled for an advanced degree (National Center for Education Statistics, 1999). Males were more likely than females to enroll in business; medicine and dentistry; engineering, mathematics, and computer science; and life and physical sciences. Females were enrolled in education, allied health sciences, and social and behavioral sciences. Enrollment rates in law and arts and humanities were not significantly different by gender. About one-half of students enrolled for a first professional degree were studying law, and nearly one-third were studying medicine or dentistry (National Center for Education Statistics, 1999). The longitudinal study also reported a relationship between students' undergraduate major and their field of graduate study. For example, undergraduate business majors tended to pursue a degree in business, education majors in education, and engineering majors in engineering, math, or computer science (National Center for Education Statistics, 1999).

Degree Completion

Far fewer graduates complete a graduate degree than aspire to one. Alumni reported that 18% had completed a two-year degree, 87% completed a B.A. or B.S., 19% completed a master's degree, and 5% completed a six-year specialist, doctorate, or professional degree at this school or another school (ACT, 2003b). "At the time of the 1997 follow up, 21% of the 1992–93 graduates had either attained an advanced degree or were enrolled. The rest had left without a degree. Of the 21% who persisted, about half (10%) had attained a degree and were no longer enrolled. Another 1% attained one degree and were enrolled for additional education, and the remaining 10% were enrolled but had not yet earned the degree" (National Center for Education Statistics, 1999, pp. 34–35).

Researchers have largely ignored persistence rates and success of graduate and professional school students. Recent studies (Lovitts, 2001) focus on the alarming attrition rate of doctoral students. Lovitt's two campus case study showed fairly strong persistence of law and medical schools students (only about 10% attrition) but attrition in other programs ranged from 40% to 80%.

The Gap Between Expectations and Experiences

The attrition rate of doctoral students mentioned earlier is one example of the gap between expectations and experiences. Another example is the change in expectation or lower aspirations. Why do expectations change? For many college seniors, the decade after college is spent launching a career, building a long-term romantic relationship, and coordinating the demands of two careers (Barnett, Gareis, James, & Steele, 2003). As college seniors or recent graduates, they may not yet be as aware of the complexities of these tasks and may therefore overestimate the likelihood of earning advanced degrees.

As we discuss in the next section, labor force changes will continue to require advanced degrees and/or new forms of professional development, certificate, and training programs.

Skilled Workers

Most Americans have come to expect that a college degree leads to more career options, better promotion opportunities, higher earnings, and lower unemployment (Dohm & Wyatt, 2002). Increasingly, workforce development has become an important objective for higher education (Hamrick et al., 2002). Most institutions, including liberal arts colleges, offer some type of practical internship experiences for students, and career development and placement programs are considered an essential service.

Student Expectations

Overwhelmingly, for the past 20 years the major reason for college attendance is to get a better job and to be able to make more money. Seventy percent (70%) of the entering freshmen decided to go to college in order to get a better job and to be able to make more money, and 71% attend to get training for a specific career (Astin et al., 2002). Expectations about employment also influence a student's choice of a particular college. More than half of the entering freshmen selected their college because "this college's graduates get good jobs" (Astin et al., 2002). One-half of entering freshmen expect college to emphasize developing vocational and occupational competence (Kuh & Gonyea, 2003).

Students' career plans are heavily dependent upon current economic and social conditions. For example, interest in careers in business has peaked and declined depending on current events. In a time of scandals, declining interest in careers in business has resulted in a decline in business majors (Astin et al., 2002). Science, engineering, and computer science majors have also experienced patterns of growth and decline over the past 35 years. Relatively few entering freshmen expect to change their major (15%) or career choice (14%) (Astin et al., 2002). In reality, between one-third and two-thirds of all students change their career choice in college (Astin, 1977; Long, Sowa, & Niles, 1995).

Entering freshmen place a high value on achieving success in their future career endeavors. For example, 60% consider it important to become an authority in their field; 51% to obtain recognition from colleagues for contributions to their field; and 40% to be successful in their own business (Astin et al., 2002). Smaller percentages consider it important to make a theoretical contribution to science (17%), to write original works (15%), or to create artistic works (15%) (Astin et al., 2002). Freshmen expectations appear to be more like seniors' than they differ, except that freshmen have higher expectations of starting salaries, expect to get a job related to their degree, and earn a higher degree (Heckert & Wallis, 1998).

Student Experiences

Collectively, college graduates fare very well in the employment setting, and the value of higher education has been documented in numerous reports. About three-fourths of alumni reported that their college experiences prepared them adequately or better for their current job. The majority also felt that their educational experiences had a major impact on helping them develop employment-related skills such as developing original ideas and/or products, analyzing and drawing conclusions from various types of data, recognizing and using effective verbal communication skills, and defining and solving problems. One-half believed that their college experience helped them learn about existing and emerging career options (ACT, 2003b).

College seniors also reported significant gains or progress in several key areas associated with skilled workers. More than two-thirds reported at least quite a bit of gain in their vocational preparation, skills associated with a professional career, gaining a range of information that may be relevant to a career, writing and speaking effectively, using computers and other technology, getting along with different kinds of people, functioning as a team member, thinking analytically, synthesizing ideas, and adapting to change. One-third did not have that experience. Slightly more than half reported quite a bit or greater progress in analyzing quantitative problems (Gonyea et al., 2003). Fewer than half of seniors reported gains in understanding the nature of science and experimentation, understanding new developments in science and technology, and becoming aware of the consequences of new applications of science and technology.

Employment Experience

Table 8.3 summarizes the data from several different surveys asking respondents to describe their current employment status.

Males were more likely than females to be employed (91% versus 88%), and women were more likely to be working part time (11% versus 6%). Women were also slightly more likely than males to have held four or more jobs since graduation (30% versus 26%).

Employment rates for college graduates generally are high but differ according to major field of study. Students who majored in a professional field of study were employed at higher rates than students who majored in the arts and sciences (92% versus 84%) and were more likely to say that their jobs were closely related to their major field of study (National Center for Education Statistics, 1999). At least one-half reported that their job was closely related to their degree or that it had career potential (National Center for Education Statistics, 1999, p. 65; ACT, 2003b). The group most likely to say that their job was closely related to their degree was the health profession majors (85%), followed by those majoring

Table 8.3 College Graduate Employment Statistics

	Bacca-laureate & Beyond 92–93 Cohort 1997	ACT Alumni Outcomes Survey	ACT Alumni Survey Four-Year Schools	ACT Alumni Survey Two-Year Schools
Employed full time	81%	70%	71%	65%
Employed part time	8%	6%	6%	—
Continuing education	18%	8%	5%	22%
Employed and enrolled	13%	—	6%	—
Unemployed	2%	—	3%	4%

Sources: National Center for Education Statistics (1999); ACT (2002, 2003a, 2003b).

in education (68%), engineering (61%), public affairs/social services (60%), and business (58%). Among those who had majored in arts and sciences, the mathematics and other sciences majors were most likely to say their job was closely related (66%), followed by biological sciences (49%), and social science majors (31%) (National Center for Education Statistics, 1999).

Reasons for Taking Current Job

When asked four years later, 20% of the 1992–93 graduates indicated that they took their job because it was related to their field of study, 20% because it was interesting work, 9% because it was intellectual work, and 8% because they had prior work experience in the field. Females were more likely to say it was related to their major and because it provided interesting work. Financial reasons also played a role in why graduates took their jobs. Sixteen percent (16%) said the job had advancement opportunities, 10% because it provided a good income, 10% because it had good income potential, and 5% because the job provided good job security (National Center for Education Statistics, 1999). Males were more likely than females to take their current positions because of advancement opportunities or income potential (National Center for Education Statistics, 2001).

Occupation Types

In 2000, 72% of all college grads were employed in two major occupational groups—management, business, and finance fields and professional and related fields. The potential number of job openings in these two groups is nearly 13 million, or 22% of the job openings stemming from employment growth and net replacement needs. These 13 million potential job openings exclude college graduates in some increasingly college-preferred occupations, particularly sales. With 37% of the 25–34-year-old college graduates holding jobs in this category, "sales is becoming a career choice for many college graduates" (Dohm & Wyatt, 2002, p. 13).

There were some differences by occupational type in the number of jobs held since graduation. Business and management employees had held an average of 2.6 jobs, while educators or those in service positions had been employed in an average of 3.2 jobs. Those working in engineering had held fewer jobs than those working in education or service roles (National Center for Education Statistics, 1999).

Salary

Not surprisingly, research indicates that the combination of experience and a degree leads to higher salaries (Dohm & Wyatt, 2002, p. 5). The Employment Policy Foundation calculates that a college degree is worth, on average, an extra $875,000 in lifetime earnings (Kauffman, 2004). Hiring practices increasingly reward employees with college-level math and verbal skills. In 1978, male college graduates aged 25–34 earned about 15% more than recent high school grads. By 1999, the gap was 50% (Weinstein, 1999). Salaries are determined by factors other than just having a degree. Other factors include student major, location, size of company, and whether the job is in the public or private sector.

While the data suggest that students' choice of college can have an effect on lifetime earnings, their choice of major field of study has the most substantial impact on later labor market outcomes (National Center for Education Statistics, 2000). The National Center for Education Statistics (2001) confirms that college graduates who major in the applied fields of engineering, business, computer science, nursing, and other health fields earn higher than average full-time salaries. In contrast, education and humanities and arts majors experience lower salaries (Berger, 2003).

After controlling for major, background characteristics, college grade point average, and work experience, men earned considerably higher salaries than women in 1997 (Boushey & Cherry, 2003; National Center for Education Statistics, 2001). For both men and women, choice of a major was associated with later earnings (National Center for Education Statistics, 2000). For men, attending a selective institution results in higher incomes. Attending a selective liberal arts college and attending a mid-Atlantic or New England institution accounted for higher earnings for women (National Center for Education Statistics, 2000).

Unemployment

Unemployment is not considered to be a major problem for most college graduates. In 2002, the unemployment rate for college graduates was 2.9%, compared with 4.6% for the general population. However, the unemployment rates for college graduates differ significantly by race. Unemployment among white college graduates is 2.7%, compared to 4.2% among blacks and 3.4% among Hispanics (U.S. Census Bureau, 2003).

Satisfaction with Employment

About two-thirds of the alumni were satisfied with the challenge, location, and working conditions. About half were satisfied with salary and benefits and career potential, and about 40% were satisfied with advancement potential (ACT, 2003a).

The other social benefits of higher education beyond income are discussed in the following sections on democratic citizens and life skills managers.

The Gap Between Expectations and Experiences

While a college education is still viewed at the best bet for secure employment, it is also apparent that "it all depends." The evidence demonstrates that for the majority of workers, a college education has a significant positive impact over time (Malveaux, 2003; Syverson, 2002). However, one cannot generalize easily about the impact of higher education on an individual's personal employment experience. A great deal depends on several factors, including the current national and international economic, political, and social conditions, location, the individual's major, and their employment experience prior to or while completing their education. For example, the Bureau of Labor Statistics (2002) concludes its projections for 2000–2010 with an endnote indicating that its projections were completed prior to September 11, 2001, and at press time it was impossible to know how individual occupations and industries would be affected (p. 42).

The discrepancy between an individual's expectations about the economic value of college and their actual experience also results from several factors. The cost of education, delay entering the workforce, and the impact of indecision in selecting a major can all contribute to a discrepancy in expected and actual earnings. Gaps or discrepancies are also reported in the daily media. A columnist recently notes that "no one does better than America's college graduates" but cautions that "the percentage of college graduates 25 and older who hold jobs declined from just over 87% in 2000 to under 76% in 2003" (Uchitelle, 2004, p. BU3).

Inequities Based on Race and Gender Persist

"For many—especially the white, experienced, and highly educated portions of the population—jobs are readily available, though they may not be as desirable as those of their predecessors. For others— youth, blacks, and the less-educated—jobs are scarce" (Hill & Yeung, 1999, p. 33). "A Latina woman with a master's degree earns about the same as a white male high school graduate" (Malveaux, 2003, p. 2). African American and Latino men earn about $10,000 less than a white male with the same education. The rate of unemployment also differs by race. Education and career aspirations have been found to be indicative of later achievements. Chung, Loeb, and Gonzo (1996) suggested the development of educational and career aspirations may be a different process among black college students.

Smith and Powell (1990) found evidence to suggest some discrepancies among college students' perceptions about the income effects associated with a college education. These college seniors had a reasonable understanding of the value of a college education. However, their propensity to self-enhance earnings was strong, especially among the men. Sex differences in income expectations were small when other college graduates were the referent group.

However, the sex difference was large when the expectation was for their own income. Given equal levels of family income, seniors from backgrounds with lower parental education foresee a greater return on a college degree than do those whose fathers have higher levels of educational attainment (Smith & Powell, 1990).

Another potential gap is between those who have made a career decision and those who have not. Students who have made a career decision tend to be clear about their educational goals, are active self-directed learners, and have an awareness of the world of work. As a result they may experience less of a discrepancy between expectations and their actual experiences (Long, Sowa, & Niles, 1995). This may pose special challenges for liberal arts colleges to consider.

A gap also exists between the increasing demands for a high tech workforce and entering students' low expectations and college seniors' reported low gains during college in areas related to understanding science and technology and in understanding the consequences of science and technology (Gonyea et al., 2003; Kuh & Gonyea, 2003).

Life Skills Managers

Hamrick et al. (2002) and others have outlined many of the effects of college that accrue directly and indirectly to the individual as a result of the total college experience. They assert that "life skills management, perhaps more than any other general outcome of higher education, is a function of the seamless learning experience of the student" (p. 303). In the previous section on skilled workers, we discussed the data on earnings for college graduates in different majors. However, college has important implications for other areas associated with successful adult lives, such as financial security, health management and fitness, participation in civic and charitable activities, attendance at cultural activities and programs, and enhancing family life and parenting, among others.

Student Expectations

Financial Security and Income Expectations

The decision to attend college often hinges on a number of factors, including the desire for self-improvement, an interest in acquiring knowledge, and the wealth of experiences that accompany leaning. However, when personal goals include high earnings, careful planning is required (Fleetwood & Shelby, 2000).

As mentioned earlier, 70% of freshmen are going to college in order to be able to make more money (Astin et al., 2002), and nearly 74% of the entering freshmen consider it essential or very important to be well off financially (Astin et al., 2002).

Some research also notes that there are differences in expectations between racial groups. For example, Placier, Moss, & Blockus (1992) reported "minority students were more likely to give personal betterment reasons for attending college while Anglo students more often emphasized gains in their earning power" (p. 468).

Adult Competencies

While income and employment are important considerations influencing college attendance, not all recent graduates see their education as simply a means to earn money (Institute for Higher Education Policy, 1997). The Cooperative Institutional Research Program (CIRP) survey indicates that 60% of freshmen believe it is very important to become an authority in their field, 51% consider recognition from colleagues for their contributions to the professional field to be important, and 43% consider developing a meaningful philosophy of life to be important (Astin et al., 2002). Other evidence to support their broader interests in higher education are that slightly more than 40% consider it important to integrate spirituality into their life and to improve their understanding of other cultures and countries (Sax, Lindholm, Astin, Korn, & Mahoney, 2002). Almost three-fourths of entering freshmen believe that it is essential or very important to raise a family, and only 21.5% agreed that the activities of a married woman are best confined to the home and family. This expectation for broader roles for married women has changed significantly since the 1960s, when more than half of the respondents agreed with it.

College freshmen come with somewhat low expectations about their participation in the arts, but more than three-fourths expect to use campus recreational facilities and two-thirds expect to exercise regularly. Sixty percent (60%) of freshmen expect to attend a concert, 42% expect to attend an art exhibit, and 31% expect to attend a lecture or panel discussion, and fewer than one-half expect to have conversations about the arts (Kuh & Gonyea, 2003).

Student Experiences

College Graduate Earnings and Career Satisfaction

A detailed discussion of the salaries associated with college is included in the previous section on skilled workers. The ACT Alumni Outcomes Survey (2003b) data indicate that about two-thirds of the respondents are satisfied with the challenges and job security provided by their employment. However, only about 50% are satisfied with their salary, fringe benefits, and the potential for career or professional advancement.

Savings and Other Financial Transactions

Seventy-one percent (71%) of college graduates are saving money for a "rainy day," education, retirement, home purchases, or other reasons. This savings rate is above the national average of 55% for all families who save (Institute for Higher Education Policy, 1997). Individuals with a college degree are more likely than those without a degree to manage their finances using technology such as ATMs, debit cards, direct deposit, automatic bill paying, and smart cards (U.S. Census Bureau, 2003).

Adult Competencies

Overwhelmingly, college graduates agree that their college education improved their quality of life (ACT, 2003a; Institute for Higher Education Policy, 1997). College seniors reported significant gains in several areas related to the development of adult competencies. For example, more than 70% reported quite a bit or very much gain in learning to adapt to change, functioning as a team member, and getting along with different kinds of people. Nearly 60% reported quite a bit of gain in becoming aware of different philosophies, cultures, and ways of life, and about 40% reported quite a bit of progress or more in developing an understanding and enjoyment of art, music, and drama, broadening their appreciation of literature, seeing the importance of history, gaining knowledge about other parts of the world and other people, and developing good health habits and physical fitness (Gonyea et al., 2003).

More than 70% of the alumni indicated that it was of moderate or major importance for them to develop the ability to think objectively about beliefs, attitudes, and values; to be able to access and use a variety of information sources; and to understand international political and economic issues (ACT, 1993b). In addition, 90% thought it was of moderate or major importance to make and exercise a lifelong commitment to learning.

Attendance rates at a wide variety of arts activities consistently demonstrate that a greater proportion of attendees have college or other advanced degrees. Similarly, those with a college education participate to a greater degree in various leisure activities, ranging from viewing movies, attending sporting events, and participating in physical activities. College graduates also participate to a greater extent in charity work and volunteering. In 2001–02, 44% of college graduates volunteered a median 60 hours per year, compared with 21% of high school graduates who volunteered a median of 50 hours per year (U.S. Census Bureau, 2003).

Participation in community service during college is associated with important outcomes, including development of leadership skills, social self-confidence, donating money to one's alma mater, and participation in service after college (Astin & Sax, 1998; Astin, Sax, & Avalos, 1999).

Finally, there are benefits that accrue to the children of college graduates. "One of the most powerful effects of the college experience is on parenting skills" (Hamrick et al., 2002, p. 311). For example, a higher proportion of the children of college graduates in grades 6–12 participate in community service activities. Children of college graduates were consistently more likely to have been read to, told a story, taught numbers or letters, or to have visited a library. In 2000, children of college graduates had greater access to computers than did the children of high school graduates (90% versus 30%) and use of the Internet at home (47% versus 11%) (U.S. Census Bureau, 2003).

Gaps Between Expectations and Experiences

In the area of life skills management, experiences after college seem to exceed the expectations of students. The challenge appears to be how to socialize students early in their college careers to increase some of their early expectations in order to take advantage of opportunities afforded by many campus programs that will lead to significant opportunities in later years. This has important implications for advising programs, particularly in the first two years of college.

Self-Aware and Interpersonally Sensitive Individuals

Hamrick et al. (2002) highlight that college provides an opportunity to develop in numerous ways, including establishing "personal and professional identity; knowledge of their learning, working, and interaction styles and capacities; knowledge of and about other people; and a sense of self as an integral part of such collectives as the work group, family, community, or network" (p. 135). The study of self-awareness and intrapersonal development includes the development of moral reasoning, spirituality, and expanding one's personal capacity to function autonomously with efficacy to handle various life tasks. Research has changed how educators view autonomy to include the closeness and support of family (particularly for women and students of color) as a foundation from which to function autonomously, not as the traditional construct meaning independence from family (Hamrick et al., 2002).

Student Expectations

The CIRP and CSXQ report on a number of areas of the college experience that would likely relate to the development of self-awareness and becoming interpersonally sensitive individuals. Thinking ahead to their first year in college, more than three-fourths of entering students expect to make friends with students of different interests, students of different family social or economic backgrounds, and students of different racial or ethnic background. Friend-making includes an active commitment to others, and it is encouraging to see the high percentages of students who are open to friendships with others different from themselves in such critical areas. About 60% expect to have serious discussions with students with a different philosophy of life or personal values, students of different religious beliefs, students with different political opinions, and students of different racial or ethnic backgrounds. However, only about 40% expect those conversations to be about social issues such as peace, justice, human rights, equality, and race relations; and just over 50% expect those conversations to be about different lifestyles, customs, and religions (Kuh & Gonyea, 2003).

Student Experiences

Although the CSXQ and the CSEQ are not matched case data, they do provide insight into the experience of students at two key points in time.

Interpersonal Skills Are Complex

The CSEQ gives us some insight into students' capacity in this area. Student patterns of telling a friend or family member why they reacted to them the way they did changed little during college and may reflect a personality characteristic influenced by culture or gender that stays stable over time. Across all classifications (freshman to senior), about 30% never did or do so only occasionally, and 40% do so very often. Likewise, about 30% of each class never or only occasionally discussed why people get along smoothly and others do not with another student, friend, or family member, while 36% did so very often. Students slightly decrease in asking a friend for help over college: about 66% do so in the first and second years, while only 60% do so in their junior or senior years. Over time in college, students ask friends less to tell them what they really think of them (40% of first-year students do this often or very often, compared to 31% of seniors).

Patterns during the senior year reflect that more than 60% became acquainted with students with different interests (a similar pattern in the other three years), with those of a different economic and social background (slightly lower that the first-year student high of 74%); of a different race; and about 40% from another country. Nearly 50% of students do have serious discussions with students who have a different philosophy of life or different values, different political opinions, different religious beliefs, and different race or ethnic backgrounds (43%).

During their senior year, 60% of students report outside the classroom conversations with others (such as students, family, coworkers, and such) on such topics as peace, justice, human rights, equality and race relations, and lifestyles, customs, and religions. Seniors report this frequency about 7% more than first-year students.

College Gains

Students in the CSEQ data report a stable amount of gain each year of college on becoming aware of different philosophies, cultures, and ways of life, with seniors reporting a mean of 2.72 out of 4.0, reflecting between some and quite a bit of gain. Students report a small, steady gain throughout college on developing their own values and ethical standards. A similar progression is reported for a gain in understanding oneself. Students report steady, small gains on developing the ability to function as a team member (ranging from first-year students' assessment of 2.78 to the senior high of 3.07). Students do not change dramatically on their gains in their ability to get along with different kinds of people, perceiving themselves to do this quite a bit across all classifications.

College students show greater gains in moral reasoning compared to their non-college high school graduate peers (Pascarella & Terenzini, 1991, cited in Hamrick et al., 2002).

Alumni Perspectives

Alumni (ACT, 2002) of all ages report similar levels of satisfaction with human diversity in the workplace. Among men and women who were over and under 30 years of age, 54% were satisfied or extremely satisfied, and only 6% were dissatisfied or very dissatisfied. While as many minorities were similarly satisfied (52%), more were dissatisfied (10%).

Women alumni attribute greater gains in their understanding and capacity to work with others different from themselves than do men alumni. More than three-fourths of alumni report that college had an impact on their ability to think objectively about beliefs, attitudes, and values. Alumni attribute nearly 70% of their ability to get along with people from various cultures, races, and backgrounds as a major or moderate impact of their college experience (with men reporting 64.6% and women reporting 71.7%; minorities report 72.8%; those under 30 report 4% more attribution than do those over 30). Similarly, alumni attribute 63% of their understanding and appreciating cultural and ethnic differences between people as a major or moderate impact of their college experience (10% more for female alumni than male alumni; 68.7% for minority alumni). Alumni attribute 67.5% of their ability to get along with people whose attitudes and opinions are different from theirs as a major or moderate impact of their college experience (8% higher for women than men; 70.4% of minorities).

More than three-fourths of alumni report that college had a major or moderate impact on their ability to work cooperatively in groups or as a team member. Women attribute more of their relational capacities with others to their college experience than do men.

Regarding their satisfaction with their campus acceptance of individuals regardless of their sexual orientation, 39% were satisfied or very satisfied, while 5.3% were dissatisfied or very dissatisfied and a large group of nearly 27% reports no opinion.

The Gap Between Expectations and Experiences

Women attribute more of their relational capacities with others to their college experience than do men. While this finding supports gender stereotypes, it must be noted that men therefore do not seem to attribute their relational empathy or capacity to work with others different from themselves to their college experience. Men may develop this capacity, but it is interesting that it is not attributed to college and to the degree it develops may be attributed to other factors like personal or family relationships. More study is needed in this area.

College clearly provides the environment for students to learn about others different from themselves. While there were few gaps in expectations and realities, it appears possible that colleges could augment the effect with more intentional and meaningful interaction among diverse students. Students appear to want this benefit from college.

Only a few alumni were dissatisfied with how their campuses responded to sexual orientation, but a large number of alumni reported no opinion on this item. Sexual orientation continues to appear to be a largely unaddressed area of student diversity.

Democratic Citizens

Hamrick et al. (2002) define citizenship as "actively attending to the well-being, continuity, and improvement of society through individual action or actions or civic and social collectives; the learning outcome is therefore the development of a personal commitment to identify and advance social interests" (p. 183). In the broadest sense, this outcome includes the communitarian concept of a "heightened sense of responsibility to one's communities that leads to active participation with others for the common good" (Komives & Appel Silbaugh, 2004, p. 12). This concept goes well beyond voting and holding public office, although those are indicators of citizenship, to include such indicators as active involvement in one's residence hall, work site, or church and being informed about shared campus and community issues.

Student Expectations

College has been regarded as one among a number of social institutions that prepare young adults for concerned and involved citizenship. Research data and the contemporary press provide evidence that there is an expectation that college attendance will influence and enhance graduates' interests and abilities to be engaged citizens and democratic leaders (ACT, 2003a,b; Malveaux, 2003; Pascarella, Ethington, & Smart, 1988). As noted in the previous section, there is also considerable evidence that higher education provides a social benefit beyond those that accrue to the individual (Institute for Higher Education Policy, 1997; Malveaux, 2003; U.S. Census Bureau, 2003).

About a third of entering college freshmen consider it to be very important to influence the political structure, to influence social values, to become involved in programs to clean up the environment, to participate in community action, to help promote racial understanding, to keep up to date with political affairs, and to become a community leader (Astin et al., 2002). Nearly two-thirds believe it is important to help others in difficulty, and one-fourth expect to participate in volunteer community service (Astin et al., 2000).

Sixty percent (60%) of freshmen expect to be engaged in conversations about current events, but fewer than 40% expect the conversations to be about the social-ethical issues related to science and technology, the economy, or international relations. Slightly more than one-half expect to talk about social justice and peace issues.

The vast majority of alumni considered it to be of moderate or major importance to live their personal and professional life according to their own standards or ethics, to appreciate and exercise their rights, responsibilities, and privileges as a citizen; and, to develop and use effective leadership skills (ACT, 2002; ACT, 2003a; ACT, 2003b).

Student Experiences

The evidence supports the belief that education has both an individual and a social benefit. College graduates are more likely to participate in the electoral process, public meetings, and community service; run for office; volunteer more hours; make more charitable contributions; read the newspaper; and participate more fully in the education of their children (Institute for Higher Education Policy, 1997; Malveaux, 2003; National Center for Education Statistics, 1999).

College seniors report significant gains in several areas that are related to the characteristics of democratic citizens, including developing values and ethical standards, developing the ability to get along with different kinds of people, functioning as a member of a team, and adapting to change (Gonyea et al., 2003).

Alumni also reported that their education contributed to their personal growth in several areas that are associated with engaged democratic citizens. The vast majority of alumni considered it of moderate or major importance to live their personal and professional life according to a personal standard or ethic, and two-thirds thought their education had a major impact in this area. One-half reported that their education had a moderate or major impact on their appreciating and exercising their rights, responsibilities, and privileges as a citizen, and 11% reported no impact at all. About two-thirds thought that their education had a moderate or major impact on their developing and using effective leadership skills (ACT, 2003b).

Among the two-year college alumni, one-fifth thought their education contributed very much to their recognizing their rights, responsibilities, and privileges as a citizen, and another one-fifth reported that this outcome did not apply to their personal growth. Sixty percent thought their education contributed somewhat or better to their learning to lead or guide others (ACT, 2002).

Almost three-fourths of alumni at four-year and two-year colleges thought their education contributed somewhat or better to their persistence at difficult tasks—a behavior often associated with many aspects of a successful adult life and an asset for those trying to influence political or social change (ACT, 2002, 2003a). Three-fourths of alumni felt college had a moderate or major impact on their ability to work cooperatively in groups and as a team member. Two-thirds felt college had a moderate or major impact on their ability to get along with people whose attitudes and opinions are different and to get along with people from various cultures, races, and backgrounds. One-half thought their college experience had a moderate or major impact on their understanding the interaction of human beings and the environment.

Voting

Three-fourths of the voting age population with four or more years of college registered to vote in the 2000 presidential election, compared to 64% of the general population and 60% of high school graduates, and 72% of the college graduates voted in the 2000 presidential election compared with 55% of the total population and 49% of high school graduates (U.S. Census Bureau, 2003).

Other

In the earlier section on life skills managers, we reported on college graduates' participation in charitable work and their involvement in their children's education, which are also relevant to the outcome of democratic citizen.

The Gap Between Expectations and Experiences

College is only one of several social institutions that influence the development of the values and characteristics associated with democratic citizenship. Other influential forces are the family, religious institutions, and the work setting, among others. However, it is surprising to see the mixed expectations that students have for how college will impact their understanding of their rights and responsibilities.

This is another area where colleges must be more intentional in helping entering college students to develop clearer and higher expectations in order to eventually influence the outcomes.

Recommendations

1. The overarching recommendation signaled by this chapter is that higher education must conduct local and national longitudinal studies on college outcomes and on the impact of college on the alumni experience. It is essential to understand what dimensions of the college experience contribute to lives well lived by alumni. It is also important to document and understand the similarities and differences between high school graduates who are college bound and those who are not.

2. Regular student assessment must be used as a pedagogy. It was almost sad that fully one-fourth of seniors (Gonyea et al., 2003, p. 92) report that they never took a test to measure their abilities, interests, or attitudes while in college. Assessments serve at least a two-pronged purpose of providing data needed by colleges to assess their impact and are a powerful pedagogy for students to learn to promote their own growth. Creative forms of assessment might include electronic portfolios and other forms of competency demonstration.

3. Campuses must ratchet up the emphasis on the importance of diversity. Students perceived a small, steady decline over time in how much the college environment emphasized developing an understanding and appreciation of human diversity (Gonyea et al., 2003). While the ACT Alumni Survey (2002) reports that nearly 60% of their alumni agreed that their campus had an atmosphere of ethnic, political, and religion understanding, this means that 40% did not think so, and minorities represented 5% more disagreement than majority students. Research presented in the Michigan cases affirmed the educational and developmental benefits of diversity for all students (Gurin, 1999), and colleges must continue to design meaningful diversity engagements of students across the environment.

4. The experiences of students of color; lesbian, gay, bisexual, transsexual (LGBT) students; and others for whom the traditional campus culture may be a chilly climate should be assessed and interventions designed that support the success of these students. Sedlacek's (2004) large body of research on factors that predict college success for students of color has direct links to interventions during college that would support that success. His work

demonstrates the importance of a positive self-concept, realistic self-appraisal, success at handling the system (particularly racism), preference for long-term goals, availability of a strong support person, leadership experience, involvement in community, and knowledge acquired in any field. These eight factors would benefit any student but have proved particularly salient to the success of students of color.

5. Life and career planning should be emphasized for all students. While most students have career goals in coming to college, life and career exploration is an option on most campuses, but it is not part of the experience for all students. Special attention to career and life goals is essential at liberal arts colleges and for those with liberal arts majors. Professional staff needs to work intentionally with juniors and seniors on graduate education goals. Their readiness to consider graduate degrees increases closer to degree attainment. Life planning would include designing programs that emphasize multiple role acquisition so that traditional-age undergraduates anticipate roles of being partners, parents, workers, caregivers, and community members.

6. We encourage a transformation of the advising role to be the touchstone for all students in their quest to design a college experience linked to key outcomes. Reflecting on her longitudinal study of college students eight years after their graduation, Baxter Magolda (2000) observed that all colleges should intentionally seek to help students develop an internal foundation so central to self-authorship. The role of academic advisors (Light, 2001) as good companions on that journey (Baxter Magolda, 2000) is critical. Changing the nature of advising relationships may alter other aspects of the organizational structure of colleges, but it would involve change that is necessary. Learning experiences must be enriched through powerful pedagogies (Marchese, 1997; Hamrick et al., 2002). Making learning an active process will broaden and deepen college outcomes and have greater transference into alumni life. Knowing how to apply and use information learned in college is central to that transference. Studies regularly support that engagement in service learning relates to and predicts future service involvement (Eklund-Leen, 1994, cited in Hamrick et al., 2002). Establishing patterns of good campus citizenship are central to being engaged in later civic life

(Kuh & Lund, 1994). Such powerful pedagogies as service learning, action research, leadership experience, meaningful part time work, internships or cooperative experience, problem-based learning, and portfolios or case study methods will support the application of that learning in post-baccalaureate life.

7. Explore the gaps in expectations and gains in areas related to understanding science and technology. All evidence suggests that informed citizens must be able to understand the implications and tradeoffs associated with new technologies—from computer privacy issues, voting technologies, and human cloning, to public investments in large research projects in science and technology.

8. Meaningful ways for students to be involved in their educational experiences must be identified. Involvement has been a goal for student affairs staff for decades and must continue to be a foundation of student affairs practice. We must expand students' concept of civic engagement and citizenship to include all the communities of practice where they share a responsibility with others for community outcomes. This campus-based responsibility can be built in work sites, residence halls, student organizations, and service sites, or by building learning communities in classes and in one's major, which in turn build commitment to professional associations, involvement in parent-teacher associations, neighborhood associations, and other shared community, regional, national, or global issues.

9. Universities must expand their focus to include the success of graduate and professional students. The *Chronicle of Higher Education* increasingly has focused on the persistence and degree attainment of graduate students (Jacobson, 2001), and there is some evidence that this focus with campus-based interventions will continue. Student affairs divisions in universities need to expand their services to graduate students and advocate for the success of these students (Woodard & Komives, 2003). Local studies of degree completion are a first step, but far more needs to be done to ensure degree completion for these students.

10. Colleges must redesign post-baccalaureate educational opportunities to support lifelong learning. Colleges should continue to expand alumni programs that promote lifelong learning, including creating more creative options like certificate programs, online coursework, discipline-based Web pages, and job-related professional development.

Conclusion

The question for this decade will become "What about alumni's attitudes and behaviors can be attributed to their college experience?" We know that college is not just the locus of the change, but is the source of many changes. What experiences particularly contribute to postcollege achievement and success of alumni will increasingly be a question asked of colleges in this expanding accountability era.

The evidence clearly suggests that the benefits of higher education for life after college go well beyond those that accrue to the individual. Public policymakers should carefully consider the implications for providing greater access and support programs for those populations that are underrepresented in college today. Higher education leaders must work to shape these initiatives.

References

American College Testing Service. (2002). *Alumni survey (2 year college form) normative data report*. Iowa City, IA: Author.

American College Testing Service. (2003a). *Alumni survey normative data report*. Iowa City, IA: Author.

American College Testing Service. (2003b). *Alumni outcomes survey normative data report*. Iowa City, IA: Author.

Astin, A. W. (1977). *Four critical years*. San Francisco: Jossey-Bass.

Astin, A. W., Oseguera, L., Sax, L. J., & Korn, W. S. (2002). *The American freshman: Thirty-five year trends*. Los Angeles: Higher Education Research Institute.

Astin, A. W., & Sax, L. J. (1998). How undergraduates are affected by service participation. *Journal of College Student Development, 39*(3), 251–263.

Astin, A. W., Sax, L. J., & Avalos, J. (1999). Long term effects of volunteerism during undergraduate years. *Review of Higher Education, 22*(2), 187–202.

Barnett, R. C., Gareis, K. C., James, J. B., & Steele, J. (2003). Planning ahead: College seniors' concerns about career-marriage conflict. *Journal of Vocational Behavior, 62*, 305–319.

Baxter Magolda, M. (1999). Defining and redefining student learning. In E. J. Whitt (Ed.), *Student learning and student affairs work: Responding to our imperative* (pp. 35–50). Washington, DC: National Association of Student Personnel Administrators.

Baxter Magolda, M. (2000). Interpersonal maturity: Integrating agency and communion. *Journal of College Student Development, 41*, 141–156.

Baxter Magolda, M. B., & King, P. M. (Eds.) (2004). *Learning partnerships: Theory and models of practice to educate for self-authorship*. Sterling, VA: Stylus.

Berger, L. (2003). The undecided. *New York Times*, August 3, p. 4A.

Boushey, H., & Cherry, R. (2003). The economic boom (1991–1997) and women: Issues of race, education, and regionalism. *NWSA Journal*, 15(1), 34–52.

Bureau of Labor Statistics. (2002). Special edition: Charting the projections: 2000–2010. *Occupational Outlook Quarterly*, 45(4), 1–42.

Chung, B. Y., Loeb, J. W., & Gonzo, S. T. (1996). Factors predicting the educational and career aspirations of black college freshmen. *Journal of Career Development*, 23(2), 127–135.

Council for the Advancement of Standards in Higher Education. (2003). *Standards and guidelines*. Washington, DC: Author.

Dohm, A., & Wyatt, I. (2002). College at work: Outlook and earnings for college graduates, 2000–2010 (Special Edition). *Occupational Outlook Quarterly*, 46(3), 2–15.

Fleetwood, C., & Shelby, K. (2000). The outlook for college graduates, 1998–2008: A balancing act. *Occupational Outlook Quarterly*, 44(3), 2–9.

Gonyea, R. M., Kish, K. A., Kuh, G. D., Muthiah, R. N., & Thomas, A. D. (2003). *College student experiences questionnaire: Norms for the fourth edition*. Bloomington: Indiana University, Center for Postsecondary Research, Policy, and Planning.

Gurin, P. (1999). Expert report of Patricia Gurin. In *The compelling need for diversity in higher education*. Part of expert testimony prepared for *Gratz et al. V. Bollinger et al.*, no. 97-75321 (E.D. Mich), and *Grutter et al. V. Bollinger et al.*, no 97-75928 (E.D. Mich.). Ann Arbor: University of Michigan.

Hamrick, F. A., Evans, N. J., & Schuh, J. H. (2002). *Foundations of student affairs practice: How philosophy, theory, and research strengthen educational outcomes*. San Francisco: Jossey-Bass.

Heckert, T., & Wallis, H. A. (1998). Career and salary expectations of college freshmen and seniors: Are seniors more realistic than freshmen? *College Student Journal*, 32(3), 334–340.

Hill, M. S., & Yeung, N. J. (1999). How has the changing structure of opportunities affected transitions to adulthood? In A. Booth, A. C. Crouter, & M. J. Shanahan (Eds.), *Transitions to adulthood in a changing economy: No work, no family, no future?* (pp. 3–39). Westport, CT: Praeger.

Institute for Higher Education Policy. (1997). *Now what? Life after college for recent graduates*. Boston: Education Resources Institute.

Jacobson, J. (2001, June 1). Why do so many people leave graduate school without a Ph.D.? *Chronicle of Higher Education*. Retrieved March 23, 2004, from http://chronicle.com/prm/weekly/v47/i38/38a01001.html.

Kauffman, M. (2004). Learn median pay for 104 occupations. *Baltimore Sun*, February 29, p. 3D.

Komives, S. R., & Appel Silbaugh, C. (2004). Leadership for civic engagement. *Concepts and Connections, 12*(1), 12–14.

Kuh, G. D., Douglas, K. D., Lund, J. P., & Ramin-Gyurnek, J. (1994). *Student learning outside the classroom: Transcending artificial boundaries.* ASHE/ERIC Higher Education Report, no. 8. Washington, DC: George Washington University.

Kuh, G. D., & Gonyea, R. M. (2003). *CSXQ: Tentative norms for the second edition.* Bloomington: Indiana University, Center for Postsecondary Research.

Kuh, G. D., & Lund, J. P. (1994). What students gain from participating in student government. In M. C. Terrell & M. J. Cuyjet (Eds.), *Developing student government leadership* (pp. 5–17). New Directions for Student Services, no. 66. San Francisco: Jossey-Bass.

Light, R. J. (2001). *Making the most of college: Students speak their minds.* Cambridge, MA: Harvard University Press.

Long, B. E., Sowa, C. J., & Niles, S. G. (1995). Differences in student development reflected by career decisions of college seniors. *Journal of College Student Development, 36*, 1, 47–52.

Lovitts, B. E. (2001). *Leaving the ivory tower: The causes and consequences of departure from doctoral study.* Lanham, MD: Rowman & Littlefield.

Malveaux, J. (2003). *What's at stake: The social and economic benefits of higher education.* Research Report 2. Plano, TX: The College Board, National Dialogue on Student Financial Aid.

Marchese, T. J. (1997). The new conversations about learning: Insights from neuroscience and anthropology, cognitive science and work-place studies. *Assessing Impact: Evidence and Action* (pp. 79–95). Washington, DC: American Association for Higher Education. Retrieved August 14, 2004, from http://www.aahe.org/pubs/TM-essay.htm.

Moss, G. (2003). Intellectualism vs. career preparation: A comparative assessment of self reported growth among graduating college seniors. *College Student Journal, 37*(2), 309–320. Retrieved January 28, 2004, from EBSCOHost Research Database, pp. 1–8, http://www.ebsco.com/home/.

National Association of Student Personnel Administrators/American College Personnel Association. (2004). *Learning reconsidered: A campus-wide focus on the student experience.* Washington, DC: National Association of Student Personnel Administrators and the American College Personnel Association.

National Center for Education Statistics. (1999). *Life after college: A descriptive summary of the 1992–93 bachelor's degree recipients in 1997, with an essay on participation in graduate and first-professional education* (NCES 1999-155). Washington, DC: U.S. Department of Education.

National Center for Education Statistics. (2000). *College quality and the earnings of recent college graduates* (NCES 2000-043). Washington, DC: U.S. Department of Education.

National Center for Education Statistics. (2001). *From bachelor's degree to work: Major field of study and employment outcomes of 1992–93 bachelor's degree recipients who did not enroll in graduate education by 1997* (NCES 2001-165). Washington, DC: U.S. Department of Education.

National Panel. (2002). *Greater expectations: A new vision for learning as a nation goes to college.* Washington, DC: Association of American Colleges and Universities.

Pascarella, E. T., Ethington, C. A., & Smart, J. C. (1988). The influence of college on humanitarian/civic involvement values. *Journal of Higher Education, 59*(4), 412–437.

Placier, P., Moss, G., & Blockus, L. (1992). College student personal growth in retrospect: A comparison of African American and white alumni. *Journal of College Student Development, 33,* 462–471.

Sax, L. J., Lindholm, J. A., Astin, A. W., Korn, W. S., & Mahoney, K. M. (2002). *The American freshman: National norms for fall 2002.* Los Angeles: Higher Education Research Institute.

Sedlacek, W. E. (2004). *Beyond the big test: Noncognitive assessment in higher education.* San Francisco: Jossey-Bass.

Smith, H. L., & Powell, B. (1990). Great expectations: Variations in income expectations among college students. *Sociology of Education, 63,* 194–207.

Syverson, P. D. (2002). What's it worth? New analysis from Census Bureau shows higher degrees yield higher earnings. *Communicator, 35*(7), 5–7.

Uchitelle, L. (2004). In this recovery, a college education backfires. *New York Times,* March 14, p. BU3.

U.S. Census Bureau. (2003). *Statistical Abstract of the United States: 2003.* Washington, DC: U.S. Department of Commerce.

Weinstein, M. M. (1999). Problems tarnishing a robust economy. *New York Times,* January 4, p. C10.

Woodard, D., Jr., & Komives, S. R. (2003). Shaping the future. In S. R. Komives & D. B. Woodard, Jr. (Eds.), *Student services: A handbook for the profession* (4th ed.; pp. 637–655). San Francisco: Jossey-Bass.

Chapter Nine

The Influence of Selected Students' Characteristics on Their Expectations of College

*Gwendolyn J. Dungy, Patricia A. Rissmeyer,
and Gregory Roberts*

The heterogeneity of the student population enrolled in colleges and universities is one of the greatest strengths of higher education in the United States. If high school students can demonstrate some promise for success in postsecondary education, there will be an institution that will accept them. With various federal loan and assistance programs helping students to pay for school, and many students opting to enroll in public two-year colleges with relatively low tuition expenses, a broad spectrum of the population has the opportunity to participate in higher education. While students may enroll in the same school and even the same classes, their expectations of the college experience can vary greatly. The purpose of this chapter is to focus on the nature of student expectations of college and how they differ depending on their age, gender, race/ethnicity, employment status, and whether or not they are the first generation in their family to attend college.

Note: The editors acknowledge a contribution to this chapter by Elizabeth Spear, of Central Connecticut State University.

Data for this chapter are drawn from descriptive statistics collected through the College Student Expectations Questionnaire (CSXQ), which assesses new students' goals and motivations (Kuh & Gonyea, 2003). We will also consider data gathered from the administration of the College Student Experiences Questionnaire (CSEQ) described in Chapter 3.

Gender Differences

In order to meet student expectations and educational goals, we must consider the multiple characteristics of enrolled students. The interactions of men and women in their social contexts, for example, influence their expectations as college and university students. In most categories for which statistics are collected by the CSXQ, men and women generally have similar expectations of their college experiences. There are some areas, however, where there are differences in expectations, seemingly based on gender, that are interesting to consider. A change in aspirations for pursuing graduate degrees, for example, appears to have reversed for men and women over the past 30 years (Astin, 1998). While women's interest in pursuing graduate degrees, especially in doctoral or advanced professional degrees, grew substantially, men indicated only a slight increase in the same categories. In 1966, Astin reported that 58% of the men and 40% of the women were interested in pursuing graduate degrees. Thirty years later, 68% of the women were interested in graduate education, compared with 65% of the men (Astin, 1998, p. 116). As Astin (1998) found in his survey of 9 million first-year students at more than 1,500 institutions, women students today have "much higher educational aspirations and are much more interested in careers in traditionally 'male' professions (business, law, medicine, engineering)" (p. 10).

One study on teaching practices and classroom climate suggests that "gender was significantly associated with only one self perception: confidence in one's ability to become an engineer. Even when controlling for SAT scores, educational aspirations, and class year, male students were more likely than female students to report confidence in their ability to become engineers" (Colbeck, Cabrera, & Terenzini, 2001, p. 183). This finding raises the question about whether or not there are differences in expectations about one's ability to succeed academically based on gender.

CSXQ data suggest that male students are more likely to expect that they will socialize with faculty outside of class. Thirty-four percent (34%) of women and 25% of men said that they never expected to socialize with faculty outside of class. Boyer (1987) concluded that women participated less in class than men. This finding is consistent with more recent research on students' perceptions of classroom participation. Male students reported significantly higher levels of class participation than did females (Crombie, Pyke, Silverton, Jones, & Piccinin, 2003). Not surprisingly, men expect to spend their leisure time in a different manner than women. According to the 30-year trends CIRP survey, the largest reported gender difference in leisure activities pertained to the amount of time students spent playing video games. A much higher percentage of men (59.5%) than women (18.3%) spent at least some time playing video games. Thirty-six percent (36%) of men versus 6.2% of women are likely to spend at least one hour per week playing games, and 8% of men versus only 0.7% of women are likely to spend six hours or more per week playing games (Astin, 1998).

How might these findings inform practice in higher education? Knowing that the expectations of college vary by gender is no real surprise, but the differences between men and women in intellectual confidence levels may inform academic advising practices. In addition, the variance by gender in expectations for advanced degrees may create a need for different approaches in career planning.

Employed Students

Astin's (1998) study of 30-year trends demonstrated that "record-high percentages of freshmen say that they will have to 'get a job to help pay for college expenses'" and "record numbers say they plan to work full time while attending college" (p. 128). These estimates are extrapolated from data collected between the late 1980s and 1996.

Data collected for the CSXQ indicated that 60% of the respondents expected to work either on or off campus between 11 and 20 hours a week while they were enrolled. Whether a student expected to work or not seemed to have little effect on expectations for good grades, plans to pursue an advanced degree, major field of study, and experiences with faculty. Research on cognitive development finds no significant differences "on any of the three cognitive outcomes [reading comprehension, mathematics, and critical thinking] among students who worked on campus, students who worked off campus, and students who did not work their first year" (Pascarella, Bohr, Nora, Desler, & Zusman, 1994, p. 368). In addition, even though research has found that students who work off campus spend less time studying (the more hours worked, the fewer hours spent in study), and typical measures of scholastic achievement (that is, grades, degree attainment) may be negatively affected, there was no evidence that "off campus work of any amount had deleterious consequences for overall cognitive development" (p. 369). Pascarella et al. (1994) suggest that because the students in their sample who work off campus tend to be older, available study time may be used in a "more mature and efficient" manner (p. 369). Male (44%) and female (45%) students were virtually the same in expecting their families to provide for the majority of their expenses while in college.

Students who are working while attending college can have different experiences depending on the nature of the work experience. "The impact on persistence and educational attainment of working on-campus appears to be just the opposite for off-campus employment" (Pascarella et al., 1994, p. 364) in that "part-time employment on-campus positively influences both persistence and degree completion" (p. 364).

The CSXQ data further indicate that differences in expectations of students who worked on campus as opposed to off campus emerged in the following areas: (1) students who worked on campus were more likely to live in campus housing, (2) students who worked on campus expected to take higher credit loads than students who worked off campus, (3) students who worked on campus reported higher expectations regarding engagement in all areas of course learning, and (4) students who worked on campus expected to use campus facilities to a greater degree than students who worked off campus. Additionally, students who expected to work on campus had high expectations pertaining to their involvement in clubs, organizations, and service projects. This information suggests a beneficial relationship between intentions for on-campus employment and expectations regarding engagement in the learning process and in campus life. Higher education leaders may consider expanding on-campus employment opportunities for students, since those who anticipate the experience of working on campus seem to also anticipate a more significant involvement in campus life and the learning experience.

Age and Student Status

According to the National Center for Education Statistics (2002), in the year 2000, more than half of undergraduates were what most consider "traditional" college age, 23 years old or younger. Seventeen percent (17%) were in their mid- to late twenties. About one-quarter were 30 years of age or older, including 14% who were 30–39 years of age and 12% who were 40 years of age or older. The average age of all undergraduates was 27, and the median age was 22. The wide range in age of the college-going population presents challenges when attempting to identify and meet student expectations.

In looking at students' characteristics, a positive correlation existed between students' income and their age. Undergraduates who were 30 years of age or older were less likely to be in the lowest income quartile than other undergraduates and more likely to be in the highest quartile. It is reasonable to expect that, for the most part, these are the same students who are gainfully employed while enrolled in a degree program.

Distinct differences based on students' expected place of residence also emerged. Eighty percent (80%) of respondents 19 years old and under expected to live in college residence halls, while 29% of 20–23-year-olds and 15% of those over 24 years of age expected to live on campus. Of those students who were 20 years of age and older, 38% expected to live within walking distance of school. The fact that 38% of "older" students expected to live within walking distance combined with the fact that 80% of "younger" students expected to live on campus suggests that residence hall living continues to have greater appeal to first- and second-year students. Providing attractive, affordable on-campus living options for older students presents an ongoing challenge for college planners in developing housing options.

In exploring the relationship between age and academic performance, 13% of students 19 years old and younger expected to receive

an A average, while 45% of students 20 years old and older anticipated earning an A. It may be that students with more maturity have
a greater sense of focus and academic purpose and a more accurate
expectation regarding their ability to succeed. When one considers
the field of study that students expect to pursue, the results are quite
specific. Seventeen percent of 19-year-olds and under expected to
major in business, while 40% of those 20 years old and above expected to major in business. Ten percent (10%) of respondents who
were 19 years old or younger planned to major in education, while
19% of those who were 20 years of age or older expected to major
in education. Older students are more confident in their expectations of academic concentration than younger students. The focus
by older students on the business and education disciplines seems to
suggest an orientation to pre-professional programs, where they can
finish an undergraduate degree and proceed directly to a professional position in the work setting.

There has been a national 20-year trend of increasing enroll-
ments of returning learners (Aslanian & Brickell, 1980). Their expectations as consumers, not surprisingly, are higher than those of
younger students. As suggested by Cross (1980), adult learners are
motivated, goal oriented, and expect their colleges and universities to operate in a flexible fashion to meet the needs of their demanding and complicated lives.

First-Generation College Students

In a study that focused on the characteristics of first-generation college students, the report found that the respondents "were more
likely to be ethnic minority students, to come from a lower socioeconomic background, to speak a language other than English at home
and to score lower on the SAT than were the other students" (Bui,
2002, p. 20). First-generation college students in the UCLA-based
study expressed a greater fear of failing, even though survey results
indicated that they did not differ from later-generation college students in feeling comfortable making decisions related to college on
their own, knowing about the academic programs at their university
prior to enrollment, and feeling accepted at their university.

Many first-generation college students begin their course work
and pursue degrees at a community college because of costs and

because their expectations of their ability to do well in college are often tempered by a fear of failure. Data suggest that "first generation college students have lower self-images of their academic ability than those who come from families with college experience" (Hellman & Harbeck, 1997, p. 165).

Data gathered from the CSXQ demonstrate that first-generation college students have expectations of college that are generally similar to the perceptions of all students. There are some measurable differences between the groups that may be useful to consider in planning campus programs. Many first-generation students who come from a lower socioeconomic background have fewer financial resources, have to work more hours, and have fewer available hours for study and participation in the co-curriculum. Despite these challenges, 76% of first-generation students included in the CSXQ data report that they expect to enroll in graduate school. Despite such aspirations, "low SES [socioeconomic status] students have lower incomes, lower levels of educational attainment, and lower levels of educational aspirations than their peers from higher social strata nine years after college entry" (Walpole, 2003, p. 63).

The consequences of having fewer financial resources for many first-generation students are evident. Fewer first-generation students opt to reside in residence halls (71% versus 82%); first-generation students expect to have a job on campus (57% versus 45%); and, as a result of employment commitments, they are twice as likely to enroll part time as other students, and they are less likely to become engaged in campus programs and co-curricular activities. According to the CSXQ data, twice as many first-generation students expected never to be acquainted with students whose socioeconomic and ethnic backgrounds were different from their own. Herter's (2002) study of first- and second-generation students found that "second-generation college students reported significantly more social adjustment than first-generation college students" (p. 13). This research supports previous studies that indicate that the most salient factor in the social adjustment of first-year students is involvement in social activities.

For many first-generation students, college is more of a means to a very practical end—they often don't have the luxury of enjoying the collegiate experience. Instead, they are motivated to earn the credential that will enable them to seek and obtain a job that will improve their families' socioeconomic status.

The results of a more recent study of college experiences and end of second year outcomes indicate that the experiences are different for first-generation students. The researchers found that "across two years of the study, first-generation students: completed fewer credit hours; studied less; took fewer courses in the natural sciences, mathematics, and the arts and humanities; had lower college grades; were less likely to join a Greek organization; and worked more hours per week than their classmates whose parents had both completed a bachelor's degree or above" (Pascarella, Wolniak, Pierson, & Terenzini, 2003, p. 425). The researchers acknowledge the resilience of first-generation students while asking the important question, whether or not the different experiences "translate into disadvantages in the outcomes of college" (p. 426).

College administrators can employ strategies to address the differences between students whose parents went to college and those who are first-generation college students. One approach may involve stronger interactions with parents. One obvious characteristic of the parents of first-generation students is that they do not have firsthand knowledge of the college-going experience. Parent orientation programs and activities that engage parents in the college atmosphere may help them to become comfortable and informed about the experiences of their sons and daughters. Special, direct support for first-generation students should also be designed. On-campus employment opportunities may help them to connect to the campus; further, targeted academic advising and career planning support directed to them may also make a difference.

Racial Differences

There are numerous factors that could be considered when studying the expectations of students based on ethnicity. For the purposes of this chapter, we focus on the reported higher expectation to pursue an advanced degree by black and Latino students and the unmet expectation of white students who had anticipated having more interaction with students from different races and national origins.

Comparatively speaking, a higher percentage of black and Latino students intend to enroll for an advanced degree, 83% and 80% respectively compared to the 79% Asian/Pacific Islander and 70%

white (CSEQ data). From their first year of enrollment to their senior year, this interest remains constant for black and white students and decreases slightly for Asian/Pacific Islander students and for Latino students (CSEQ).

This finding is broadly consistent with the findings of other studies that identify higher expectations for pursuing a graduate degree for black students (Carter, 1999; van Laar, 2000) and for black and Hispanic students (Kao & Tienda, 1998). High aspirations for economic success, however, are not necessarily correlated with strong grades among minority students (Eskilson & Wiley, 1999).

A greater aspiration for graduate school attendance has not been realized, however, through the matriculation and persistence rates of black and Hispanic students, which are comparatively lower than those of Asian/Pacific Islander and white students. A theoretical explanation for the gap between educational aspirations and actual achievement has been sought, but remains unresolved. Particularly absent has been the nature of the responsibility that the college or university must take. Carter (1999) suggests, "Theoretical conceptualizations of college students' degree goals have been lacking in terms of the role of institutions in the development of students' aspirations" (p. 38).

Clearly one approach to close the gap between the expectation for and the achievement of an advanced degree for black and Latino students would be to strengthen the academic and research skills of undergraduates to prepare them for the rigors of graduate education. Additionally, high school and college programs that provide anticipatory socialization and research opportunities can provide critically important experiences to help students consider graduate school as a realistic education option.

Increasing the number of graduate and professional school degree holders in the black and Latino populations would be invaluable not only to the individual but to society as a whole. Wilson (1996) applauds the notion suggested by Oden and others that "America's future depends on our having a highly educated and skilled work force, and to accomplish this, we must exploit previously untapped potential" (p. 7).

So what should higher education professionals do to address the gap between expectations and achievement for African American/black and Hispanic/Latino students? Given the need for an educated workforce that is able to create and disseminate new knowledge to address society's greatest challenges, it is incumbent upon higher education institutions to increase the pool of graduate and professional students from diverse ethnic backgrounds. Developing creative and effective strategies to overcome barriers to matriculation and graduation of black and Hispanic students in graduate programs is a national imperative that must be vigorously pursued. At the same time, students of color should not be led to think that a bachelor's degree is not valuable or a laudable accomplishment. The aspiration for advanced study should be encouraged and enabled, but students who do not achieve those degrees should be empowered and valued for the accomplishment of an undergraduate degree.

Multicultural Experiences of White Students

All students participating in the CSXQ survey indicated a similar level of interest in making acquaintances with students who differ from themselves in race or national origin. This expectation, however, does not seem to be comparatively realized by white students, according to CSEQ data. Of the white students responding in the CSEQ, 40% indicated that they have infrequent interactions with students whose racial backgrounds were different from their own. In contrast, 23% of the Asian/Pacific Islander, 21% of the black, and 20% of the Latino respondents reported that their interactions with students who were different from themselves were infrequent. Similarly, white students reported having fewer interactions with international students when compared with the responses of Asian/Pacific Islander, black, and Latino students.

A possible explanation for the comparative lack of interaction of white students with students from different races or countries is the actual ratio of enrolled white students to those of other races. According to the National Center for Education Statistics (2002), 67% of students on college and university campuses identify themselves as white, non-Hispanic. As majority students, white students are comparatively more easily able to live, study, and socialize within same race and national origin circles. Experientially, the predominantly white institution of higher education does not, for the most part, seem to be providing sufficient opportunities for students to meet, interact with, and befriend students who are different from them.

The lack of cross-cultural interaction is not only disappointing for the individual white student whose expectations are not being met, it is unfortunate given the commitment of most colleges and universities to promote multiracial and global understanding as part of their institutional mission. Many in higher education share the view of King (1996) that, "Given the changing demographics of the twenty-first century, a college education must include learning to live and work effectively with people whose experiences and cultures are different from one's own" (p. 3).

During a discussion in what had been institutionally perceived as an all-white honors colloquium at a small, private college in the Northeast, a self-identified biracial student weighed his words carefully as he tried to articulate an honest response to the dean of students' positive characterization of teamwork among students across different racial groups. Speaking with a level of frustration in his voice, the student said, "Administrators like you will always think that cross-racial socializing is happening on campus. I can tell you that it isn't. Nor is it likely to happen. There are too many obstacles" (Rissmeyer, 2004).

The intellectual and interpersonal benefits of cross-racial dialogue and relationships are increasingly becoming identified for majority students. In a longitudinal study involving more than 1,000 students in 18 colleges and universities, Pascarella, Palmer, Moye, and Pierson (2001) found a significant and positive relationship between making friends with racially diverse students and the development of critical thinking skills for white students. Pascarella et al. (2001) conclude, "Finally, we note with some irony that White students in this study benefited the most from racially oriented diversity experiences. Contrary to some of the conservative rhetoric that opposes affirmative action policies, White students, not students of color, may be experiencing a richer and more intellectually challenging college experience because of current efforts to recruit a racially and ethnically diverse student population" (p. 270).

In a study involving more than 50,000 full-time undergraduates at 124 institutions, Hu and Kuh (2003) reported that on most outcome measures, particularly those that related to human relations and the ability to work with different people, white students benefit from interacting with students from diverse backgrounds. Chang (1999) suggests that a diverse student body is a significant "compelling interest" for higher education: "Institutional efforts to create a racially diverse student population, whereby opportunities for cross-racial issues are optimized for all students, is sound educational practice and can potentially enhance student development. When campuses genuinely value diversity and take it seriously, at all levels and in all parts of the campus, the quality of the environment is improved and benefits accrue not only for underrepresented students but for all students" (p. 393).

Cotton, Kelley, and Sedlacek (2000) suggest that rich dialogue across different racial and ethnic groups can occur successfully in four arenas: (1) in safe classroom environments, (2) in campus employment environments that promote the opportunity for students across races to work on a common goal, (3) in residence halls where organized activities can provide opportunities for interaction among students from different races, and (4) at large social events that draw students from different races together for social interaction.

Particular care must be taken to foster dialogue across student groups over the entire span of the college career—not only during orientation, welcome week, and the first-year experience (Hu & Kuh, 2003). As students progress in college, become focused on their postcollege lives, and are less engaged with the activities of the school, they are less likely to be influenced by the programs that seek to foster an understanding of diverse cultures (Hu & Kuh, 2003). The most significant learning is likely to occur when colleges and universities intentionally structure experiences that promote quality in-class and out-of-class involvement and interactions (Pike, 2000).

There have been many creative and strategic institutional initiatives to enhance diversity across the United States in the past several decades. These and other programs must continue to be developed and funded if American higher education is to realize its dream of educating its citizenry for the 21st century.

Conclusion

Higher education in the United States draws together men and women from different ethnic, racial, and socioeconomic backgrounds, students of varying ages and with individual aspirations. As educators, we are called upon to heed our responsibility as outlined in *Learning Reconsidered: A Campus-Wide Focus on the Student Experience.* "Regardless of our past accomplishments or disappointments, we are all, as colleagues and educators, now accountable to students and society for identifying and achieving essential student learning outcomes and for making transformative education possible and accessible for all students" (Keeling, 2004, p. 3).

College administrators should know how students with different characteristics have varying expectations of college. There is much more to be learned about these variances. Knowing about the unique expectations of students with disabilities, commuting students, student athletes, and others representative of the whole range of student subcultures will inform the higher education community and enhance its ability to serve students and further their learning experiences.

References

Aslanian, C. B., & Brickell, H. M.(1980). *Americans in transition: Life changes as reasons for adult learning.* New York: College Entrance Examination Board.

Astin, A. W. (1998). The changing American college student: Thirty-year trends, 1966–1996. *Review of Higher Education, 21,* 115–135.

Boyer, E. L. (1987). *College: The undergraduate experience in America.* New York: Harper & Row.

Bui, K.V.T. (2002). First-generation college students at a four-year university: Background characteristics, reasons for pursuing higher education, and first-year experience. *College Student Journal, 36,* 3–12.

Carter, D. F. (1999). The impact of institutional choice and environments on African American and white students' degree expectations. *Research in Higher Education, 40,* 17–39.

Chang, M. J. (1999). Does racial diversity matter? The educational impact of a racially diverse undergraduate population. *Journal of College Student Development, 40,* 377–393.

Colbeck, C. L., Cabrera, A. F., & Terenzini, P. T. (2001). Learning professional confidence: Linking teaching practices, self-perceptions, and gender. *Review of Higher Education, 24,* 173–191.

Cotton, V., Kelley, W., & Sedlacek, W. (2000). Situational characteristics of positive and negative experiences with same race and different race students. *Diversity on campus: Reports from the field* (pp. 16–17). Washington, DC: National Association of Student Personnel Administrators.

Crombie, G., Pyke, G., Silverton, S. W., Jones, A., & Piccinin, S. (2003). Students perceptions of their classroom participation and instructor as a function of gender and context. *Journal of Higher Education, 74,* 51–76.

Cross, K. P. (1980). Our changing students and their impact on colleges: Prospects for a true learning society. *Phi Delta Kappan,* May, 630–632.

Eskilson, A., & Wiley, M. G. (1999). Solving for the X: Aspirations and expectations of college students. *Journal of Youth and Adolescence, 28,* 1–14.

Hellman, C., & Harbeck, D. (1997). Investigating self-regulated learning among first-generation community college students. *Journal of Applied Research in the Community College, 4,* 165–169.

Herter, J. B. (2002). College student generational status: Similarities, differences, and factors in college adjustment. *Psychological Record, 52,* 3–18.

Hu, S., & Kuh, G. D. (2003). Diversity experiences and college student learning and personal development. *Journal of College Student Development, 44,* 320–334.

Kao, G., & Tienda, M. (1998). Educational aspirations of minority youth. *American Journal of Education, 106,* 349–384.

Keeling, R. (Ed.). (2004). *Learning reconsidered: A campus-wide focus on the student experience.* Washington, DC: National Association of Student Personnel Administrators and American College Personnel Association.

King, P. (1996, May-June). The obligations of privilege. *About Campus, 1*(2), 2–3.

Kuh, G. D., & Gonyea, R. M. (2003). *CSXQ: Tentative norms for the second edition.* Bloomington: Indiana University, Center for Postsecondary Research.

National Center for Education Statistics. (2002). *Profile of undergraduates in postsecondary institutions: 1999–2000.* Washington, DC: U.S. Department of Education, Office of Educational Research and Improvement.

Pascarella, E., Bohr, L., Nora, A., Desler, M., & Zusman, B. (1994). Impacts of on-campus and off-campus work on first year cognitive outcomes. *Journal of College Student Development, 35,* 364–370.

Pascarella, E. T., Palmer, B., Moye, M., & Pierson, C. (2001). Do diversity experiences influence the development of critical thinking? *Journal of College Student Development, 42,* 257–271.

Pascarella, E. T., Wolniak, G. C., Pierson, C. T., & Terenzini, P. T. (2003). Experiences and outcomes of first-generation students in community colleges. *Journal of College Student Development, 44,* 420–429.

Pike, G. R. (2000). The effects of students' backgrounds and college experiences on their patterns of interaction and acceptance and appreciation of diversity. *Diversity on campus: Reports from the field* (pp.

38–39). Washington, DC: National Association of Student Personnel Administrators.

Rissmeyer, P. A. (2004). Sophomore honors class discussion. Unpublished conversation notes, Boston, MA.

van Laar, C. (2000). The paradox of low academic achievement but high self-esteem in African-American students: An attributional account. *Educational Psychology Review, 12,* 33–61.

Walpole, M. (2003). Socioeconomic status and college: How SES affects college experiences and outcomes. *Review of Higher Education, 27,* 45–73.

Wilson, R. (1996, May/June). Educating for diversity. *About Campus, 1,* 4–9.

Chapter Ten

Institutional Type and Students' Expectations

Wilma J. Henry, Penelope H. Wills, and Harold L. Nixon

Fueled by issues involving equal access, accountability, social justice, and the quest for academic excellence, higher education in the United States has been described as the most diverse educational system in the world (Brazzell, 1996). Students can pursue a college education at a vast array of institutional types, taking into consideration such factors as size, location, and their own personal characteristics and career aspirations. The Carnegie Foundation for the Advancement of Teaching (2000) reports that there are 3,941 institutions of higher education in the United States, including public and independently supported schools, two- and four-year colleges, multipurpose research universities, military academies, historically black colleges, Hispanic-serving institutions, women's colleges, religious institutions, and professional schools. The purpose of this chapter is to examine how the expectations that students have regarding their college experience vary by institutional type. We analyze data from multiple sources to identify the most noticeable differences in students' expectations as a factor of the type of college and university they attend. The data studied included The American Freshman: National Norms for Fall 2002, a survey administered by the Cooperative Institutional Research Program (CIRP) (Sax, Lindholm, Astin, Korn, & Mahoney, 2003), which provides national normative data on the characteristics of students attending American colleges and universities as first-time, full-time freshmen. We also considered reports from the administration of the College Student Expectations Questionnaire (CSXQ) (Kuh & Gonyea, 2003), which assesses new students' goals and motivations and is administered through the Indiana University Center for Postsecondary Research. The 1996/01 Beginning Postsecondary Students Longitudinal Study (BPS) (Hoachlander, Sikora, & Horn, 2003) and the National Education Longitudinal Study 88 (NELS: 88) (Ingels, Scott, Taylor, Owings, & Quinn, 1988) were also data sources. The chapter concludes with a discussion of the implications for institutional policies and practices.

Two-Year Versus Four-Year Colleges

The variety of options for enrolling in postsecondary education in the United States provides extensive opportunities for almost everyone with the potential and commitment to attend college. There are more than 1,100 community colleges, enrolling more than 10 million students (American Association of Community Colleges, 2004), and their significance in the higher educational community is powerful. Two-year colleges are especially designed to provide open access for students who may face multiple challenges, including financial hardships, limited high school academic preparation, basic skills deficiencies, and geographic restrictions. Two-year institutions generally provide a broad curriculum through both credit and noncredit course offerings. Matriculation and degree completion generally result in students' earning an associate's degree, and/or a certificate for a particular field.

Students who attend community colleges have expectations that are distinct from those enrolling at four-year institutions. Students' goals in the community college setting are distinct when compared with those of students attending institutions of other types. A significant group of community college students never intend to complete a formal degree. Many plan to purposefully upgrade their job skills by enrolling in select courses. Others pursue personal enrichment classes, while another segment plans to transfer to other colleges without attaining their associate's degree. The 1996/01 Beginning Postsecondary Students Longitudinal Study (BPS; Hoachlander et al., 2003) described that 16% of first-year students attending community colleges reported no intentions of earning a degree or transferring to a four-year college. Another 60% indicated that they planned to earn a degree or a certificate but not to transfer to a senior college. Of those hoping to transfer to a senior college, only 22% planned to receive a degree or a certificate before doing so.

Student success is commonly measured by persistence rates and graduation rates. The data in the BPS study (Hoachlander et al., 2003) demonstrate that students' initial goals must be considered when assessing the effectiveness of attending a two-year college. Without doing so, it is not possible to accurately describe the extent to which they have met their goals. When factoring in their goals, 51% of community college students who intended to earn a degree or to transfer to a four-year institution had met their expectation or were still on track toward that goal within six years of their initial enrollment (Hoachlander et al., 2003). In another study, the 1998 National Education Longitudinal Study (NELS) (Ingels et al., 1988), the success rate increases to 63%. This latter study focused on a cohort of students who graduated from high school in 1992 and were last interviewed in 2000.

When comparing the success rates of two-year college students with students enrolled at baccalaureate institutions, it is important to consider the differences in the personal characteristics of the two groups. As found in the BPS study (Hoachlander et al., 2003), there are two major factors that influence degree completion: part-time enrollment and delayed entry into postsecondary education after high school, both common characteristics of community college students. Community college students are more likely to be described as nontraditional students. In addition to delaying enrollment, community college students may not possess a traditional high school diploma and therefore have to enroll in appropriate courses to earn an equivalency certificate. They may have children, be single parents, financially independent, or working full time while enrolled. Students who began their studies at a four-year college typically have entered without delay from high school; most were dependent on parents, had no dependents of their own, and did not work full time. It is not surprising to conclude that two-year college students, compared with their counterparts at four-year institutions, were less prepared for college and were less likely to be continuously enrolled.

The key distinction between expectations of students enrolling in two-year institutions and those at four-year schools is the intent to attain degrees. The objectives of community college students are less likely to focus on degree or diploma attainment. This is consistent with the purpose of community colleges and their role in providing access and equity and supporting community-based educational interests.

Public Versus Private Institutions

The distinctions between public and private higher educational institutions are substantial, and it is not surprising that students enrolled in those respective sectors have varying expectations of their institutions. When studying the differences between public and private colleges, the influence of governmental control and support is an essential discerning factor. However, there are many other aspects that impact students that distinguish these two major types of institution. The American Freshman: National Norms for Fall 2002 (CIRP; Sax et al., 2003) is rich with data that suggest that students' expectations vary widely between these sectors. For all students, regardless of the college's source of support, the institution's academic reputation was the most influential factor in choosing a college. However, this factor was of greater significance for students attending private colleges (68%) than public college students (52%).

Size is a key distinguishing factor between these sectors. Private institutions account for more than 70% of the four-year institutions in this country but enroll only 35% of students in the four-year sector. Private institutions are inclined to be smaller, and the largest of institutions are public universities (Carnegie Foundation, 2000). College students at independent institutions reported that they enrolled in their schools because they were comfortable with the size of the college. Only 27% of students attending public colleges responded in the CIRP study that size was an attractive factor of their enrollment choice. Given these findings, perhaps new students in public institutions are affected prior to enrollment by their expectation that the size of the postsecondary school is larger than they prefer.

One contrast between student expectations at public or private college students is the highest academic degree that they anticipate earning. Students enrolled at public colleges have a greater expectation of their highest degree received being a bachelor's degree

(25.3%) as compared to their counterparts at private colleges (17%), and they are less inclined to express interest in advanced degrees. Private college students consistently reported that they expect to earn a degree beyond the bachelor's degree, either a Ph.D. or a degree in medicine or law. The aspiration for advanced study is another significant distinction between those students in private higher education and those enrolled at public schools. This was discussed in more detail in Chapter 8.

Data from the National Center for Education Statistics (NCES) (Hoachlander et al., 2003) regarding graduation and persistence rates for students attending public and private colleges show a related difference in degree attainment. Over a six-year period, students who began their studies at private colleges were more likely to attain a bachelor's degree (72%) than those first enrolled at public colleges (55%). If students at private institutions are more likely to aspire to advanced degrees and also more likely to complete their undergraduate degrees, it is a telling difference.

From the CIRP study, students enrolling at private institutions consistently had higher expectations regarding aspects of college life that relate to engagement, such as "obtaining a B average," "playing a varsity sport," "being satisfied with their college," and "socializing with other racial groups." The differences between public and private college students are further apparent when comparing the response that 21% of students at public schools and 34% at independent institutions expect to participate as community volunteers in some capacity. Another area with marked difference is the expectation that they will study abroad. Only 17% of public students anticipate that they will participate in international programs, while 31% of students at private schools estimate that they probably will do so. Fifty percent (50%) of students at private colleges expect that they will participate in student clubs, compared to 37% of the respondents from public institutions. Finally, 43% of private college students have higher expectations that they will communicate with their professors compared with the 32% of respondents who indicated such an expectation at public schools.

In summary, it seems that private college students anticipate a high level of interaction and involvement in their college experience. From their interest in volunteering to their expectation of getting good grades and playing sports, they appear to enter college with confidence in their engagement and involvement. This may relate back to the matter of size, where smaller institutions stimulate and encourage levels of involvement and interaction with college life at different levels than at larger institutions. This premise bears more careful research.

Historically Black Colleges Versus Other Institutions

Historically black colleges and universities (HBCUs) were initially church-related private institutions established in the mid-1800s and evolved after the post–Civil War era into primarily public colleges and universities. These institutions helped prepare black leaders for participation in the "political economy of the New South" (Anderson, 1988, p. 239; Whiting, 1991). For approximately 125 years, until the civil rights movement of the 1960s, the majority of African American college students attended HBCUs (Wilson, 1994). The desire to share in America's dream of the "good life" was chief among the reasons African Americans challenged racial segregation in public higher education (Nixon, 1988). As a result, historically black institutions have been credited for creating America's black middle class (Gurin & Epps, 1975). According to Freeman and Thomas (2002), by 1980, HBCUs enrolled only 20% of all African American college students. Today, "African American students can attend college anywhere their test scores, grades, talents, and interest will take them" (Thomas, 2004, p. 1). Consequently, African American students have more enrollment options available to them, and HBCUs are not necessarily the primary college and university choice for many students.

When comparing institutional factors that influence the success of African American freshmen attending HBCUs and other types of institutions, researchers have discovered several differences in outcomes for students. For example, African American students tend to be more satisfied with their overall college experience at HBCUs than their peers at other schools (Astin, 1993). African American freshmen enrolled in HBCUs are also more likely to persist until graduation than their peers at non-HBCUs (Allen, 1991). Additionally, among African American freshmen, those attending HBCUs enter doctoral programs more frequently than do their peers attending other institutions (Gray, 1997). Researchers suggest that these types of positive outcomes result from experiences and interactions at HBCUs that encourage and motivate African American students to achieve (Astin, 1993; Freeman & Thomas, 2002; Wilson, 1994), experiences that are not provided at non-HBCU schools (Latiker, 2003).

The influence of family on first-year students seems to be greater for those enrolled at HBCUs. According to the CIRP study in 2003, freshmen at HBCUs were almost twice as likely to have been influenced by relatives (16%) as freshmen enrolling in all other types of universities (9%) (Sax et al., 2003). These findings are consistent with earlier studies (Freeman & Thomas, 2002; Nixon, 1988; Robinson & Shearon, 1978) that suggested that African American students were greatly influenced by parents, family members, teachers, or other personal acquaintances to enroll in an HBCU. Recognizing the influence of family on students' college selection, the fact that more than one-half of all African American professionals are graduates of HBCUs (Gray, 1997) further underscores the dedication to community that is engendered in undergraduates at HBCUs. Students attending HBCUs are more likely to indicate that they chose the institution because relatives wanted them to, and that may have a relationship to some other differences in those expectations. Compared with those at other institutions, students enrolling at HBCUs were more likely to indicate that they may transfer to another institution and less likely to indicate that they expected to be satisfied with their college. Those students seem, in this regard, to have lower expectations for their happiness and fit with the HBCU. The fact that satisfaction and persistence rates are higher than for other institutions is an intriguing contrast with this expectation (Allen, 1991).

Historically, many of the activities that black students have enjoyed and sponsored at colleges and universities across the country started at HBCUs. The original black Greek organizations, for example, were founded on the campus of a private black college (Kimbrough, 2003). Greek-letter organizations continue to be responsible for many of the social activities and programs on private black campuses (Latiker, 2003). The gospel choir, a student organization that exists at HBCUs and many other institutions, is another example of a culturally significant student activity.

Another noteworthy finding from CIRP (Sax et al., 2003) data indicated that freshmen attending HBCUs expressed interest in special educational programs with greater frequency (32%) than students attending other four-year colleges (22%). That students choose HBCUs for special career or major choices is not surprising, because CIRP data also demonstrate that students enrolled at HBCUs are less likely to predict that they will change majors or career choices. Students go to HBCUs, it seems, with a sense of purpose and focus.

The American Freshman Survey: National Norms for Fall 2002 surveyed new freshmen regarding their expectations for needing special tutoring in the following subject areas: English, reading, mathematics, social studies, science, foreign language, and writing. Consistent with an earlier study of the Characteristics of the Black Undergraduate by Astin (1990), CIRP (Sax et al., 2003) data indicated that freshmen at HBCUs reported with greater frequency the expectation of needing academic assistance relative to their counterparts enrolled in other four-year colleges. It is not just in the academic arena that students enrolling at HBCUs predict a need for extra support. They also reflected a greater inclination to expect to seek personal counseling while in college. This inclination to seek support may relate to the particular needs of students, but it may also reflect an indication of support offered at HBCUs and an acceptance of that support by enrolling students.

Research indicates that black students tend to have high educational aspirations (Astin, 1990; Astin & Cross, 1981). Findings from CIRP (Sax et al., 2003) data revealed freshmen attending HBCUs reported with greater frequency that they intended to obtain a doctoral degree (22%) compared with all four-year colleges (17%), and a concurrent indication that they were less likely than other students to end their educational experience with a bachelor's degree. Antoine Garibaldi (cited in Thomas, 2004), Chief Academic Officer at Howard University (a private HBCU), suggested, "The connections African American students make with their professors is part of the extensive mentoring facilitated by HBCUs and is a key factor in the high percentage of HBCU graduates who go on for their doctorates" (p. 2). Extensive mentoring that reaches beyond the classroom may account for related CIRP (Sax et al., 2003) findings. Students who enrolled at HBCUs were more likely (16%) than students at all universities (11%) to report spending three or more hours per week with teachers outside of class during their last year in high school. At the same time, those students were more likely to indicate that they expected to communicate regularly with their professors. The relationships with teachers in high school may produce expectations for similar connections with faculty in college.

Mayo, Murguía, and Padilla (1995) noted the importance of social integration in a study that compared the college experience of African American students and white students. These authors found that formal social integration (contact with representatives such as faculty members) had a greater effect on African American students' academic performance at both historically black and traditionally white institutions. Furthermore, the data suggest that daily interactions and contact with members in the dominant campus culture (for example, African American faculty mentors and role models) help to inspire African American students to want to obtain doctoral and other professional degrees (Gray, 1997). Clearly, at HBCUs the campus culture is African American, and African American students may be more likely to find support from persons similar to themselves, enhancing their prospects for success.

According to the CIRP results, more than 20% of freshmen attending HBCUs reported working more than 20 hours per week during their last year in high school, compared with only 14% enrolled in all other universities. Although they are more likely to work during high school, students who attend HBCUs are less likely than students at other institutions to anticipate working during college to help pay their expenses. It is not clear why this is the case, but it may relate to perceptions of other commitments and obligations during the college years.

More than 10% of enrolling freshmen at HBCUs reported that they watched 20 or more hours of television per week during their last year of high school, and this is disproportionate with the responses from students attending other institutions. Watching television is perhaps the preferred form of entertainment in many homes today. Some high school students watch television while engaging in a variety of activities, including eating and studying. Accordingly, it is not surprising that some enrolling freshmen at HBCUs indicated that they spend a large number of hours per week watching television. Many freshman students at HBCUs are first-generation college students and may have been exposed to only a limited number of venues for entertainment. Compared with other entertainment choices (for example, concerts, theater), television remains relatively low cost and widely accessible. We do not know how much television these students watch during college, but their expectations seem to reflect an intention to spend their time in another way. They are substantially more likely to indicate an intention to join social fraternities or sororities, participate in intercollegiate athletics, and participate in student government. It is likely that the time they spent watching television in high school is replaced by such other activities, more engaged in campus life.

Finally, enrolling freshmen at HBCUs were more than twice as likely to pray compared to students at other colleges and all universities. When asked the number of weekly hours spent in prayer during their last year in high school, only 11% of HBCU freshmen reported "none." This is a lower percentage compared with freshmen entering Catholic four-year colleges (27%) and all other universities (36%). This is consistent with the expectation of students going to HBCUs that, more than other students, they anticipate strengthening their religious beliefs during the college experience. There is a strong religious influence within African American culture. Several HBCUs were founded by religious organizations wherein prayer is a part of the institutions' practices. For example, required attendance, especially for freshman students, at chapel or convocations was common at some private and public HBCUs. Religion and the act of praying or giving thanks to a supreme being are woven into the fabric of African American culture.

Conclusion

This chapter explored student expectations as they vary by certain institutional types, and a number of observations can be made in summary. Clearly there are differences between the expectations of students going into community colleges and those at four-year institutions. Central among those differences is their anticipation of degree attainment. That students at community colleges are less likely to expect to complete degrees is a useful context for understanding how that sector of American higher education is different from others and should relate to how community colleges are evaluated and measured.

The differences between the public sector of higher education and private institutions are as significant as between community colleges and four-year schools. Much of private higher education is comprised of smaller institutions, so some differences in expectations arise from perceptions of size. Students enrolled in private institutions are more likely to expect to participate in behaviors that engage college life, things like volunteering in communities, joining organizations, and studying abroad. The size of the institutions they are attending may contribute to those expectations. It is easier for students at large, public institutions to disengage and not be noticed, but at smaller, private institutions students are recognized and more easily become familiar and comfortable with the scale of the institutions they attend. The persistence rates at private schools may be accounted for in the same fashion, as might the intention to pursue advanced degrees.

Regarding the expectations of students enrolled at historically black colleges and universities (HBCUs), some differences arise from the same contrasts, because few HBCUs enroll as many students as the larger public universities. Nonetheless, some of what was demonstrated about HBCUs comes from their predictability and well-known and established purpose. Students enrolled at HBCUs seem to have more accurate or reasonable expectations of the experience, and this may be due in part to their known and predictable culture and purposes. Students enrolled in such institutions ought to be able to take an accurate measure of their experiences to come, because the way in which they will fit in should be predictable.

This latter point may be instructive. The more clear that an institution's purpose is and the more distinct and demonstrable is its culture and mission, the more reasonable and accurate student expectations can be. For special-nature institutions similar to HBCUs, like women's colleges, Bible colleges, tribal colleges, military academies, and Hispanic-serving institutions, the clarity with which they communicate their nature and culture will probably relate to the accuracy and reasonableness of student expectations. These types of institutions have been recognized for their ability to provide a uniquely supportive climate with mentors and role models who encourage and inspire students to achieve academically and professionally. This may pose difficulty for the larger public or multipurpose private institutions, which have many missions, constituencies, and values, since they serve broader functions. It does serve to alert us to be sensitive to ways to help students make connections to aspects of our institutional communities that make sense for them.

Knowledge of students' expectations can contribute key information to university administrators as they plan and implement student programs. The existing pool of data pertaining to students' expectations would be complemented by the addition of future research that has a focus on other institutions for special populations (that is, women's colleges, Hispanic-serving institutions, tribal colleges, and so on). In addition to the expansion of data collection among special populations, an assessment of expectations among students enrolling in professional institutions (engineering schools, medical schools, military academies, and so forth) may find substantial contrast to the expectations of those students attending other professional or specialty institutions, not to mention the large, general purpose institutions. Future research exploring professional institutions would provide a specific profile that characterizes their students' expectations. Additionally, future research that would bolster the existing literature should include survey instruments that are administered longitudinally, thus allowing for the detection of trends over time of other special populations and professional institutions.

References

Allen, W. (Ed.). (1991). *College in black and white: African American students in predominantly white and in historically black public universities*. Albany: State University of New York Press.

American Association of Community Colleges. (2004). *Community college fact sheet*. Retrieved May 14, 2004, from http://www.aacc.nche.edu.

Anderson, J. (1988). *The education of blacks in the south, 1860–1935*. Chapel Hill: University of North Carolina Press.

Astin, A. W. (1990). *The black undergraduate: Current status and trends in the characteristics of freshmen*. Los Angeles: University of California, Higher Education Research Institute, Graduate School of Education.

Astin, A. W. (1993). *What matters in college? Four critical years revisited*. San Francisco: Jossey-Bass.

Astin, H. S., & Cross, P. H. (1981). Black students in black and white institutions. In G. E. Thomas (Ed.), *Black students in higher education: Conditions and experiences in the 1970s* (pp. 11–17). Westport, CT: Greenwood.

Brazzell, J. C. (1996). Diversification of postsecondary institutions. In S. R. Komives & D. Woodard, Jr. (Eds.), *Student services: A handbook for the profession* (3rd ed.; pp. 43–80). San Francisco: Jossey-Bass.

Carnegie Foundation for the Advancement of Teaching. (2000). *The Carnegie classification of institutions of higher education.* Retrieved April 12, 2004, from http://www.carnegiefoundation.org/Classification/index.htm.

Freeman, K., & Thomas, G. E. (2002). Black colleges and college choice: Characteristics of students who choose HBCUs. *Review of Higher Education, 25*(3), 349–358.

Gray, W. H. (1997). The case for all black colleges. *ERIC Review, 5*(3), 21–23.

Gurin, P., & Epps, E. G. (1975). *Black consciousness, identity and achievement: A study of students in historically black colleges.* New York: Wiley.

Hoachlander, G., Sikora, A. C., & Horn, L. (2003). Community college students: Goals, academic preparation, and outcomes. *Education Statistics Quarterly, 5*(2), 121–128.

Ingels, S. J., Scott, L. A., Taylor, J. R., Owings, J., & Quinn, P. (1998, May). *National education longitudinal study of 1988* (Issue Brief No. NCES 9806). Washington, DC: U.S. Department of Education, Institute of Education Sciences.

Kimbrough, W. M. (2003). *Black Greek 101: The culture, customs and challenges of black fraternities and sororities.* Madison, NJ: Fairleigh Dickinson University Press.

Kuh, G. D., & Gonyea, R. M. (2003). *College Student Expectations Questionnaire [CSXQ]* (2nd ed.). Bloomington: Indiana University, Center for Postsecondary Research.

Latiker, T. T. (2003, April). *A qualitative study of African American student persistence in a private black college.* Paper presented at the Annual Meeting of the American Educational Research Association, Chicago, IL.

Mayo, J., Murguía, E., & Padilla, R. (1995). Social integration and academic performance among minority university students. *Journal of College Student Development, 36,* 542–552.

Nixon, H. L. (1988). *Factors associated with enrollment decisions of black students and white students in colleges at which they are in the minority.* Unpublished doctoral dissertation, University of North Carolina, Chapel Hill.

Robinson I. A., & Shearon, R. W. (1978). *Black students in the North Carolina community college system: Implications for educational programming.* Raleigh: North Carolina State University, North Carolina Research Coordinating Unit in Occupational Education.

Sax, L. J., Lindholm, J. A., Astin, A. W., Korn, W. S., & Mahoney, K. (2003). *The American freshman: National norms for fall 2002.* Los Angeles: University of California, Higher Education Research Institute, Cooperative Institutional Research Program.

Thomas, C. (2004). *Here's why many African-American students are choosing HBCUs.* Retrieved April 19, 2004, from http://www.petersons.com/blackcolleges/choice3.asp?sponsor=13.

Whiting, A. N. (1991). *Guardians of the flame: Historically black colleges yesterday, today, and tomorrow* (ERIC Document Reproduction Service No. ED340334). Washington, DC: American Association of State Colleges and Universities.

Wilson, R. (1994). The participation of African Americans in American higher education. In M. J. Justiz, R. Wilson, & L. G. Bjork (Eds.), *Minorities in higher education* (pp. 195–209). Phoenix, AZ: Oryx.

Chapter Eleven

Expectations of Multiple Publics

*Barbara E. Bender, John Wesley Lowery,
and John H. Schuh*

Perceptions of higher education, if one is to believe the movies, have changed only marginally over the years. Contrast the themes of the Marx Brothers' 1932 spoof *Horse Feathers* (McLeod) with the 1978 parody on campus life *Animal House* (Landis) and the four *Revenge of the Nerds* (Kanew, 1984; Roth, 1987; Mesa, 1992; Zacharias, 1994) films. The films, released over a 60-year period of time, portray campus life as centering on parties, pranks, and high jinks. College administrators and faculty, when portrayed, are often shown as deceptive, manipulative, pompous, incompetent, and lecherous. If all that higher education leaders had to worry about was how colleges and universities are depicted for entertainment purposes, then they would have few concerns. Over the years, and we would argue at an increasing pace, multiple publics are paying increasing attention to colleges and universities, and they are exerting pressure on how colleges and universities ought to conduct their business. This pressure ranges from who is admitted to study, to how institutions provide for student safety, to how much colleges and

The editors acknowledge a contribution by Harvey Waterman of the Graduate School–New Brunswick, Rutgers University to this chapter.

universities should charge for their services. It is also important to point out that in general, higher education is highly valued by members of the public (The Chronicle Survey of Public Opinion on Higher Education, 2004). In this survey, 93% of the respondents strongly agreed or agreed with the statement, "Colleges and universities are among the most valuable resources in the U.S." The poll that also revealed that "college officials need to stop being so 'arrogant' in answering the public's legitimate concerns" (Selingo, 2004, p. A10). This chapter considers the perceptions of multiple stakeholders and external constituencies and their expectations, reasonable or otherwise, for institutions of higher education.

Who Are Higher Education's Stakeholders?

The answer to this question is "Virtually everyone"; we all benefit from the research, teaching, service, and recreational outlets provided by colleges and universities. Certainly there is no question that public institutions have broad constituencies. However, private institutions, too, have broad constituencies, since most participate in programs created and financed by the federal government, state aid programs, and so on. With this wide array of constituents, higher education is faced with serving many masters who may have competing goals for colleges and universities.

Another way of thinking about higher education's stakeholders is to consider the extent to which colleges and universities must respond to their many constituencies. Presumably, higher education has a different level of responsibility to current students and their parents than to the person who attends a concert on campus or occasionally uses the services of the institution's extension office for advice on how to remove weeds from a garden. It is impossible to develop a complete list of constituent groups for institutions of higher education (IHEs), but the following illustrates how complex such a list might be:

- Students
- Students' parents and relatives
- Graduates
- State legislators
- State governmental agencies

- Members of Congress
- Federal agencies
- Members of the local community
- The media
- Organizations that employ graduates
- Donors
- Organizations that provide goods and services to IHEs

Members of these constituent groups may not have similar goals, or even opinions, on the various decisions that IHEs make. Consider the many points of view that could emerge surrounding the following decision: A national television network asks the athletic department to reschedule a football game from Saturday afternoon to Thursday night. The athletic department will receive several hundred thousand dollars for rescheduling the game as compensation from the television network. In tight budget times, the additional revenue is welcome. Not every constituent, however, will applaud this decision. Ticket holders who have to travel to get to town may not be able to attend a weeknight game. Students, who want to attend the game, may not be able to do so if they have classes on Thursday night. If they miss class to attend the game, their professors will not be happy. Local hotel and motel owners won't like the change because people will not take advantage of the weekend room packages they offer built around football games. Restaurateurs may be divided, since some people may come to town early, eat dinner, and go to the game, but the usual postgame business may not materialize, since the game will end after 10:00 P.M. Leaders at local schools won't like the change since it conflicts with their events, and people who would normally participate in school programs, such as open houses, parent-teacher conferences, or musical presentations, also may have game tickets and skip the school's offerings to attend the football game. Changing the game has implications for law enforcement and traffic control, which are designed to manage an afternoon game. Parking may become a problem, since those attending the game will compete for parking with evening commuter students. And on it goes. Whose needs take precedence? What is the process for making a decision such as the one described? Who needs to be consulted? The complexity of this seemingly simple decision, moving the date of a football game, illustrates the complexity of several multiple stakeholders.

What Do Stakeholders Expect? An Example

Stakeholders have very different expectations for IHEs, and often those expectations conflict with one another. Using the football game illustration, those associated with the athletic department's financial administration want to maximize revenue. They expect that faculty who teach Thursday night courses will be sympathetic to the students who either play in or want to miss class to attend the game. They want those students whose normal Thursday night parking will be changed to be flexible, since their temporary parking will require just an extra 10-minute walk, which shouldn't be all that difficult in the balmy weather the region currently is experiencing. They would like the local merchants to understand that the amount of revenue generated by the television appearance will ease the budget strains the department is experiencing. They would like the ticket holders to balance their inconvenience with the benefits from the exposure that the evening game will provide for the football program and the university, which may help in recruiting players and students in succeeding years. They would like the local school leaders to understand that this game is a one-time proposition and that while attendance may decline at other competing events, the athletic department has no plans to play home games regularly on Thursday nights. Stakeholders, on the other hand, expect just the opposite. That is, the faculty want the athletic department to understand that holding classes with the distraction of a concurrent football game will impede student learning. The commuting students, many of whom are enrolled in evening graduate programs, really don't want to take an extra-long walk from temporary, satellite parking spaces. They are not interested in football games, and they are only focused on getting to and from class as quickly as possible, particularly after a full day of work.

So, what do stakeholders expect? In general, what stakeholders want is for colleges and universities to act in their best interests. When IHEs do not act in their best interests, stakeholders react in a variety of ways, none of them favorable. Typical responses from unhappy stakeholders include:

"They [the IHE's leaders] just don't understand our point of view."
"They don't listen."

"They have other priorities."

"They don't consider our perspective valuable."

"They only pay attention to the big shots."

"If you don't give a lot of money, they don't care."

The fact is, IHEs simply cannot respond to the needs of all of their stakeholders simultaneously. But that does not mean that their stakeholders will not hold IHEs to a high level of accountability and responsiveness.

What About the Role of the News Media?

Most of what goes on in IHEs is not newsworthy in the sense that the broad array of stakeholders would not be interested in the activity or event. Consider the following daily occurrences on the campus of a typical IHE:

- Virtually all classes meet as scheduled for the appointed length of time.
- Thousands of people access the resources of the library.
- Students study.
- Faculty members evaluate papers, presentations, and other student work products carefully.
- Dozens of committee meetings are convened, during which the business of the institution is conducted.
- The food service operates efficiently and serves thousands of customers.
- Various organizations hold meetings, events, and other activities.

The following occurrences do not happen:

- No one gets hurt (faculty, staff, or students) while traveling on official business of the IHE community.
- There are no crimes committed. There are no arrests.
- No one engages in sexual harassment.
- There are no laboratory accidents.
- There are no protests.

It is unlikely that any of the activities listed would make the news. The answer as to why they would not make the news is obvious: these activities are part of a routine day on a college campus. When a crime is committed, or someone gets hurt, or money is spent inappropriately, it makes the news. For example, CNN.com reported on the increasing costs of higher education on September 30, 2003. After reporting that in-state tuition increases had ranged from 4.6% to nearly 40% for the 2003–04 academic year, the story focused on the 28% increase in tuition levied by the State University of New York (SUNY) (Nissen, 2003). The story did not report that SUNY charges below the national average for tuition and fees. Nor did the story report that the average increase at SUNY's two-year colleges was 13.8% or $231, and that while the increase at four-year public institutions was 14.1%, what that number really meant was a total of $579 (The College Board, 2003). The story also did not report that SUNY institutions are located in one of the most expensive regions of the country, a fact reflected in their tuition rates. The media helps shape perceptions of higher education as well as other societal institutions, and, in the case of college costs, prospective students and their parents consistently overestimate the cost of attendance, according to the most recent study conducted by the U.S. Department of Education, even when they have obtained information about college costs (U.S. Department of Education, 2003).

It is easy to blame the media when people do not understand complex issues. The responsibility for the public's lack of understanding about college costs could just as easily be assigned to higher education leaders who may not be communicating in terms that can be understood by members of the public. What is clear is that there is plenty of blame to go around, and the public does not understand why college costs what it does.

How Is College Depicted to Mass Markets?

This chapter was introduced with references to how selected films have represented college life over six decades. None of the Hollywood depictions was especially correct, as we can verify from volumes of research data on the student experience (see, for example, Astin, 1993; Pascarella & Terenzini, 1991). Frankly, movies or television series about the lives of undergraduate students, or faculty members for that matter, would not be very interesting.

The television show *Saved by the Bell: The College Years* (Higuera & Melman, 1993) consisted of 19 episodes, mostly focusing on social relationships and student escapades. Among the story lines of the episodes were a Friday night poker game, fraternity rush, plans for Thanksgiving, and a social relationship between a faculty member and a student. Precious little airtime was devoted to classroom, laboratory, or library activities, students studying, preparing papers, or participating in service learning activities. We do not propose that a television show focusing on students studying or writing would be a good idea. And, we have no idea how influential this television show was on shaping the views of the general public as to what college life really entails. What we are more confident of is the fact that a television series about the routine life of most college students and their colleges and universities would help to enhance the accuracy of the public's understanding of the collegiate experience, but we doubt that there would be much of an audience for such a show.

Other Ways Expectations Emerge

A variety of sources contribute to how expectations and perceptions of the college experience are formed. Water cooler conversations at work, conversations with neighbors, one's own experiences as a college student, conversations with current college students, and other bits of anecdotal information help frame perceptions and expectations. None of these is complete, but they reflect how perceptions of institutions evolve. Expectations for college are framed in many of the same ways that they are for other institutions. How many citizens have actually dealt with the local fire department in the past year? Most citizens, if they are lucky, have never dealt with their local fire department, but they still have a sense of how this public service works. Or consider the state police, local hospital, or the airlines. The point is obvious. We all have perceptions of various organizations framed by our direct or indirect experiences with them.

Periodically, polls are conducted to ascertain the perceptions of the public of various institutions and occupation groups. The *Chronicle of Higher Education* reported in its May 2, 2003, issue on the level of confidence respondents expressed in selected societal institutions. Topping the list was the U.S. military (65% of the respondents indicated "a great deal" of confidence in the institution), followed by four-year private colleges and universities (51%), the local police force (48%), and four-year public colleges and universities (46%). The U.S. Congress (14%), lawyers (9%), and large corporations (6%) represented institutions in which the public had the least confidence (The Chronicle Survey of Public Opinion on of Higher Education, 2003).

Various professions are also evaluated periodically though public opinion polls. In November 2001, a poll rated fire fighters, nurses, and members of the military at the top, while labor union leaders, insurance salesmen, car salesmen, and those working in advertising were at the bottom (The Most Hated and Admired Professions, n.d.). A more recent poll released in 2003 reported that the most admired professionals in terms of ethics and honesty were nurses, followed closely by doctors and veterinarians (who tied), pharmacists, dentists, and in a tie came engineers, police officers, and college teachers (Those Angels in White, 2003).

Whether or not those who participated in the polls actually had dealt recently with these professionals is unknown. However, people have their perceptions, and some professions consistently are at the top of the list, while others remain at the bottom. With this overview, we will now consider, more specifically, the expectations that specific stakeholder groups have for IHEs.

Higher Education and Government

The expectations of federal and state governmental agencies of higher education must be a priority if IHEs are going to continue to expect to receive funding from them. For nearly 40 years, however, both nationally and at the state level, legislators have expressed concerns about IHEs not meeting society's expectations. In 1979, Furniss and Gardner described the relationship between higher education and the government as an uneasy alliance and the balance between control and accountability continues to shape the relationship between government and higher education today. Kerr (1991) observed that there had been a fundamental shift in the power struggle between IHEs and external constituencies to a point where "now it is the campus asking for autonomy from the government" (p. 213). Rosenzweig (1979) noted: "It is very difficult to come to grips with this condition [government intervention in education] because it is a condition that no one intended to produce. If institutions of higher education were the victims of a conspiracy, or of an ideology, or even of a coherent set of policies, they could perhaps, understand their source and their purposes and begin to deal with them. But none of those is in fact the case. Instead, those institutions are the victims of the least glamorous and most characteristic affliction of modern society—the unintended consequence" (pp. 92–93). Although Rosenzweig offered these comments 25 years ago, they still aptly describe the government's regulation of higher education.

Michael (1998) discussed numerous factors that have contributed to a loss of the traditional autonomy and independence that higher education had enjoyed in American society. One element has been a changing view of higher education from one of a societal benefit to an asset that primarily benefits the individual. Such a fundamental shift has had clear consequences for the role of higher education in our society (Layzell & Lyddon, 1993). Gehring (1998) warned the net effect of these changes may ultimately be a federalized system of higher education. This would arise not out of any one factor, but rather, Gehring (1998) warned, "Autonomy, like liberty, is not lost in one massive stroke, nor does it come crashing down at one time. It falls victim to a slow chipping process in which a little autonomy is lost here and then a bit there until finally control is lost entirely and no one even realizes that it has happened until it is too late" (p. 11).

The most recent issue that has gained significant interest in Congress and threatens the autonomy of higher education institutions has been the issue of rising tuition costs. Representatives Boehner (R-Ohio) and McKeon (R-California) (2003) issued a report that described America's higher education system in a crisis caused by "decades of uncontrolled cost increases" (p. 1); the authors attributed these rising costs in part to "wasteful spending by college and university management" (p. 2). Many within the higher education community, however, were highly critical of the document. In his own characteristically blunt way, Stanley Fish (2003) described the report as "bereft of anything like an argument, the report instead offers a couple of overheated and unnuanced assertions: Higher education costs are 'skyrocketing' and the reason is 'wasteful spending' by colleges and universities" (p. C3). Comparing the report to a paper written by an undergraduate student, Fish gave Boehner and McKeon failing grades. Fish (2004) has urged higher education officials to take the offensive, noting "my experience suggests that it might just be worth a try to stand up for ourselves unapologetically, and to comport ourselves as if we were formidable adversaries rather than easy marks" (p. C4).

Representative McKeon also introduced legislation called the Affordability in Higher Education Act of 2003 (H. R. 3311) which would have penalized institutions of higher education financially for excessive tuition increases. In response to a chorus of complaints from the higher education community and members of Congress, including a number of Republicans, McKeon announced in March 2004 that he would not pursue the penalty provisions (Burd, 2004). He attributed this decision, however, to "the voluntary steps taken recently by a number of major colleges and universities to curb tuition growth for students and parents as a result of the national debated triggered by the introduction of the Affordability in Higher Education Act."

Winston (1993) argued that the unfriendliness which has been visited upon higher education is due, at least in part, to higher education's own actions:

> We've let an unseemly interest in revenues—in income, making money—erode the public's trust in higher education. Other things may have contributed—like rising public expectations, opulent college building programs, and a competitive pursuit of "institutional excellence" that has bid star faculty salaries well into the six figures—but our collective attention to institutional income is surely central. (The major contribution of public universities to the erosion of trust has probably been—cold fusion aside—their promotion of a blatantly professional athletic-entertainment industry under the fig leaf of scholar athletics, with attendant self-promotion, big money scandals, and corruption.) (p. 406)

Even as this chapter was being written, the University of Colorado was being rocked by allegations of rape by football players and the provision of sexual favors to recruit athletes. Sperber (2000) argued that college athletics are the blame for much of higher education's woes. To our many publics, these scandals are a reflection on higher education in general—not just athletic departments. Higher education administrators must understand that, while from within higher education institutions are understood as loosely coupled systems with significant autonomy, to outsiders higher education institutions are perceived as tightly coupled organizations similar to many large businesses. Discussing the problems at the University of Colorado as well as several scandals at San Diego State University involving that institution's football team, Canepa (2004) observed, "Today, the ivy on the walls of higher education is coated with slime, deceit and alcohol. Pick your poison."

There has been a fundamental shift in the issues addressed by the federal government in the regulation of higher education. Prior to 1974, federal regulation of higher education, other than financial aid, was focused upon preventing discrimination in higher education (Bills & Hall, 1994). More recently, however, Congress has shifted its attention to creating laws that seek to protect students from harmful campus conditions for which institutions should be responsible (Gehring, 1994). Legislation of this type has been successful because of the general mistrust of higher education in Congress. The cumulative effect of the financial, athletic, and other scandals described by Layzell and Lyddon (1993) and Winston (1993) has been the creation of an environment in which seemingly every allegation against the higher education community is accepted as gospel and requires a legislative response.

Parents and Families of Students

In recent years, the parents and families of college students have begun to play a more active role in working with colleges and universities as advocates on behalf of their children. While their interests may vary from such issues as rising college costs, the relationship of a college education to finding a job, or campus safety and security, for example, the parents of college students have become a vocal constituency that higher education leaders cannot afford to ignore.

The role of parents in decisions made by students extends to most aspects of the college experience. More than one-third of respondents to the Cooperative Institutional Research Program (CIRP) indicated that the wishes of their parents were very important in their decision to attend college (Sax, Lindholm, Astin, Korn, & Mahoney, 2003). The triangular relationship among parents, students, and institutions might have its start in the decision to go to college, but it hardly ends there; parents have become powerful forces in setting expectations and, as informed consumers, they hold their child's institutions accountable for providing the education and services that were promised in the recruitment literature.

One aspect of the relationship between parents and institutions that has received special attention and heightened tensions between the two pertains to circumstances when students are in difficulty and parents expect to be informed. The Family Educational Rights and Privacy Act of 1974 (FERPA), which governs the nature and amount of information that colleges and universities can release about enrolled students, was amended in 1998 to allow institutions to inform parents or guardians if their children have been found responsible for violating regulations pertaining to alcohol or drug use. Prior to the 1998 amendment of FERPA, routine parental notification of student conduct violations was not permitted; institutions were vigilant in protecting the confidentiality of student disciplinary information, even from parents. Federal legislation supporting institutional interaction with parents signaled a sea change that is still in transition regarding role of parents in the affairs of higher education.

As reported in the popular press, parents expect to be informed by college officials when their children are experiencing problems, are under duress, or have health problems. In recent years, there have been several incidents in which students have been victimized by others or even taken their own lives, resulting in parents' initiation of legal actions in response to their perception that the college or university failed to serve their children in a fiduciary fashion (Farrell, 2002; Okrent, 2003; Security on Campus, 2004).

Administrators are not alone, however, in feeling the effects of parental intervention. Faculty members report that the numbers of parents who contact them regarding students' grades and progress have increased significantly. This has become even more noticeable as students maintain routine contact with their families via low-cost cell phones and electronic mail use. One parent has even created a Web site to serve as a forum for students and others to express concerns about their experiences when college courses or programs have been used as a forum for "social or political propaganda" (Wright, 2004).

The influence of parents goes beyond the jurisdiction of individual campuses. An organization called College Parents of America has been an active force representing the interests of parents of college students in the development and passage of federal legislation. Representatives of this membership-based organization have testified before Congress and become active in the formation of public policy that relates to the interests of the parents of college students. Clearly, the notion that parents drop off their sons and daughters during new student orientation and next appear on campus for parent's weekend or commencement is long gone.

To serve parents' concerns more effectively, some institutions have created and staffed offices to provide designated liaisons to meet their needs (Hoover, 2004). In reality, assigning staff to this function can be an effective method to enhance the quality of the relationship between parents and the colleges and universities where their students are enrolled. An organization of administrators involved in serving the parents of college students, Administrators Promoting Parent Involvement, has seen its membership grow almost threefold since its creation in 1998 (Johnson, 2004). By formally recognizing the role of parents and understanding their expectations, it should help both students and their families tackle the many bureaucratic hurdles pertaining to matriculation and adjust to the rigors of college life.

Special Interest Groups

Another factor that has shaped the public perception of higher education over the past decade has been the emergence of special interest groups whose sole focus is higher education. One example is Security on Campus (2004), which was founded by Howard and Connie Clery after the rape and murder of their daughter at Lehigh University. Security on Campus was the driving force behind the passage of the Jeanne Clery Disclosure of Campus Security Policy and Campus Crime Statistics Act and subsequent amendments to that legislation. Another recent example is the Foundation for Individual Rights in Education (FIRE, n.d.), which was founded by Harvey A. Silverglate and Alan Charles Kors to protect the individual rights of students and faculty. Both Security on Campus and FIRE have been successful in shaping the discourse in the media and in Congress on their respective issues.

What Colleges and Universities Can Do

For more than 300 years, colleges and universities enjoyed a special niche in American society. Respected for their collective expertise and their contributions to strengthening the quality of life across the country, higher education institutions were viewed as having the knowledge and skills to solve the most difficult problems faced by the nation. As suggested in this chapter, however, the perceptions of colleges and universities have changed dramatically in the past 40 years.

There are several reasons for the erosion of public confidence in the academy. Perhaps with greater access and a much greater proportion of the populace enrolling in postsecondary education, the mystique of the college experience has disappeared. It may be that the escalating costs of college attendance without a guarantee of a golden postgraduate future have tarnished the possibilities that higher education can bring. Still another reason may be that of a collective disappointment in the academy as a result of well-publicized incidents such as ethical failures by presidents and faculty, scandals in athletics, and unruly student behavior.

Questions about how colleges and universities spend money on research were raised by former Senator William Proxmire of Wisconsin and captured national attention. Senator Proxmire was committed to saving federal monies, and he may have added to the public's wavering belief in the work of the academy through his leadership of the well-advertised "Golden Fleece Awards." The tongue-in-cheek awards highlighted what Senator Proxmire believed to be wasteful government spending on useless research and federal projects, many of which were university sponsored (Taxpayers for Common Sense, n.d.).

On a local level, the struggles between "town and gown" have existed since the founding of the colonial colleges and continue today as colleges seek to expand their classroom, research, residence hall, cocurricular, and parking facilities. While colleges and universities may strive to be good neighbors, permanent residents directly experience the noise and late-night student behaviors that can disrupt otherwise quiet communities. Higher education institutions do change the nature of a neighborhood and can increase the financial burdens on already strapped municipal governments. Describing the pressures of university expansion, the *Chronicle of Higher Education* noted the particularly difficult problems that George Washington University has had with its neighbors. "Over time, the university has steadily encroached on Foggy Bottom, the District of Columbia neighborhood surrounding its campus. Now residents there say they have no option but to sue to preserve what is left of their shrinking community. 'We're getting shafted,' says Ron Cocome, the president of the Foggy Bottom Association, a residents' group that supported attempts to contain the university. 'They're gutting our neighborhood'" (Gomstyn, 2003, p. A23).

While changes in the public's attitude are frustrating and demoralizing for those working in the academy, the current views of higher education and uncertainty about the role of colleges and universities in our society can be changed. Various efforts can and should be undertaken to build more positive relationships with the external constituencies with whom we work. With proper planning, commitment, resources, and sustained creativity, a renewed confidence in the academy can be achieved. The remainder of this section considers methods that institutions can employ to strengthen its relationships with its multiple and varied constituencies.

Make the Case

Nationally, independent and public colleges and universities need to do a better job to "make the case" regarding the purposes of their institutions and how they work to achieve their missions. Increased demands for accountability are not unreasonable, but quantifying and describing the results of our work have not been a strength of institutions of higher education. IHEs are very effective at preparing lists to demonstrate grant attainment, patent development, degrees granted, and jobs secured by recent graduates, for example, but they must also be able to describe and demonstrate the differences our institutions make for individual students, communities, states, and institutional stakeholders. Especially important to consider is the fact that higher education leaders have a long history of asking for money, but only in recent years have funding agencies asked for formal ways to measure whether or not the funds have been put to good use.

Colleges and universities must devote greater energies to developing allies—individuals and groups who will be ready to provide assistance in good and bad times. The more people understand what IHEs are trying to accomplish, the greater the likelihood that the academy will be perceived in a positive light, worthy of both moral and financial support. Comprehensive partnerships that foster a public interest in what colleges and universities actually do need to be developed. A recent example of such an effort is "Rutgers University's collaboration with the Stephen Low Company, with major funding from the National Science Foundation, to produce 'Volcanoes of the Deep Sea,' the first higher education sponsorship of an IMAX film" (M. Breton, personal communication, December 22, 2003). The movie chronicles extraordinary oceanographic research findings in an educational and entertaining movie that will expose millions of viewers not only to the mysteries of the ocean, but to the nature of the research process and the contributions that comprehensive research universities can provide.

Public relations efforts with external constituencies should be ongoing and sustained to insure that our multiple publics receive frequent communications regarding accomplishments and challenges. Developing electronic mailing lists for specific external constituencies, for example, is a particularly useful and inexpensive way of keeping a wide range of people up to date about the work of our institutions. Such efforts have been in place for years with graduates, trustees, and donors, but with easy Internet access, informing a wider public of the work of IHEs can strengthen ties to local, state, and national legislators, as well as to local communities.

Mass mailings and electronic communications are essential, but the personal contacts that members of our institutional communities make with the public are critical for building the partnerships that will maintain the vitality of higher education in this country. In the end, nothing is as useful as building a group of "friends of the university" and meeting personally with individuals in various community settings. While preparing this manuscript, one of the authors of this chapter was asked by a participant at a community function why the costs of college attendance always went up. The person posing the question understood issues related to salary increases, but he admitted he never had considered the costs the colleges and universities incur to pay for insurance, supplies, technology, and fuel. At the same time, the author, somewhat surprised at the question from a person who read local and national newspapers daily, recognized that the university in question clearly had not informed the public when announcing tuition and fee increases about why such decisions were necessary.

Form Personal Contacts

Personal contacts with the local community can be particularly effective when made by students through volunteer programs and service learning functions. Students have been shoveling snow and assisting community members for years, but the enhanced and formalized programs resulting from President Bill Clinton's service learning initiatives have been particularly fruitful in building campus-community partnerships. Across the country, students are volunteering in health care settings, libraries, government agencies, and myriad arenas combining their practical assignments with the theoretical background that they are learning in the classroom.

Equally important are the contacts made by faculty in their role as experts in their fields and as members of their local and extended communities. Faculty are the critical advocacy group for an institution; their work at the local, state, national, and international levels provides the fundamental core of teaching, research, and service. Their contributions, therefore, are essential in helping multiple constituencies understand the mission, goals, and activities of our colleges and universities. Such efforts can help to ameliorate legislators' perennial perceptions that faculty positions are "cushy jobs" that require only as many hours a week as are mandated to be in the classroom. To prepare faculty to consider the importance of accountability, they should receive an orientation to the realities of documentation requirements and be taught the various strategies to demonstrate their work in service and teaching, just as they provide cogent and detailed reports relating the status of their research projects (Layzell, Lovell, & Gill, 1997, p. 332).

Enlisting graduates broadens greatly the ability to contact multiple publics. From institutions with hundreds of thousands of living alumni to those with only a few hundred graduates, their participation as advocates for their alma maters greatly expands an institutional voice, locally, nationally, and around the world.

Use National Associations

The role of national higher education organizations is a critically important one in presenting the issues and "making the case" to legislators. While many colleges and universities have their own lobbyists in Washington, D.C., the national associations can present a collective and unified voice on some of the most vexing challenges facing the academy. Financial aid allocations, regulations affecting international students, and legislation affecting institutional reporting requirements are just some of the selected issues that national associations tackle on behalf of institutional members. Of particular importance in maintaining contacts with national associations is that they enjoy a perspective on the issues that can inform institutions in charting their own legislative agenda.

Plan, Evaluate, Adapt

To make the appropriate connections and communications and have systems in place for working with external constituencies requires comprehensive planning and oversight. The right staffing patterns and personnel need to be in place to ensure that appropriate programs and services are positioned to work with multiple constituencies. In the planning process, institutional leaders should consider both daily communications and those necessary to deal with emergencies and crises. Depending on the nature of either a routine matter or a crisis, local officials may need to be informed and enlisted to address the issue. Emergency communication information, for example, should include appropriate leaders of local municipalities to insure that they are informed about the status of the problem and their role in the matter.

Coupled with an effective planning process, ongoing evaluation processes can help to strengthen the bonds with various constituencies. Asking questions about whether they are receiving the information they need in a timely fashion and then adapting programs to address their responses can help to ensure the effectiveness of advocacy efforts. These efforts can be time consuming and labor intensive, but well worth the effort as IHEs work to forge bonds that will strengthen their specific position and higher education in general.

References

Astin, A. W. (1993). *What matters in college? Four critical years revisited.* San Francisco: Jossey-Bass.

Bills, T. A., & Hall, P. J. (1994). Antidiscrimination laws and student affairs. In M. D. Coomes & D. D. Gehring (Eds.), *Student services in a changing federal climate* (pp. 47–66). San Francisco: Jossey-Bass.

Boehner, J. A., & McKeon, H. P. (2003). *The college cost crisis: A congressional analysis of college costs and implications for America's higher education system* [Electronic version]. Washington, DC: U.S. House of Representatives. Retrieved March 5, 2004, from http://edworkforce.house.gov/issues/108th/education/highereducation/CollegeCostCrisisReport.pdf.

Burd, S. (2004, March 12). Plan to punish big increases in tuition is dropped. *Chronicle of Higher Education*, pp. A1, A24.

Canepa, N. (2004, February 20). Where did SDSU go wrong? Select your allegations. *San Diego Union-Tribune.* Retrieved February 23, 2004, from http://www.signonsandiego.com/sports/canepa/20040220-9999_1s20canepa.html.

The Chronicle Survey of Public Opinion on Higher Education. (2003, May 2). *Chronicle of Higher Education*, pp. A11–A12.

The Chronicle Survey of Public Opinion on Higher Education. (2004, May 7). *Chronicle of Higher Education*, pp. A12–A13.

The College Board. (2003). *Trends in college pricing.* Washington, DC: Author.

Farrell, E. (2002, January 24). Family of MIT student who committed suicide plans to file lawsuit. Retrieved August 9, 2004, from http://chronicle.com/prm/daily/2002/01/2002012406n.htm.

Fish, S. (2003, October 3). Grading Congress on tuition. *Chronicle of Higher Education*, pp. C3–C4.

Fish, S. (2004, March 5). Make 'em cry. *Chronicle of Higher Education*, pp. C1, C4.

Foundation for Individual Rights in Education. (n.d.). Retrieved February 24, 2004, from http://www.thefire.org.

Furniss, W. T., & Gardner, D. P. (Eds.). (1979). *Higher education and government: An uneasy alliance.* Washington, DC: American Council on Education.

Gehring, D. D. (1994). Protective policy laws. In M. D. Coomes & D. D. Gehring (Eds.), *Student services in a changing federal climate* (pp. 67–82). San Francisco: Jossey-Bass.

Gehring, D. D. (1998). The frog in the pot: External influences. In D. L. Cooper & J. M. Lancaster (Eds.), *Beyond law and policy: Reaffirming the role of student affairs* (pp. 3–13). San Francisco: Jossey-Bass.

Gomstyn, A. (2003, November 21). Turf wars. *Chronicle of Higher Education*, p. A23.

Higuera, M., & Melman, J. (Directors). (1993). *Saved by the bell: The college years* [Television series]. New York: NBC Productions & Peter Engel Productions.

Hoover, E. (2004, January 16). Parents united. *Chronicle of Higher Education*, p. A35.

Johnson, H. (2004, January 9). Educating parents about college life. *Chronicle of Higher Education*, p. B11.

Kanew, J. (Director). (1984). *Revenge of the nerds*. United States: Interscope Communications.

Kerr, C. (1991). *The great transformation in higher education, 1960–1980*. New York: State University of New York.

Landis, J. (Director). (1978). *Animal house*. United States: Universal Pictures.

Layzell, D., Lovell, C., & Gill, J. (1997). Developing and viewing faculty as an asset for institutions and states. In L. Goodchild, C. Lovell, E. Hines, & J. Gill (Eds.), *Public policy and higher education* (pp. 325–337). Needham Heights, MA: Simon & Schuster.

Layzell, D. T., & Lyddon, J. W. (1993). Budgeting for higher education at the state level: Enigma, paradox, and ritual. In D. W. Breneman, L. L. Leslie, & R. E. Anderson (Eds.), *ASHE reader on finance in higher education* (pp. 311–330). Needham Heights, MA: Simon & Schuster.

McLeod, N. Z. (Director). (1932). *Horse feathers*. United States: Paramount Pictures.

Mesa, R. (Director). (1992). *Revenge of the nerds III: The next generation*. United States: Twentieth Century Fox Television.

Michael, S. O. (1998). Restructuring U.S. higher education: Analyzing models for academic program review and discontinuation. *Review of Higher Education, 21,* 377–404.

The most hated and admired professions. (n.d.). *Strangecosmos*. Retrieved January 5, 2004, from http://www.stragecosmos.com/view.adp?picture_id=3760.

Nissen, B. (2003, September 30). *Higher costs for higher education*. Retrieved December 31, 2003, from http://www.cnn.com/2003/EDUCATION/09/30/sprj.sch.tuition.hikes/

Okrent, I. (2003, May 26). David's death doesn't have to be in vain. *Newsweek*, p. 18.

Pascarella, E. T., & Terenzini, P. T. (1991). *How college affects students: Findings and insights from twenty years of research*. San Francisco: Jossey-Bass.

Rosenzweig, R. M. (1979). Federal involvement in spending. In W. T. Furniss & D. P. Gardner (Eds.), *Higher education and government: An uneasy alliance* (pp. 91–95). Washington, DC: American Council on Education.

Roth, J. (Director). (1987). *Revenge of the nerds II: Nerds in paradise.* United States: Interscope Communications.

Sax, L. J., Lindholm, J. A., Astin, A. W., Korn, W. S., & Mahoney, K. (2003). *The American freshman: National norms for fall 2002.* Los Angeles: University of California, Higher Education Research Institute, Cooperative Institutional Research Program.

Security on Campus. (2004). Retrieved February 23, 2004, from http://www.securityoncampus.org.

Selingo, J. (2004, May 7). U.S. public's confidence in colleges remains high. *Chronicle of Higher Education,* pp. A10, A11–A12.

Sperber, M. (2000). *Beer and circus: How big-time college sports is crippling undergraduate education.* New York: Henry Holt.

Taxpayers for Common Sense. (n.d.). Retrieved January 14, 2003, from http://www.taxpayer.net/awards/halloffame/proxmire.html.

Those angels in white. (2003, December 23). *latimes.com.* Retrieved January 5, 2004, from http://www.latimes.com/news/opionion/editorials/la-edpoll23dec23,0,6179076.story?coll=1a-news-comment-editorials.

U.S. Department of Education. (2003). *Getting ready to pay for college: What students and their parents know about the cost of college tuition and what they are doing to find out* (NCES 2003-030). Washington, DC: National Center for Education Statistics.

Winston, G. C. (1993). Hostility, maximization, and the public trust: Economics and higher education. In D. W. Breneman, L. L. Leslie, & R. E. Anderson (Eds.), *ASHE reader on finance in higher education* (pp. 405–410). Needham Heights, MA: Simon & Schuster.

Wright, L. (2004). About Us. Retrieved August 2, 2004, from http://noindoctrination.org/aboutus.shtml.

Zacharias, S. (Director). (1994). *Revenge of the nerds IV: Nerds in love.* United States: Zacharias-Buhai Productions.

Chapter Twelve

Perspectives from the Field

Thomas E. Miller and Barbara E. Bender

The purpose of this chapter is to present the reactions of leaders in the higher education community to the premises explored in this text. The writing team believed that critical reflection about student expectations by persons with wide views of American higher education would shed additional light on the matter. This chapter presents a collection of thoughts by persons selected to respond to the basic notions in the text.

When the manuscript for this book was largely completed, it was distributed to a group of persons who serve leadership roles in higher education associations based in Washington, D.C., and who represent those associations on the Higher Education Secretariat, coordinated by the American Council on Education. It was also distributed to four presidents of colleges, whose insights were expected to be useful. After the responders had the chance to review the text, they were interviewed by phone, and those interviews were tape-recorded and transcribed. The transcriptions were edited to a somewhat uniform length and voice, and the responders were shown the written product and offered the chance to further edit the remarks attributed to them. This collection of short essays is the work of the writers, rather than the responders, but it is our hope that it represents their thoughts accurately.

The writing team is deeply indebted for the time and effort on this project by George Boggs, Evelyn Clements, Richard Ekman, Monika Hellwig, Richard T. Ingram, Theodora Kalikow, Clara Lovett,

Carol Schneider, Joyce Smith, Peter Smith, John Strassburger, and Christopher Thomforde. Their willingness to review the manuscript and give their time and energy to the project is greatly appreciated.

George R. Boggs
President of the American Association of Community Colleges

Community college students are especially vulnerable to a lack of information about what to expect when they enroll in college for the first time. Our students often register at the last minute, without any real planning, and some of them are the most "at-risk" students in two-year colleges. With greater percentages of high school graduates entering higher education than at any other time in the history of the United States, many of these students, especially older students, first-generation college students, students from families with low incomes, and traditionally bypassed students, will not have accurate information about what to expect from college.

Student expectations will vary, for sure, but it seems that the older they are, the greater the likelihood that they will expect our colleges to operate in a businesslike manner. Adult students don't like standing in lines, they want to be treated as customers, and they expect high-quality service. These same students are often our most goal-oriented and focused registrants. At the same time, our younger students, not surprisingly, seem to bring greater experience with technology and expect our schools to provide a full complement of electronic communications and applications.

As we consider the multiple roles of community colleges and the extent to which students succeed in achieving their goals, it seems clear that people who have more realistic expectations are generally more successful and more satisfied with their community college experience. Those with unrealistic expectations, especially about the rigor of the school, can spend an inordinate amount of time completing remedial work, lose sight of their goals, and fail to persist.

Community college leaders need to do more to inform high schools about the expectations that they have for their students. As it stands now, high school graduation requirements do not necessarily match college admissions requirements. Although community colleges are open admission, there is often the misperception that students can underperform in high school and still graduate from college without the understanding that these students may have to take extensive remedial work before they can hope to be successful in college courses.

Higher education associations would seem to be the logical group to address the dissonance between student expectations and the reality of the college experience. They could help develop public opinion research to learn about perceptions of community colleges, for example, and forge relationships with the media and with legislators and their staffs to create a more open and trusting relationship between the colleges and the public. Those of us in positions of leadership also need to write more frequently for newspapers and journals outside of higher education to inform our constituencies about our organizations, how they operate, and what students need to do to prepare for success.

Evelyn Clements
President, National Council on Student Development

This piece highlights the importance of helping students to develop accurate expectations—an absolute essential in the community college sector. With more than 10 million students enrolled in 1,100 community colleges across the nation, many of whom are first-generation college students, we must work diligently to engage students in our academic programs and support activities to increase the chances of their success.

The community college sector is an enormous portion of the higher education market in this country. Kuh's College Student Expectations Questionnaire (CSXQ) research, highlighted in Chapter 9, focused on this population, and noted that such students are less likely to become engaged in campus programs, complete fewer credit hours, study less, and, generally, enroll on a part-time basis. Kay McClenney's CSSE research confirms these data (McClenney, 2003), noting that 80% of community college students do not engage in any campus activities. When we consider this, these data make sense: community college students are working; they have families; they rush to the campus for their classes and then leave immediately afterward. In a nutshell, these factors present very special challenges for those of us working in community college student affairs positions.

This book correctly suggests that the strongest direct and indirect relationships between expectations and experience, and experience and gains, are activities such as peer discussion, diversity experiences, and similar interactions. For a commuter college population where most students are working, engaging students with the institution can be quite a challenge. One approach, suggested in this volume, is the creation of learning communities, freshman seminar programs, and as many opportunities as possible for students to engage in small group interactions. That to me is the message that really comes through loud and clear for community college personnel—that we need to develop these communities and get these students closely involved in some kind of learning community environment to make them feel a part of the college.

Low's 2000 study (Low, 2000) focusing on student expectations and institutional performance was a very pleasant surprise for those of us who work in community colleges: two-year colleges are outperforming their four-year counterparts in meeting student expectations. That was an impressive outcome for me, but it seems logical given the associations that people attach to costs and value. Lowe found that the higher the cost and the more selective the school, the higher the expectations that students had for their college. In other words, there was greater congruence for students at community colleges—their expectations were met.

Once community college students walk in the door, they are often surprised. Faculty can be incredibly caring and student oriented—one of the major strengths of the community college. Students receive attention, both in the classroom and throughout the learning environment. The academic standards remain high, but students are nurtured and cared for. Classes are often small, and academic and student support services are imbedded in the student experience. So once they're in the door, the student reaction is often, "Wow, I didn't expect this, and this is wonderful."

In my years at a community college in the Northeast, where certainly we're surrounded by many private colleges, students come from many different socioeconomic levels. Some are from affluent communities, and they think, "Well, I'm at a community college but all of my friends are going to more prestigious schools." Once they have experienced the community college, however, they are transformed, they love it, and they are our best admissions ambassadors. We often hear from our graduates when they go on to the four-year college, and they tell us that "the experience was never quite the same as it was when I was at the community college where I was cared for, I was challenged, and the experience really changed my life."

Community college students may apply without having a clearly defined sense of what to expect, but once they enroll, these students are often transformed. The community college experience, with its clear expectations and nurturing environment, enables them to thrive and grow, to develop self-confidence, and to experience academic success. It's no surprise that community colleges, as Lowe's study indicates, perform so well in meeting student expectations. They open doors of opportunity and they truly do change students' lives.

Richard Ekman
President, Council of Independent Colleges

The expectations of students, why they enroll in a particular institution, how they perceive their schools, and what interferes with their ability to graduate are questions of growing interest. Colleges and universities are working harder to understand why students choose a particular college or university and, at the same time, are looking more closely at how well they are achieving their institutional missions.

In general, students do expect more of us than what we seem to provide. It was particularly interesting to review Kuh's research indicating that, while students enrolled at the smaller private schools seem to be more satisfied, their experiences do mirror their expectations—a lesson that comes through in quite a few of the essays. Part of this satisfaction is due to the fact that private colleges pay greater attention to their students; they are "market sensitive."

At the same time, smaller schools can also be more adaptable to change. When undergraduates at small schools have concerns about a program, curriculum, or service, the governance processes can move more quickly than it might at a comprehensive institution. Added to the ease of working in smaller bureaucracies, the undergraduate experience is the focus of a small college. Issues related to setting priorities between research and teaching, or between graduate and undergraduate students, are not as prominent.

Programs at small colleges enjoy more explicit educational values, sometimes drawn from founding traditions, denominational and others, and sometimes developed as part of a successful curriculum that becomes pervasive.

A real concern for all of us in higher education is the media personnel and politicians who focus on aspects of dissonance between what students expect and what colleges deliver. In fact, there is not a significant gap. What parents and taxpayers want from the college experience is pretty much what the colleges want as well. We want students to meet their goals, succeed in college, and enter the workforce and civic life with the appropriate skills.

We need to continue to encourage colleges to communicate information that is accurate. Relations with parents can always be strengthened, and we need to continue to work closely with the media and government officials to make sure they understand what we are trying to do. Working together, we can succeed.

Monika Hellwig
President, Association of Catholic Colleges and Universities

From the perspective of the Association of Catholic Colleges and Universities, much in this work is of interest, particularly the insights offered in Chapter 3. As to particular situations and issues discussed, expectations of students and parents about campus life as discussed in Chapter 4 are very different from those we hear from our campuses, where questions arise concerning Catholic orthodoxy and parameters for morality and lifestyle in the institutional policies. Our institutions do not get many questions about the quality of life on Catholic campuses, because that is a known priority, a focus believed to be the essential component for creating a welcoming and reasonably orderly community. It would be foolish to suggest that we are not challenged by alcohol and extramarital sexual relations on campus, but they are addressed as moral issues. The focus of the expectations as well as the reality of campus life at Catholic colleges and universities is different.

On our campuses, the provision of services and meeting students' personal expectations are often addressed by campus ministries. Counseling services, for instance, are often shared by campus ministry and are heavily based in the Catholic tradition. We also try to build community around the liturgy. I do not want to suggest that the summary of the research in this volume is inadequate, but only that some of the findings are remote from issues that we more commonly face at Catholic institutions.

An important component of meeting expectations is whether students find their college community to be a comfortable and welcoming environment. It was therefore enormously interesting to read about the success of the historically black colleges in this regard, especially their wonderful track record in developing strong learning communities and graduating their students. I thought the work as a whole could have gone beyond records of graduation to explore evidence of other positive outcomes of college attendance.

Of particular interest to me was the theme that emerged in several chapters of the new and active role that parents are adopting in their children's higher education. They seem to be stepping in more than in the past to negotiate on the children's behalf. This is particularly interesting to me, as we observe in our institutions that students are trying to assert greater independence at the same time that their parents exert a conservative influence on the institutions.

It is clear that in the main, expectations should conform as closely as possible to the reality of the college experience. Therefore, either the reality must be brought to answer to the expectations, or there need to be changes in the ways programs and activities are officially or unofficially announced and portrayed.

R. Thomas Ingram
President, Association of Governing Boards of Universities and Colleges

The text represents a worthwhile endeavor and makes a useful contribution to the literature. Its undertaking was ambitious and produced a complex set of detailed discussions from available research and anecdotal speculation. As the authors acknowledge, the book is limited in that it focuses on the concerns of students at residential colleges who are recent high school graduates, which is not the full landscape of higher education today.

The book touches on how expectations vary by gender, but perhaps more could be made of this. Many of us wonder about the gender mix in higher education and what has happened to transform the college-going population from largely male to largely female. This is far different from the experiences of many trustees. The gender shift in going to college is particularly the case among African American and Hispanic populations and is worthy of our attention and concern.

From the standpoint of institutional trustees, the book has the potential to help the reader know who our students are. That is a perspective that many, probably most, trustees wish to have. University trustees often long for more interaction with both students and faculty members. Trustees regularly focus on business aspects of institutions, campus building matters, strategic plans, and the like. They yearn for opportunities to be engaged with those who bring the institution alive—our students and those who teach them. Presidents and chancellors have difficult jobs these days, but creating more opportunities to bring trustees into the life of the institution can obviously bring its own rewards.

Perhaps those who consider this text can use it to identify ways in which trustees and students can be better connected. If college presidents want to look for ways to foster interaction between trustees and students, providing exposure to and understanding of the real life of colleges, selected sections of this book should prove to be helpful.

Theodora J. Kalikow
President, University of Maine at Farmington

Examining student expectations is a fascinating notion. Typically, we don't really know what their expectations are, so it is hard for us to know if we are meeting them. While I would not suggest that we should always work to meet what they expect, especially when their wishes are contrary to the mission of the school, we do need to know what their reasonable expectations are to develop and implement appropriate programs and activities.

There is a wide variety of students who enroll across the nation, but looking at the traditional-age students, those at my institution, for example, they seem to have well-informed expectations and generally match what we offer. Certainly, and not surprisingly, there are high expectations held by the public and government and business leaders regarding workforce development and jobs—all legitimate concerns. Still, we don't want to be in danger of forgetting the traditional values of a college education, the virtues of a liberal arts and sciences education, and, in my case, the mission of public higher education.

Currently, most institutions prepare their students prior to enrollment through literature, viewbooks, and Web sites. Added to that, we have a summer orientation program that provides an in-depth credit-bearing seminar to help students prepare for the semester. The challenge of such focused experiences, however, is that the individual attention that the students receive in the summer does not really mirror the nature of the interactions and classroom experiences during the academic year. We need, therefore, to make sure that what we provide in preparing students for the actual semester is accurate, so that there will be a consonance between expectations and reality.

At my public institution, we need to be concerned about preparing a competent citizenry and educated workforce, and educating people who are going to contribute to the culture of the state in fashion that will strengthen our community. To this end, our students are clearly willing in their enthusiastic way to contribute as volunteers and be enthusiastic in their work in the surrounding community. When they participate in volunteer activities off campus, they change people's minds about higher education, usually in positive ways. This is good, because who listens to the president? Nobody. But the students who work with the local animal shelter or teen counseling center can make a real impact. Those are real voices, and they are real people, and when they affect the fabric of the community, people pay attention. And I think they are a little bit less likely to agree with all the stereotypes of *Animal House* and all those other movies.

Clara Lovett
President, American Association for Higher Education

The focus of this work, student expectations, is quite timely, but today we are also dealing with the expectations of many other constituencies as well. This was not necessarily the case 20 or 30 years ago, when higher education was a much smaller universe and played a less critical role in our society. The more important we have become, as the underpinning for the actual or perceived competitive advantage for graduates and as a vehicle for educating good citizens, the higher the expectations that people have for us. As all of higher education's functions have become more central, the level of interest with what we do is greater, the level of scrutiny is greater, and the expectations are rising. So it's not just students, it's almost everybody who has expectations of the contemporary academy.

Those of us in higher education should work to demystify our institutions so that there will be a greater understanding of what we do, why we do it, and how we do it. We need to make our work more transparent, including informing people about the curriculum, programs, and very mission of our institutions. Thinking broadly about the public's expectations and those of current students, for example, it seems that the critical factor in closing the gap, to the extent that you can ever close it or narrow it, is in making everything we do more visible and understandable. Unless we work directly and routinely with the multiple publics we serve, we will continue to make assumptions, rely on alienating jargon, and not make the connections that we need to with the people we serve. Every profession regards itself as special and sets itself apart, and every profession has its own professional language; there's nothing wrong with that. However, with the rising expectations of our many publics, it becomes extremely important for us to speak more than one language—translate, if you will, and explain our assumptions and our frameworks in ways that are accessible to people outside of higher education.

Carol Schneider
President, Association of American Colleges and Universities

This work seems to contain an internal tension about the role of expectations in a student's education. On the one hand, the several chapters provide very useful data about students' own expectations as they come to college and what role they think the college experience will play in their lives. And the authors provide interesting conceptual frameworks for why it matters to pay attention to these expectations. Several authors contend that campuses should do a better job of responding to student expectations.

On the other hand, many of the authors hold—as does the Association of American Colleges and Universities (AAC&U)—a strong conviction that the college environment at large should be shaped to guide students' use of time, talent, and interpersonal engagement with other students and with faculty. In other words, these authors imply that colleges should work to influence and change student expectations of college rather than simply respond to them. But this claim is not directly presented or fully developed.

As a result, there is a tension between a view that we should take student expectations seriously, and an alternative assumption, embedded in several chapters, that we should work to change student expectations by enlarging them. These two views aren't necessarily mutually exclusive. But the book does not suggest a way to reconcile them.

Take, as an illustration of this tension, the role of diversity in the educational environment. As a community, higher education has decided that diversity is a value and that teaching students to respect and learn from people different from themselves is one of the civic contributions we make to our democracy. This view is widely held by faculty and administrators, and was clearly spelled out in all the *amicus briefs* the academy collectively submitted to the Supreme Court while the Court was considering the two affirmative action cases from the University of Michigan.

Given this view that diversity is important, many institutions are shaping their environments not just to acquire "compositional diversity" but also to ensure that we forge new connections across the Balkanized student communities that many campuses report. Student affairs has a major role in this agenda. Throughout this book, correspondingly, several authors speak of doing a better job with one or another aspect of campus diversity.

Yet, as we all know, many students arrive on campus with no interest at all in diversity. Or they may hold well-developed stereotypes of other groups. Learning from people with different backgrounds and perspectives isn't part of these students' expectations of college. To do "a better job with diversity," colleges and universities will have to change these students' conceptions of what they expect from college. A strong "expectations" framework needs to address this clash of expectations as a dynamic in the college experience.

What I missed in this book is a recognition that our colleges and universities have been established to provide an intentional design for learning, not just a response to market wants. Society values us because we develop talent. But developing talent means that we have an obligation to help students discover what they need to know to fulfill their own aspirations.

For example, most students want to prepare for the job market. But they may not know that employers value diversity. It's our job to help students find that out. We need to help our students understand why we are committed to creating extraordinary opportunities for people to learn from people with backgrounds, traditions, and cultures different from their own. It's then up to us to show students that employers are saying: "Our customers are diverse; our workforce is diverse; the world is diverse; our new markets therefore are diverse; we want our employees to be capable of dealing with difference." I met a student on one campus who told me he loved a course he was taking on the sociology of race, but that it was not going to help him get a job. That was his misconception. Learning about diversity will help him get a job, and it will help him for his entire life after college.

This same point applies to all the goals for student learning in college. Students often have a rather vague conception of what college will really be like and what they will need to do. They may be coming to college because they want access to the job market, but they don't really understand either what employers are looking for in terms of learning outcomes or what society expects of a well-educated person. In our recruiting materials we could, and should, do a much better job of helping students clarify what we—on behalf of society—will expect of them. At AAC&U we say that we need to help students become more intentional about their own learning. But if that's a goal, the academy needs to become more intentional about learning as well.

I concur with the book's suggestion that there should be better orientation of students in the recruitment process and that the failure to do so is one of the real shortcomings of American higher education. We busily sell the buildings, the prettiness of the campus, and the vitality of the community, but we say very, very little about what students will actually be expected to accomplish in college. Therefore, it's not surprising that they come in with educational expectations that are not necessarily in their best interest.

All in all, this book seems to have a higher purpose than just promoting "reasonable expectations." I strongly believe both that you start with the students "where they are," but that you also attend to where they want to go. Society has certain expectations of a well-educated person. It is up to us to be attentive to what tradition has said on the subject, to what contemporary society is saying on the subject, and to what the evidence suggests about learning that pays benefits over a lifetime.

With this larger vision of education in view, student affairs professionals can help shape both an environment and educational programs that empower students to meet their own and the world's expectations. The key to all this, I believe, is helping students think seriously about what will be expected of them when they graduate from college.

Joyce Smith
Executive Director, National Association of College Admission Counseling

Today, we need to be concerned about pipeline issues: who is enrolling in college, and what kinds of expectations students have for their colleges. We have long been concerned about what the projections and profiles of students are like, how are they different from past generations of Boomers and X-ers, but the focus of this work—student expectations—is novel. Our constituencies focus far too much on the application to college process and not necessarily on what happens after admission. Equally important is making the leap between the differences in expectations among parents, the faculty, and their students regarding what the college experience should encompass.

Some of the traditional things that one would have expected to read in this work, the values of education, how it affects graduates' incomes and their career options, did not receive the focus that the reader would have expected from a book on student expectations. Readers also would have appreciated the opportunity to learn more about enrollment management strategies, including the perspectives of those who manage programs in residence halls, admissions, financial aid, and policymakers in general.

Clearly, the book demonstrates how different the expectations are that students have today compared with their Baby Boomer parents. Competitive colleges are changing to keep up with the changing nature of students. The changing student population, the reality of some of the educational challenges that we're facing in this early part of the 21st century, and, of course, the ever-present fiscal challenges force us to weigh priorities carefully and develop programs that will serve our multiple publics.

Many of the chapters addressed the fact there are significant numbers of first-generation college students attending college, probably more than ever before. To this end, we need to consider more coordinated and comprehensive enrollment management programs to help students adjust successfully. Orientation programs, financial aid packages, in fact all aspects of the information we provide to prospective and new students need to be prepared in a fashion to help students develop expectations that will help them to succeed. We also need to pay very careful attention to what happens in the high schools, what students are learning, and the quality of the educational experience they are receiving. This is really important as we consider what is happening with test scores, grades, and the very quality of the preparation of the applicants we receive.

If we could, it would help all higher education to inform the media and all of our publics that the greatest percentage of students attending college are doing so at public institutions. While the elite privates receive a great deal of media attention, the coverage is disproportionate to their numbers and the numbers of students enrolled in those schools. Looking at the budget processes, the interaction with legislators, and the influence of the public at large, given the sheer volume of enrollment numbers, we need to work carefully to accurately represent the populations we are serving and the important role of public institutions in this country.

Peter Smith
President, California State University, Monterey Bay

The DNA of this book, the strand that ties the chapters together, is student learning. Everything that we do needs to be planned to increase the chances that students' appreciation of the world around them will deepen, that colleges will work actively to engage students in the process, and that the likelihood that students will persist to the degree will increase. We must keep the primacy of student learning in the forefront. If we can frame our work and focus on learning, everything at our schools will come together into a meaningful educational experience for our students.

The material in the book reflected various perceptions of student expectations, but the organizing concept underpinning the essays is that we want students to learn, persist, and graduate. But, we still need to be concerned about getting students even to participate in higher education in some form. We know, statistically, that in America, out of 100 ninth graders, 18 will have a baccalaureate or an associate's degree 10 years later. Recognizing that there are people who don't get it done in 10 years who do get it done eventually, from a national perspective, the numbers wouldn't change a great deal. Additionally, we know that 32 out of 100 don't graduate from high school in four years (many more than we admitted), and we know of the 68 who do graduate from high school, 60% go to college, and we know of that number (42) 50%–60% graduate within six years. In other words, we have a national disaster waiting to happen. We're taking 68 kids that graduate from high school, and of those, only 18 are getting a bachelor's or associate's degree six years later—we need to do a lot better than that if we're going to have an educated society.

Regrettably, right now, we're not moving forward on the objective of fostering greater participation; we're right now moving backward. Higher education leaders simply know too much about good practice, and there's too much research on these issues for us to pretend that it's not essential. What we are describing is all aimed collectively at keeping kids in school, strengthening the value and quality of their learning, and getting them into society as functioning success stories. We know how to do this; we know better how to accomplish our goals. Now we need to do our work.

John Strassburger
President, Ursinus College

Over the years, the one consistent gap between what students expect and the reality of the college experience seems to be the surprise they encounter when they learn how much discretionary time they have or how much of their time is subjected to their discretion. The amount of freedom they have and the huge contrast between high school and college require a great deal of adjustment. No matter what we say to them, they never fully appreciate the extent to which they really do have complete control over what they do all day, every day. They don't really believe that often attendance will not be taken, or that no one is going to care whether they spend all day (or all night) playing video games. Come exam time, the grading system will determine to what extent they have worked on their academics.

At the same time, given George Kuh's observations that students arrive at college having very high expectations for what's going to be demanded of them, we need to ensure that they are challenged intellectually to the fullest possible extent right from the first moment they are on campus, if not even before that. And when we do assign summer readings, we must make sure that the assignments are treated seriously once students arrive. One thing we all may wish to consider, continuously, is the need to provide more structured academic rigor, especially during the first six to eight weeks, when students are just beginning to adjust to the college environment. This is not to suggest that we create more busy work for them, but we should try to engage students in more writing and in more class participation right from the start. We need to create a much more demanding culture of expectations for student performance on those issues that may not automatically result in earning a grade of A in the class, but will influence how hard students are working right from the first day of college.

As we market and advertise the goals of our institutions, we also need to remember that prospective students are asking themselves important life-forming questions that will help to frame their lives. Students come to college thinking some of those questions will be informed by what they learn, and it is incumbent on colleges to create an institutional ethos that fosters such learning. It is worth having a course that all students will take called "What It Means to Be Human," and one of the reasons many colleges, including my own, have all the first-year students now clustered in housing that does not have upper-class students is that we assume that a course focusing on the best that has been thought and said on the largest issues of human existence will inform the conversations that 18-year-olds inevitably have at 2:00 A.M. Our schools must work strategically to shape the conversations of our students so that their college experiences will help them to grow as individuals who will be contributing and engaged members of their communities. It is not enough to leave life choices to them and focus only on job preparation.

Generally, higher education, across all sectors, needs to do a better job in making the case for our institutions. The whole accreditation movement and the media rankings game reflect some of the public's frustration with understanding what quality education is, where it exists, and how we define it. We need to educate the public about what we do and how successful we are in doing so. There is still too much negativity and misperception about higher education. More and more, we must work to try to find ways of distilling and publicizing what students actually accomplish. Focusing on student achievement is the real key. If some of those skeptical about what we do could see the quality of academic and scholarly work students are producing on campus after campus—work that exceeds in quality what most students anywhere were doing 40 years ago—they would be far less skeptical. In discipline after discipline, students today are doing extraordinarily good work.

Reverend Christopher Thomforde
President, Saint Olaf College

How do we balance our central academic calling and purposes with broader, reasonable, and understandable expectations about developing the whole person, making people comfortable, dealing with serious mental health issues, interpersonal relationships, all the kinds of thing that make a total human being? How we attempt to address all of these questions is our fundamental challenge and the focus of the book.

The material in this work is very, very important because there is clearly a gap among the expectations of students, the expectations of their parents, and the expectations of our society. What the authors have worked to address here is the fact that colleges have to do a better job at making clear to people that while there are many good things that can happen for young men and women while they are in college, these are academic institutions whose primary reason for being is education. Certainly the academic missions of colleges and universities are the foci of activity, but student life issues in general seem to be as important or, at some institutions, more important, and hence the confusion of expectations.

While this may vary by institutional type, the increase in intensity in recruiting students has helped to fuel the fire and raise the expectations about student development and student comfort. What colleges are trying to convey about the experiences they provide has changed a great deal from the days when deans sternly warned students about the rigors of the undergraduate experience. Indeed, we have come quite a distance in the other direction, and if there's some middle point that values the broader range of developing the whole person while providing a rigorous academic program, working toward it should be our goal.

One of the authors of this text noted that there should be some direct link among general education, a student's major, the degree awarded, and the potential for postgraduate employment. As opposed to an expectation (at least in liberal arts colleges) that one could study English and then go to medical school or study classics and join the FBI, there doesn't need to be an absolute relationship between reading Plato or studying Russian history and getting a job. Students and their parents do have the expectation that college will position them to get a job, and they are not wrong in having those expectations. On the other side of the coin, however, it is disconcerting when we are asked why we have a classics department, since it won't provide a direct link to getting a job.

The book seems to include many wonderful statements by a wide variety of people about cognitive learning, developing citizens, responding to mental health issues, and developing the whole person. There did not seem to be much emphasis, however, on spiritual formation. Colleges should not be expected to teach students how to pray or think about God, but there is a great deal of what is called spiritual yearning, exploration, and adventure. In the same way that we would want men and women to be responsible in their capacity of cognition to analyze material, and be responsible in their use of alcohol, drugs, and sexual life, an equally strong proponent of student life might also consider the creation of programs to address what it would mean to be a responsible man or woman from a spiritual perspective. Is there any way that we could help students think through what it means to be a man or woman who had some appreciation for wonder or the sacred? There must be something to studying the spiritual aspects of life that is worth thinking about and studying, much like we study Plato or organic chemistry.

The book appropriately covers student expectations and parent expectations and so forth, but what are faculty expectations of students? The silence on this issue is an important one, given the reality that there can be such a major gulf in expectations. The men and women who make up the faculty of our colleges and universities in many ways had a very different undergraduate experience than today's undergraduates. Most were very much focused on their own academic and professional pursuits and didn't play sports or weren't part of a fraternity or didn't take part in many other aspects of college life that are important to today's students. How many faculty have made such comments as "Why don't students study more?" or "Let's just close down all the fraternities" or "Let's do away with all athletics like the University of Chicago did"? The faculty don't always understand how hard it would be to accomplish some of these changes, or they don't appreciate the value of some of those activities if they themselves never participated in them. This is not to suggest that faculty members' expectations are wrong, but in the same ways one of the chapters of this volume dealt systematically with how we can or how we should respond to student expectations or parent expectations, we also need to look closely at the expectations of faculty, and certainly have them read these essays as well.

References

Low, L. (2000). *Are college students satisfied? A national analysis of changing expectations.* Indianapolis: USA Group.

McClenney, K. (2003). Engaging community colleges: A first look. In K. McClenney (Ed.), *CCSE Highlights* (pp. 1, 2). Austin, TX: Community College Survey of Student Engagement.

Chapter Thirteen

Conclusion

Thomas E. Miller

One of the core premises of this project has been that the interaction between colleges and students can fairly be characterized as a relationship. That relationship has a beginning, and, over time, its nature changes. Sometimes, the relationship comes to an end. We do not mean to imply that the "end" comes with graduation, because institutions hope for lifelong relationships with their alumni. However, some students leave a particular college with a disaffection and unhappiness that severs permanently their relationship to the institution.

If we look at the student and college interaction as a relationship, it helps us understand the power of expectations in driving some of the characteristics of the relationship. In most of our relationships we had expectations, for the relationship and for the other party, as the relationship began. Whether we consider our spouses, our new neighbors, or an employer, all of the significant relationships into which we have entered have been framed, in the beginning, by the expectations we had for each other. If we have been careful, the most important of those relationships have generated carefully negotiated expectations. Regarding going to college, it would seem as though the student-institutional relationship might benefit from the same sort of negotiation.

Colleges do not usually ask students what they expect from the experience, but they seem effective at communicating their own expectations of students. Institutions explain what they expect of students in the form of course catalogs, course syllabi, and student codes of conduct. In the same fashion, institutions usually spell out some of what students can expect of the college. Institutions also explain what effort or result they expect from students, to an extent, but often not in much detail. It is much less common for institutions to survey students or interview them or otherwise ask them what the students expect of the college-going experience and their relationship with the institutions.

Actually, in some classrooms, faculty members have addressed student expectations. One of our interviewed responders recalled being surveyed about his expectations as a freshman at a large public institution decades ago. He recalled being unsure about what he expected of himself and wondered about the extent to which students have an informed notion of the quality and nature of their investment and their experience in higher education. Another of the responders, in a more recent application, surveyed his students at the start of a class on what they expected of the religion course he was teaching. He found a wide range of expectations from a small group of student participants.

The notion explored by this book has been that colleges should be doing exactly that sort of thing. They should be attempting to gather information about student expectations. They should be doing so in an aggregate way to help explore systems and program adjustments to respond to general student expectations.

They should also do it on an individual basis, exploring with students their aspirations and hopes and what they anticipate regarding college. It is on the individual basis that the negotiation of expectations can take place. It is in the academic advising session or in the career exploration meeting or in the private discussion with the faculty member that such conversations can have the most meaning. This type of thinking is addressed when we ask students to be reflective about their futures and their purposes and we give them the tools and teach them how to be reflective. It is good strategy to ask students to explore why they are in college and why they exist, what their aspirations are, their purpose for being, and where they are headed.

The responder referenced earlier, who was not sure what his expectations were when he was surveyed decades ago, was challenged by the notion. However, that sort of challenge can only be good for students; to explore their purpose, their future, their reason for being in college or anywhere can produce insight and personal growth that can be life changing. These personal explorations do not most usefully take the form of survey completion, but are better when they are private reflections in written form or in conversational encounters. It can be a way in which expectations can be comprehended and, as appropriate, adjusted.

Walk the Talk; Talk the Walk

We do not suggest that there is little that colleges can do before those first encounters with students on campus. Those early interactions produce rich opportunity for engaging students about their expectations, but other interactions present good chances for engagement, too. There is no doubt that some of the difficulty we have described about unreasonable expectations is attributable to the enrollment management phenomenon and the intense pressure that colleges feel to manage the size and nature of their student bodies. Too few admissions recruiters are tasked with finding the best student-institution fit ahead of meeting their recruitment goals. The competition for students drives our marketing of colleges, and too many institutions recruit on a basis that is inconsistent with the realities of their campuses. We do not conclude that colleges should not attempt to recruit across a wide span of talent and interest and attract student bodies that are diverse and representative of the range of nature in our society. However, if they are to do so, then they should do more to ensure the chances of success of all students whom they recruit, not just some. Peter Smith argues that it is the failure of higher education to respond to student learning needs that is at the core of our current set of problems in American higher education (Smith, 2004).

Part of the solution is finding a good student-institution fit, but the other part is that, once the relationship begins, a large burden falls on the institution to make it work. In other words, we need to think about creating a good fit where one might not naturally occur. If we have recruited students on the premise that they can succeed, then we need to do what we must to see that they do. When students fail, it is consequential for all, and institutions need to explore what they need to do to enhance student success.

Why do student athletes find success at a rate greater than predicted? Might it be because institutions spend time, effort, and energy to give them support and structure to enhance their chances of success? What would happen if we did that for all students? In the alternative, it seems rather Darwinian for higher educational institutions to recruit students and then somehow expect them to figure out what they need to do in order to satisfy their expectations of themselves and their institutions.

Institutions need to be the institutions they claim to be, and they need only to claim to be what they are. To the extent that students have unrealistic expectations of the college experience, colleges need to do what they can to help students acquire accurate impressions of college and negotiate expectations that are attainable and reasonable.

As much as institutions need to "walk the talk" and be the institutions that they claim to be in their marketing and in student recruitment, there is also value in acting on the premise to "talk the walk." As described by Susan Komives and Liz Nuss in Chapter 8, there are outcomes and important life-changing experiences and developments that will occur in college, due directly to the college experience, but institutions do not describe them. They should.

They ought to explain to students that they intend to make them more appreciative of diversity and help them acquire better citizenship skills and make them more accepting and tolerant. The ways in which a college education changes an individual ought to be a full component of the description of the college experience.

Students should expect to have a greater appreciation of diversity through the college experience, and that is central to their future success. Many students do not expect that, nor aspire to it, but it is a very important outcome of the college-going experience. Because of their involvement in college, students are going to become better citizens, better parents, better neighbors, and have more stable marriages. These outcomes all have to do with the acquisition of a better life through the college experience, and they should be as important to the college student as acquiring a chance to make a better living. The vocational interests of students are key drivers in the college choice process, but these other, as (or more) important, outcomes should be part of the message in the negotiation of expectations.

Institutions and those served by them benefit when they define their purpose and for whom they exist. These can be complicated, unwieldy, or high-sounding statements of mission, or they can be clear, user-friendly clarifying assertions that allow those reviewing them to gain perspective and understanding. If we are clear about who we are, those with whom we relate—students, for the purpose of this project—can better understand us.

However, this may sound simpler than it is. The more complex the institution, the more difficult it is to describe exactly what expectations are reasonable. The more focused and clear the institution's purpose, the more accurate student expectations will be. As described in Chapter 5, Lipsky's account of life at West Point is instructive (2003). Most of us understand what the United States Military Academy is, so the West Point experience is clear to us. Many smaller private institutions are clearly understood, too, and they often are the more nimble and adaptable organizations. Religiously affiliated schools have clear purpose, as do community colleges, to an extent.

However, it is not as easy when an institution is large and complex, as one would describe most research universities. They have many purposes, many functions, and many different relationships with society, so it is not surprising that persistence rates at such institutions are not as high as for the smaller, more focused institutions. It is harder for the student coming into a large, research institution to have a clear notion of what he or she can reasonably expect of the learning experience.

Sources of Expectations

Where do unreasonable expectations arise? It might be argued that, unless institutions are the cause of them, it does not really matter what is their source. As previously described, when admissions recruiters are responsible for creating student expectations that are not likely to be met, institutions are not free from duty, but they need to try to figure out how to help students achieve the goals they have set.

However, even when expectations come from other sources, be they parents, the media, popular entertainment, or the fanciful imaginations of persons aspiring to better lives, colleges still have performance duties. Those duties go back to the negotiation process, to engaging students in discussion about what colleges can do to help them succeed, so they see what course makes the most sense.

Some expectations arise from the published rankings of institutions, which, of course, feed the notion of competition among schools. When a national publication generates a list of schools in some rank order, there is established a top, middle, and bottom on that continuum, and few institutions are comfortable settling at the bottom. Students trying to make comparisons among the institutions they may attend might be influenced by such rankings, and their expectations for the experience may be affected.

Another challenge facing institutions is that tangible matters, like the physical quality of campus and the cost of attendance—things one can see and measure—often have a greater impact on expectations than do those matters that are less tangible, like the quality of learning or the level of student engagement and participation. When expectations are more affected by the look of buildings, the size of residence hall rooms, or the equipment in the weight rooms, the real effects of college are devalued. Learning and the quality of educational programs can be positively affected by physical structures and comfort, but often less than their importance in the college choice process and, hence, the development of expectations.

Research Tools

As this project has attempted to demonstrate, higher educational institutions have much to gain by exploring the expectations of students and determining the extent to which those expectations are met. Careful consideration of what students think will happen in their college experience is a key first step. This project has pointed toward the available research tools and their value to understanding student expectations.

The College Student Expectations Questionnaire (CSXQ) is intended for the explicit purpose of gathering information about student expectations prior to their matriculation. Collecting data about expectations through the CSXQ allows administrators and faculty members to consider program and instruction adjustments to respond to student beliefs about what they will encounter in college.

It also permits institutional personnel to consider strategies for re-framing student expectations when they are determined to be un-reasonable.

The CSXQ, when combined with its sister instrument, the College Student Experiences Questionnaire (CSEQ), allows institutions to consider how expectations of students match with their real experiences on the same basic set of considerations: how they use the library, how they interact with faculty, their course learning, their writing experiences, their use of facilities, their involvement with student organizations, the nature of their student relationships, and their scientific and quantitative experiences. Of the research tools available to study expectations and experiences of students, the CSXQ and CSEQ tools are the most elegant available.

As described in this book, the Cooperative Institutional Research Program (CIRP) is another appropriate instrument for assessing student expectations. CIRP has value beyond the measure of expectations, because it broadly surveys students about their values, intentions, aspirations, and backgrounds. Although it has that important advantage, its study of expectations is not as thorough as is the CSXQ.

Those research tools can prove useful for institutions, but institutional design of instrumentation can be just as effective. What is lost with that strategy is the ability to compare institutional results with national norms, but what is gained is focused and well-targeted research. Institutions that develop their own research instruments can study specific institutional aspects of the student experience and consider unique cultural and organizational characteristics.

Key Issues

Among the central discoveries from this project has been that student expectations seem to be an underutilized aspect of understanding the relationships between students and institutions. Although there exists some measure of normative research, it is not generally characterized as institutionally specific or as applied by colleges and universities.

We have generally concluded that more accurate communication about the college experience would be a useful approach in helping students to frame expectations that are reasonable. We found differences between institutions and across individual type, but far too little research was available for our conclusions to be representative of the full range of American higher education.

Colleges usually are able to help those with the highest aptitude and greatest potential to succeed. The students with the best grades and the highest scores on standardized tests usually make their way through higher education with a measure of success and attainment. It could be that students with weaker academic track records have the same aspirations and expectations as those with greater promise. Few institutions treat them differently, but few are surprised when the lesser prepared student fails. When institutions succeed with those who are virtually predetermined to thrive, it is no great accomplishment, but when institutions can be the deciding difference, the determining factor for those who are struggling, a more genuine success is the result. Institutions need to work hard to see that all whom they admit are able to succeed, and they need to give support and whatever resources are necessary to ensure that result.

Entire institutions need to invest themselves in understanding student expectations and how they compare with real experiences. This is not just the purview of institutional researchers or of academic officers or student affairs staff. These matters need consideration across the full range of institutional operations, because expectations of students intersect with every aspect of the college, from bill paying, to student activities, to security, to the cleanliness of the buildings.

The managers of this project did not study what institutions (and faculty) can reasonably expect of students, but the American Association of Colleges and Universities' (AAC&U) Greater Expectations project (National Panel, 2002) is a worthy example of such an effort. Actually, it could be that clear and careful articulation of expectations of students can help them frame expectations of themselves and of institutions that are based on reason and perspective.

A final point for consideration relates to capacity issues. This relates to institutions, large and small. Colleges need to take care to admit only up to their capacity, both in numbers and in qualitative programming. The victims of institutions that admit more students than they can comfortably accommodate are those students. When classrooms are too small or the curriculum is inaccessible or students cannot get to see their instructors, students are disserved and are unlikely to have their reasonable expectations met. Such size issues often affect large public institutions. However, smaller institutions face capacity issues, too, often in the form of the limits of their programs and services. If institutions admit students with special needs or who require enhanced support, those needs should be addressed and that support provided. Capacity for supporting learning is something that limits many institutions, and students with reasonable expectations may be left unsatisfied.

Still to Come

There are key matters still to be understood about student expectations, and the greatest part of this has to do with studying the full range of the college-going population in the United States. Too much of what we were able to uncover was limited to descriptions of the expectations of students recently graduated from high school and enrolled on residential campuses or campuses with a residential sphere. We hope, as future research is configured, care will be taken to pursue perspective about the full range of characteristics of those attending college. We found some helpful studies about the expectations of college students, but far too little about older students, part-time students, graduate students, married students, students who are parents, and so forth.

Another central aspect of diversity in American higher education has to do with the differences not just between individuals, but between institutions. More study needs to be conducted about two-year institutions, women's colleges, tribal colleges, Hispanic-serving institutions, proprietary schools, trade schools, and all of those types of institutions where individuals pursue postsecondary experiences to help them engage society and realize their dreams and aspirations and their expectations.

As noted earlier, this project did not address the expectations that institutions have or should have of students. The original product did (National Association of Student Personnel Administrators, 1994), and the Association of American Colleges and Universities Greater Expectations panel (National Panel, 2002) did, also. The relationship between students and colleges has two sides, and each has expectations of the other—some reasonable, some not, some clearly articulated, some not.

This project leaves us with a clear understanding that student expectations play an important part in students' relationships with institutions. Colleges should study those expectations and use them to inform practice, whether it takes the form of improving performance or of informing students about what is reasonable and negotiating adjusted expectations. We hope for more discourse on the subject and urge colleges to take student expectations seriously.

References

Lipsky, D. (2003). *Absolutely American: Four years at West Point.* New York: Houghton Mifflin.

National Association of Student Personnel Administrators (1994). *Reasonable expectations.* Washington, DC: National Association of Student Personnel Administrators.

National Panel. (2002). *Greater expectations: A new vision for learning as a nation goes to college.* Washington, DC: Association of American Colleges and Universities.

Smith, P. (2004). *The quiet crisis.* Bolton, MA: Anker.

Index